P9-ARQ-848

THE ABSENT MOTHER

Alix Pirani is a psychotherapist and writer. She was born in London and educated at Cambridge, and has four children. A teacher and lecturer in English and Creative Writing for twenty-five years, she has written and published poetry, drama, fiction and essays; much of this work is concerned with feminine spirituality and interfaith tension. Her book *The Absent Father: Crisis and Creativity* appeared in 1989. She runs workshops in Creative Mythology and seminars in Christian-Jewish relations, and finds inspiration in Kabbalah and Reform Judaism. She is on the training staff of the Bath Counselling and Psychotherapy Courses and has been practising humanistic and transpersonal psychology since 1971.

THE ABSENT MOTHER

Restoring the Goddess to Judaism and Christianity

Edited by ALIX PIRANI

Illustrations
by Foosiya Miller
and Abi Pirani

Mandala

An Imprint of HarperCollinsPublishers

Mandala
An Imprint of Grafton Books
A Division of HarperCollins*Publishers*
77-85 Fulham Palace Road,
Hammersmith, London W6 8JB

Published by Mandala 1991
1 3 5 7 9 10 8 6 4 2

© Alix Pirani 1991

Alix Pirani asserts the moral right to
be identified as the author of this work

A catalogue record for this book
is available from the British Library

ISBN 1 85274 099 X

Printed and bound in Great Britain by
Biddles Ltd, Guildford and King's Lynn

All rights reserved. No part of this publication may be
reproduced, stored in a retrieval system, or transmitted,
in any form or by any means, electronic, mechanical,
photocopying, recording or otherwise, without the prior
permission of the publishers.

CONTENTS

For Michael, Katherine, John, Sarah and Jo

ACKNOWLEDGEMENTS

The playlet *In the Beginning* by Janet and Stewart Farrar was first published in their book *The Witches' Goddess* (Robert Hale, 1987). The extract from Gloria Orenstein's 'Gender Politics and the Soul', which originally appeared in *A Modern Jew in Search of a Soul* (ed. Spiegelman and Jacobson, Falcon Press 1986), is printed here by permission of the publishers. The poem 'His Madwoman' was originally published in *Encounter* magazine, under the pen-name Alix Frank. 'Mary – Receptive Woman' was first given, in a slightly altered form, as a talk by Vera von der Heydt at St James's Church, Piccadilly, in 1985.

INTRODUCTION

This book aims to re-introduce the Goddess to Jews and Christians for whom she has been absent. It has been inspired by devotion to the Shekhinah, the feminine aspect of the Jewish God, whose role is to find form for the divine presence on earth. Can she become a Goddess we are prepared to accept? We are never sure, yet she challenges our imagination to give her that form without betraying what she is. The implications and complexities are vast: we seek to contain them in a vision of her wholeness.

There were goddesses, before monotheism took over: feminine deities of great power and creativity. They originated in the Great Earth Mother, begetter of all natural and human life and all religions, Matrix and Nurturer. Recently many women have sought them out in their search for spiritual and political identity, for creative womanhood. Men are following in that quest. Once called on, the Goddess begins to manifest in her own way, which is mythological, imaginal, somatic, magical: a vital complement to the rational, logical, superconscious ways of God.

The Goddess takes many forms, but she is eminently local and familiar. The Goddess of the Hebrews, once the awesome Canaanite Asherah had been officially suppressed, seemed to disappear. But she was in fact kept alive in oral legend, and then revived and preserved secretly in Kabbalistic writing (which was not available to women), described in rich detail by the rabbis of the twelfth and sixteenth centuries. They gladly imagined the Shekhinah, Lilith, the Shabbat, the Matronit, as deities. And Hochmah, goddess of wisdom, already had a place in the Bible. They stopped short at 'worship', or overt prayer, but their devotion and reverence was as wholehearted as it was concealed. The chief characteristic of the Shekhinah and Lilith was their being in exile or banishment, concealed from view. This reflects the condition of the Jewish people, exiled and obliged to hide from those who envied and sought to destroy their spiritual power. For Christians, blessed with the opportunity to celebrate the feminine in Mary, the connection with the Goddess was hidden from consciousness.

The Goddess's power can now come out of hiding. In the 1990s it is needed more than ever before, as established religions lose their hold and the world, in its near-suicidal state and dire need for peace and collaboration, is in crisis.

The solely patriarchal nature of those religions and the societies they cultivated have brought us to this crisis. The appalling holocausts of the Second World War were the outcome of centuries of Christian anti-semitism, ruthless patriarchal warmongering and the rule of vengeance, and still we seem not to have learned how to curb the rampant destructiveness that now threatens to annihilate the whole planet. Only by returning to the roots of those religions and the original sources of their inspiration in matriarchy can we hope to heal our woundedness and begin to recover what we can of our images of 'human divinity'.

Edward Whitmont, in his *Return of the Goddess*, a work of major importance, stresses that we must expect no paradise, no permanent peace: 'polarity and conflict is the dynamic, evolutionary movement of Life. . . . While old values are breaking down, a new (feminine) consciousness is also being born .... but compared to the past, the new consciousness will have to be endowed with greater clarity, freedom, self-awareness, and a new and different capacity to love.' With these as our guidelines, we look to the Goddess, who is concealed within us. Since she has been without overt, established and therefore corruptible power, she can offer us a way to visualize afresh what religion is, and what we may be. She is of her essence creative.

The teachings of the mystical tradition are fundamental to the work. In mysticism and its careful, protected cultivation there has always resided a 'feminine' intelligence of a kind that cannot be enshrined in synagogue or church structures. Hochmah is the wisdom goddess of the Kabbalah, the guardian of the mystery. Our souls will indeed be lost if we ever let the mystery go out of religion.

The contributors to this volume have all been made aware of the Goddess's need to return, through diverse experience:

imaginative, theoretical, physical, psychic, visionary. You will find here complementary and contradictory opinions and perspectives, ideas that may shock, unfamiliar dimensions. There are three extended essays: by Asphodel Long on the history of the Goddess in Judaism, Roger Horrocks on the divine feminine in Christianity, and my own on the psychic-creative manifestations of the Goddess. These, and the shorter contributions, offer their viewpoints in a variety of forms. The writers' ages range from 30 to 90, and this accounts for significant differences of approach.

I have said that goddesses are eminently local, and I must identify the location of this work, compiled in England in 1990. Raphael Patai's classic book *The Hebrew Goddess* was first published in America in 1967 at a time when the women's movement, the human potential movement, and transpersonal psychology were gathering momentum. Feminine spirituality and the Goddess have flourished there, through theology, psychology, poetry, dramatic activity and art. British perspectives are different. Orthodox – constitutionally established – religion still holds out against fully recognizing women's spiritual power, and those who pursue New Age spirituality are viewed with caution. Most significant is the revival of interest in Celtic religion and the Arthurian background to Christianity in Britain.

To give readers some impression of the culture of the Goddess in the USA I have included extracts from one American writer; but there is a wealth of material to be consulted, as indicated in the bibliographies. I believe we have a particular view and responsibility in our spiritual work in Europe. All the contributing writers are of European or British origin and live in the British Isles. Their combined work has an immediacy and an impulse to integrate the dark and light aspects of the Goddess, effectively focus her energies, and reconcile her with the God. For we are very close to Germany and to Poland, to the Middle East, the Gulf, Russia; destructiveness, past and present, haunts and threatens us, even while there are many dramatic heartening and liberating changes in these areas. The shadow of the dark goddess still looms. At the same time, Britain's depression and insularity, her loss of imperialist power, challenge us to restore the humanity and fineness of English-speaking civilization and culture. We have had a unique experience of ten years of political domination by a woman: this asks of us that we find a healthier, holier view of womanpower, a redemptive image of a modest harmonious goddess energy to complement what has often felt like a ruthless and destructive goddess energy.

The task of restoration has its dangers. Synagogue and Church authorities may look askance, with disapproval or mild tolerance, at the interest in Eastern religions and mysticism which is now common among spiritual seekers, the going after strange gods and goddesses. It is quite another thing for them to let in their own Goddess and allow their own mystical traditions the power that has for so long been misinterpreted and maligned. I hope they can respond to this book in the spirit of revival with which it has been written, and be alive to its aliveness. 'For everything that lives is Holy.' So said William Blake, the great English visionary who, in spite of his heterodoxy, was ultimately given a place in Westminster Abbey, his head marvellously sculpted by an iconoclastic Jew who made icons in defiance of his aniconic religion: Jacob Epstein.

The Shekhinah has been with me all the way in my task of editing this book, sending me appropriate messages and formative suggestions through dreams, synchronicities, the I Ching, chance meetings, and the Tree of Life. Help has been given by innumerable people. I am particularly grateful to Marion Russell, my editor at Mandala, for her consistent encouragement; to Asphodel Long, who has been in stimulating and supportive dialogue with me ever since the project was conceived, and to Rabbi Zalman Schachter-Shalomi and Eve Ilsen, whose expansive wisdom, partnership, and passion for learning have offered an inspiring model of integrity and spiritual commitment.

Alix Pirani

NOTES ON CONTRIBUTORS

Ruth Barnett is an analytic psychotherapist in private practice in London and an active member of the London Centre for Psychotherapy. She is married to a psychoanalyst and they have three young adult offspring. In the 1960s she was active in NAWCH (National Association for the Welfare of Children in Hospital) pressing for implementation of the 1959 Platt Report recommendations for visiting children in hospital. In the 1970s she trained with the NMGC and worked as a marriage counsellor, writing several articles for the MG quarterly journal. As a secondary school teacher for 19 years she played a major role in gaining recognition for Child Development as a GCE/CSE subject for which she was Chief Examiner (SWEB), and wrote a textbook for schools, *People Making People*, Hutchinson, 1985.

Howard J. Cooper is a rabbi, a psychotherapist in private practice, and a lecturer in Biblical, psychological and spiritual themes. He lectures at the Leo Baeck College, the Spiro Institute, the Analytical Psychology Club, and in a variety of Jewish-Christian contexts. Trained in creative group work, he has a particular interest in the contemporary use of traditional mythology, and works in therapeutic, religious and educational contexts exploring the interface between religion and psychology. He is the editor of *Soul Searching: Studies in Judaism and Psychotherapy* (SCM Press) and is co-author of a new portrait of British Jewry, *A Sense of Belonging* (Weidenfeld & Nicolson/Channel 4) to be published during 1991.

Janet and Stewart Farrar are leading figures in the world of Wicca, and have been practising witches for twenty years in the

Gardnerian tradition. They are now High Priestess and High Priest of a coven in Ireland. They have appeared frequently on television and radio, and their books have become standard reference works on witchcraft. These include *Eight Shabbats for Witches*, *The Witches' God* and *The Witches' Goddess*.

Jenny Goodman grew up in a Jewish atheist Marxist home, spent her teens in a socialist Zionist youth movement and her twenties discovering sex, feminism, the Human Potential Movement, and brown rice. She would like to spend her thirties *et seq.* reading and writing, but has to earn a living. She trained as a doctor, left medicine for ideological reasons, and now teaches the Politics of Women's Health, Radical Healing, etc. to adult education classes, and lectures on holisitc medical sciences to practitioners of alternative medicine. She helped organize the Jewish Feminist Conference in 1987, and RUACH – a gathering of the Alternative Jewish Network – in 1988. She enjoys the challenge of pursuing a Jewish spiritual path while remaining a feminist and freethinker. She has published articles in the *Guardian*, in *Greenline* and other journals. 'Jerusalem the Red' will appear in a Jewish Feminist Anthology to be published by Women's Press. She is currently writing a critique of patriarchal medicine.

Dyana Hart is an unsupported mother with a teenage and a six-year-old son. She is a healer, practises homoeopathy, and leads workshops on dance, birth, addictions, and the sacredness of the ordinary. She has been writing since the age of seven, and her poems and articles have been published in *Solstice*, *Equator*, *Film*, *Everywoman*, *inter alia*. Dyana says: 'Everything I have read by Monica Sjöö has been an inspiration and touched me deeply. But the book which was a signpost at the start of my path was by a man – Robert Graves, whose *White Goddess* was a sixteenth birthday present from my Mother. Nowadays I read less and less. Going deep within, finding my essential truth and power and trying to express them in all I do, and in my healing work being there for others to discover theirs – that is the most important thing to me.'

Jean Head was born in 1925. An only child, she grew up in rural Bedfordshire. She read Natural Sciences at Cambridge during the war, then taught briefly, in England and as a missionary in Nigeria. Her 23-year marriage with a Methodist minister broke in 1980. This sudden ending precipitated and permitted an analytical exploration. She discovered her long bondage within generational patterns, both in family and also inside, for her, a destructive church. After 29 years in Birmingham and London she now lives in the north Cotswolds, delighting in the countryside and the weaving of tapestries. Much solitude is possible, allowing nurturing of spirituality and the continuing of inner healing. Jean enjoys and values her daughter, her son, three young grandchildren and a small number of women and men friends.

Roger Horrocks is a psychotherapist in private practice. He was formerly a lecturer in psycholinguistics. He has also studied theology, and has practised contemplation extensively within a Western form of Zen, and now describes himself as an 'idiosyncratic Christian'. Over the last few years he has been increasingly interested, personally, as a therapist and as a writer, in the 'Second Coming' of the feminine, and its impact on men and women today.

Asphodel Pauline Long was born in London in 1921 of Jewish parents, refugees from Tsarist persecution. She left home at sixteen, worked all her life, became a mother/grandmother. She has always been an activist for women's equality – first in left-wing politics then, with joy, moving into the Women's Liberation Movement. She is especially concerned with the influence of traditional religions in conditioning women and men to accept stereotypes. She took a theology degree as a (very) mature student to study this. Her ongoing commitment is to women's (and men's) consciousness-raising, especially empowering women to understand and reclaim the past to inspire them in the present, and men to understand that they must change for an egalitarian society to come about. She has many publications in feminist and similar presses on Goddess material, and runs ongoing classes, workshops, etc. on Female Aspects of Deity in their many forms.

Mhairi MacMillan was born and brought up in the west of Scotland, where her family name is associated with the clergy of the Celtic Church. She currently runs the student counselling service in the University of St Andrews, and practises as a person-centred psychotherapist and supervisor. She has been a facilitator of small and large groups in workshops in Britain, Europe, Turkey and the USA for over ten years. In recent years she has had a growing interest in the myths of the occidental tradition and in the rediscovery of feminine archetypes. This interest has come to centre around the study of Kabbalah as a spiritual discipline.

Foosiya Miller was born in 1953. A mother and a sculptor, she originally trained in art, then, as part of her spiritual journey, lived in an ashram and spent several years in Africa working with the dying. She belonged for a while to a French order of nuns, then devoted herself to healing and to her art, in which she expresses the continuing struggle to find her spirituality as a woman.

Lorna Mitchell is 44 and lives in a housing co-op in the inner city of Leeds. She writes: 'I cannot describe my life in the last 18 years in straightforward Western terms, but only in the Indian term "Sanyassin" – by which I mean a person who "drops out" of straight society in order to seek enlightenment. During that time I have also engaged in a wide variety of voluntary subversive and supportive activities of the feminist and anarchist kind. In 1989 I published a novel, *The Revolution of Saint Jone* (Women's Press). At present I am working on a book of stories called *The Teachings of Barbie Finnie*, my own re-working of Norse and Celtic mythology. I hope this will be the first vehicle for putting across my own Spiritual Teachings.'

Gloria Orenstein, at the time of writing, was Associate Professor of Comparative Literature, and Director of the Program for the Study of Women and Men in Society at the University of Southern California in Los Angeles. She has published two books in 1990: *The Reflowering of the Goddess* (Pergamon Press) and *Reweaving the World: The Emergence of Ecofeminism* (Sierra Club Books).

Abi Pirani was born in 1955 to Alix Pirani and has since then followed various careers including daughter, mother, shopkeeper, student, academic, and artist. An awareness of the Goddess has influenced the writings and artworks created by Abi over the years. On good days the various aspects of the Goddess hold hands and provide nourishment and laughter; on bad days the destructive power of the Goddess is overwhelming. The images shown here are an attempt to share something of the influence of the Goddess, both benign and cruel, as seen by one woman through her hand and eye.

Fay Pomerance was born in 1912. After rejecting the

opportunity to enter the acting profession she trained at the Birmingham School of Art and devoted herself to a career as an artist. As well as the major work described here, the 'Sphere of Redemption', she completed a series of paintings based on Hebrew texts, contributed innumerable illustrations to books – mainly on occultism and mysticism – and designed a stained glass window, 'The Rebirth of the State of Israel' for Birmingham Singers Hill Synagogue. She has exhibited widely in Britain and is represented in permanent collections in the UK and overseas, and has written and lectured extensively on spiritual and psychological issues, taking an active part also in inter-faith work. She has one daughter, and lives in Sheffield with her husband Ben.

Deike Rich was educated at the Hohere Fremdsprachen und Handelsschule in Hamburg and, on moving to London, gained the Diploma of the Faculty of Astrological Studies and of the Psychosynthesis and Education Trust. She is now in private practice as psychotherapist, astrologer and rebirther. She has given many lectures and workshops in Britain, the USA and Australia, chiefly on the abandoned child, sexuality and the inner journey. She is co-author of *On the Trail of Merlin* (Collins/Aquarian, 1991), has translated Reinhold Ebertin's book *Pluto* and contributed to astrological journals and to *Harvest*, the magazine of the Analytical Psychology Club. She has undergone a Jungian training analysis and is associated with the APC, the Independent Group of Analytical Psychologists, and the Convivium for Archetypal Studies, of which she is one of the four founder members.

Valerie Sinason is a widely published poet whose work has appeared in such places as *Ambit*, *Angels of Fire* (Chatto & Windus), *Argo, Bread and Roses* (Virago), *Contemporary Women Poets* (Rondo), *Dancing the Tightrope* (Women's Press), *Iron*, *PEN* (Hutchinson), *Spare Rib*, *Literary Review*, *Poetry Review*, *In the Gold of Flesh* (Women's Press), BBC Radio 3, etc. Her full-length collection, *Inkstains and Stilettos*, was published by Headland in 1987. She was a founder member of Prodigal Daughters' Poetry Theatre Group, editor of Gallery magazine and co-founder of Poetry West Hampstead. A graduate in English Literature (London University) she is a Principal Child Psychotherapist at the Tavistock Clinic in London. She has published widely on sexual abuse and mental handicap and her book *Stupid? The*

Meaning of Mental Handicap will be published by Free Association Books in Spring 1991. A regular columnist for the *Guardian*, she is married and has two teenage children.

Chani Smith was born in Israel. She studied Jewish Philosophy and Kabbalah as well as Musicology at the Hebrew University of Jerusalem. She is married with four children, and now lives in England where she plays and teaches the flute.

Baroness Vera von der Heydt was a Jungian analyst for 50 years, and is now retired. She trained in Oxford, Zürich and London, and for seven years was a member of staff at the Davidson Clinic in Edinburgh. She is a Professional Member of the Society of Analytical Psychology, a Founder Member of the Association of Jungian Analysts, of the Independent Group of Jungian Analysts and of the Institute for Religious Psychotherapy. She is a member of the British Psychological Society, President of the Analytical Psychology Club, and Honorary Fellow of the Guild of Pastoral Psychology. She is the author of *Prospects for the Soul*, and a broadcaster on radio and television.

Michelene Wandor is a poet, playwright and critic. Her many plays and dramatizations for radio include serials of *Persuasion*, *The Brothers Karamazov*, *The Mill on the Floss* and *Kipps*. Her books on the theatre include *Carry On*, *Understudies* and *Look Back in Gender*. Her short stories, *Guests in the Body*, are published by Virago, and her selected poems, *Gardens of Eden: Poems for Eve and Lilith*, by Century Hutchinson. Her work has recently involved an exploration of Renaissance music, reflected in two programmes for Radio 3, *Ben Venga Maggio*, and a play, *The Courtier, the Prince and the Lady*. She also reviews regularly for the *Sunday Times* and for the BBC arts programme, *Kaleidoscope*.

NATIVITY
Alix Pirani

(The exiled Shekhinah will come again to redeem the
feminine. The Shekhinah mediates between God and
humankind.)

The Chinese staff nurse
And the Jamaican ward orderly
And the Irish theatre porter
All had a dream on Christmas Eve:
A divine baby girl would be born next day in Maternity Ward
  E.

Sharon Levy was rushed in after midnight
From her Euston bed-sit.
Blood everywhere.
'We must have got the date wrong,' said the midwife ruefully,
Holding the groaning girl's hand.
Her Arab boyfriend had left her five months back.
In St John's Wood Mr and Mrs Levy were still arguing.
'No daughter of mine, Rosalie ...'
'What can you do? It's a love-child, Monty. Have a heart.'

Sharon's baby arrived very quickly, howled,
And fell silent on her mother's breast.
'She's determined to live,' remarked the house-doctor.

'I had this strange dream – ,' said Sharon, sitting up in bed.
'Yes,' said the staff nurse, and the ward orderly,
And the Irish porter who came in specially to see her.

The Jewish Christmas Day volunteers
Kissed the child on the forehead.

'A little Maccabee!' joked Simon the rabbinical student.
'Then maybe the North Sea oil won't run out,' said Ruth from
    LSE.

Camden Single Mothers' Group sent in grapes, nuts and
    raisins.
The baby slept peacefully.
Sharon dozed, dreamed, stared out of the window:
Tried to foresee the next thirty years.

Mrs Levy arrived late that evening, frowning.
'Your father doesn't know I'm here.'
Held the baby's tiny strong fingers.
'She's a beauty, Sharon. Looks just like you.
Poor little thing. But I daresay you'll be as headstrong as your
    mother.'
'And grandmother,' said Sharon.

Visiting time was soon over. Lights out.

'Is she coming again?' murmured Sharon drowsily
On the borders of a dream.

THE SYMBOL OF THE SHEKHINAH – THE FEMININE SIDE OF GOD
Chani Smith

Once there was a king who had six sons and one daughter. His daughter was very dear to him, but one day when he was with her he became very angry for a moment and thoughtlessly said: 'Let the evil one take you.' That night the princess went to her chamber as usual, to sleep. But in the morning she was not anywhere to be found. And when her father, the king, realized she was missing, he was filled with sorrow and remorse, and he began to look for her everywhere. Then the king's minister, seeing that the king was in sorrow, asked to be given a servant and a horse, and enough silver for expense, in order that he might undertake the search.[1]

This is the beginning of Rabbi Nachman of Bratzlav's story of the lost princess. The motif of the king's daughter is often to be found in Rabbi Nachman's stories. She always represents the symbol of the Shekhinah.

What is the Shekhinah, and what is her function in our life? The king's minister in the story has already started his search for the lost princess ...

The word Shekhinah comes from the root SH-KH-N, which means to dwell, to be present. We find this verb in various forms in the Bible. For example in Exodus 25:8: 'And they shall build me a house and I shall dwell (*veshakhanti*) among them.'[2]

The term Shekhinah appears first in Aramaic translations of the Bible and in early midrashim. In Pirkei Avot (ch. 3.2), Rabbi Hanina ben Tradion says: 'When two people sit together and the words of Torah pass between them, the Shekhinah is in their midst.' The term Shekhinah here indicates God's presence in a certain place.

After the destruction of the temple, the name Shekhinah was used to indicate God's presence not in a certain place, but rather within the people of Israel. In Mekhilta de Rav Ishmael[3] we read the famous midrash: 'Wherever Israel was exiled to, the Shekhinah, so to speak, also went with them. They went to Egypt – Shekhinah went with them. They went to Babylon – Shekhinah went with them ...' (Megillah 29a).

At the time when this midrash was composed, the word Shekhinah was used as one of God's names, where the immanence and nearness of God to the people was expressed. At this stage there is no indication yet that the Shekhinah can be a separate feminine entity.

Some of the expressions associated with the term Shekhinah originate at that period. For example: 'The wings of the Shekhinah' – an image of God protecting Israel. Another image: 'The withdrawal of the Shekhinah.'[4] The origin of this expression is connected with the destruction of the temple. The traumatic loss of God's nearness and God's protection marked a split between God and his people. In their experience God – the Shekhinah – withdrew from them. This split, this separation, is also the beginning of intense yearning for reunification, for finding that nearness once again.

The Kabbalistic writings of the twelfth and thirteenth centuries show a revolutionary break from Rabbinic interpretation of the concept of the Shekhinah.[5] The Shekhinah is seen as a separate figure, who, while being part of the divine God, is also independent from other parts of God. She is portrayed in different names and images: a bride, a king's daughter, a matron, a mother, a point, an only one; she is the source of all new life and source of all the souls. She becomes the collective life of the community of Israel.

As a bride, the Shekhinah has a dual role. She is both God's bride and Israel's bride. When the Shekhinah is God's bride, she contains in her the Jewish people, and is identified with them.

The Biblical book Song of Songs was traditionally interpreted as the love between God and Israel. In Kabbalah the female lover in the book is a personification of the Shekhinah who is in loving relationship with God. (The community of Israel is then part of the feminine side of God.) In the second role of the Shekhinah as Israel's bride, Israel assumes an opposite masculine role of the groom.

In all these images we can identify the principle of

relatedness in the Shekhinah. The relationships that the Shekhinah forms, which are male–female relationships, are perceived as symbolic to all other relationships.

Some brief explanations of the basic Kabbalistic ideas may be necessary before we can further explore the symbol of the Shekhinah. (See diagram of the Tree of Life, p. 96.)

Creation, for the Jewish mystic, is seen as God revealing himself to the world in a process called Atzilut – Emanation. From a beginning where God is in himself and there is nothing else but him, God emerges out of himself and creates a world in which he is present. If we can imagine a ladder with ten rungs, then on top there is God as he is in himself: infinite and concealed. We do not know anything about this state of God except that it exists. As we climb down the ladder God becomes more 'revealed', and when we reach the bottom we find our world, where we are, just under the tenth rung. These ten steps are called 'the ten spheres'.

The first three spheres have the names of: (1) 'Keter' (crown), (2) 'Chokhmah' (wisdom), (3) 'Binah' (understanding). They also have other names like: (1) 'Ayin' and 'Ensof' (nothingness and infinity), (2) 'Abba' (father), (3) 'Ima' (mother). All three together represent that aspect of God which is beyond all human comprehension, yet is the source of all that we know.

From the fourth sphere to the tenth, we find the seven children of the father and the mother. They are six sons and one daughter. They form a certain Kabbalistic structure known as 'The seven spheres of the edifice'. Each has a number of names and is associated with different attributes of God.

Through these ten spheres flow the divine light and powers, from the upper worlds to the lower worlds. We mortals are under the world of spheres, but we are connected to it, influenced by it and influential on it. In fact it is often from below that the movement begins and it spreads upwards until the upper worlds get into action.

The tenth sphere is called 'Malchut' (kingdom). One of its other names is 'Shekhinah'. As mentioned above, the Shekhinah symbolizes simultaneously various feminine roles of eternal mother, bride and daughter; she is a matron, a queen and a princess. She is the feminine part of God. God has a masculine part too, which is symbolized by the sixth sphere 'Tiferet', otherwise known as 'the Holy One blessed be He' (Hakadosh Baruch Hu). The Shekhinah and the Holy One blessed be He are two opposites.

Originally the Shekhinah and the Holy One blessed be He had been in a state of union, which was a sort of total union, unifying the different conflicting elements inherent in the divine realm.

What are the qualities that our tradition relates to the Shekhinah? What is she like?

We have mentioned relatedness as one of her characteristics. Another important quality is her receptivity. She is in fact purely receptive, in the sense that she receives her light from all the other spheres. She does not have a light of her own. She is the moon reflecting the light of the sun. She is the channel through which the divine light flows. Some of the divine powers can be potentially evil. This happens when powers which stem from the sphere of 'Din' (judgment) break loose from their source and become independent. In their independence they are evil, so when they invade the Shekhinah she is dominated by evil.

Because the Shekhinah has this special role of being a channel, the ambivalence is an integral part of her nature. She is therefore described as the tree of knowledge of good and evil, since she swings from side to side: from good to evil, from mercy into judgment, from peace to war.

The Shekhinah has a central place in the universe. She is, so to speak, between heaven and earth. In the world of the spheres she is the last in the chain of emanation, but in relation to the world that we know, she is the first and foremost. She is the mother of the world and its conductor.

In the Garden of Eden the Shekhinah was united with the Holy One blessed be He as husband and wife. No evil could come between them. The Shekhinah in this paradise is symbolized by the tree of knowledge which is in union with the tree of life.

It was Adam's first sin of eating the apple which separated the two trees – the two lovers, the female and male in God. Adam's fault was that he worshipped the last sphere – the Shekhinah – on her own, rather than as a part of and in relation to the other spheres. He stopped at the bottom step of the ladder, impatient, shortsighted and greedy. Thus down fell the apple, and down fell Adam and Eve out of the Garden of Eden.[6]

The Shekhinah, having been separated from her lover, is no longer protected in the same way, and the evil forces, known in Kabbalistic terminology as 'Sitra Ahrah' (the other side), have a way in. The evil forces unite with the Shekhinah and receive their power from her, till they become the rulers of the world.

This state of inner split in the realm of the spheres is temporarily corrected for one day a week – on Shabbat. The book Zohar – a major Kabbalistic writing from the thirteenth century – contains a number of sections where Shabbat is described as the Shekhinah. The word 'Shabbat' in its Hebrew form שבת is seen as a visual image of the spheres, since every letter and word in the Torah is believed to contain esoteric meaning. The letter 'shin' with its three branches ש represents the three patriarchs (who collectively symbolize the sphere of the masculine). This letter makes the sound of 'Sha' and is combined with 'bat' בת, which in Hebrew means 'daughter'.[7]

Shabbat as an image of the Shekhinah found a home in the heart of every Jew. On Shabbat the Shekhinah, God's bride, descends from heaven to be with her people. At the same time she ascends towards the Holy One blessed be He her husband. Just for one day a week she is free from the 'other' evil side. She brings with her peace and blessing and is called 'Succat Shalom' – a Tabernacle of Peace.

The Zohar says: 'Come and see: when the people of Israel bless and invite this tabernacle of peace, the holy visitor ... sanctity from above descends and spreads her wings on Israel, protecting them like a mother protects her children ... and as she is present with them, her wings over them, she brings new souls for each one of them' (Zohar 1, 48).

On Shabbat the stern judgment stops. Even the wicked in hell have a rest from their torments. The Shekhinah opens her womb to receive God's loving forces in order to create new life. However, when Shabbat is over the harmony is lost. The Shekhinah is separated from her lover and the war between good and evil continues.

The midrashic passage, 'In every exile into which the children of Israel went the Shekhinah went with them ...' meant to say that God has not forsaken his exiled people. In Kabbalistic context the midrash implies that a part of God is exiled from God.[8] As in Rabbi Nachman's story, the king's daughter is lost to him, and he is searching for her everywhere.

In the story, the king's minister takes on the search out of love for the king and compassion for his sorrow. Does he find her?

Many things happen to the minister on his journey. He finds the princess and loses her again three times. He has to learn patience and discipline, and he must yearn for her all the time, with all his might. He must be awake and aware. Finally, he must at one point leave his servant and alone in the desert seek a mountain of gold where she is to be found.[9]

In the Kabbalah the power of redemption was placed in the hands of humanity. Through our wholehearted service of God we can change things in our world as well as the world of the divine spheres. If we transform the inclination to judgment into an inclination to mercy, we help tip the balance in the upper world in the same direction. Our job is to reconnect the Shekhinah to God and to Knesset Israel – the community of Israel. We can do that through the three major paths to God: prayer, study and keeping God's commandments. In order to do it we have to reaffirm God's redemptive power working within us.[10]

The Chassids, on commencing the performance of a 'mitzva' (a religious command), would say the formula: 'For the sake of uniting the Holy One blessed be He and his Shekhinah'.[11] In allowing love to be present in our earthly lives we assist the heavenly lovers. The Shabbat that we keep is not merely a beautiful idea. When properly kept it becomes a human reality and a divine reality all at once. Like the minister in the story we need perpetual yearning and utmost determination for this task.

Adam and Eve sinned by separating the masculine and feminine in God. Are we doing the same?

In the Jewish world of today there are many separations and divisions. We have to ask ourselves whether we, like Adam, are holding on to one aspect of Judaism while mistaking it for the whole of Judaism. I am referring to any approach to religion which does not take into account the many various needs that every human being has. These needs include the body, mind, spirit and, above all, the heart. Religion can best function in us when all the levels mentioned are involved.

An expression of a religious split, where tradition is rejected in favour of an intellectual 'enlightened' Judaism (as happened in Europe at the turn of the nineteenth century), is found in H.N. Bialik's[12] moving poem 'Alone'.[13]

Alone

The wind has carried all of them, the light has swept all of
them away.
A new song enlightened the dawn of their life
And I, a young nestling, was forgotten
Under the wings of the Shekhinah.

Alone, alone I remained, and the Shekhinah, even she
Her broken right wing on my head, trembling.
My heart knew hers: she feared for me,
For her son, her only one.

Already expelled from all corners, only
One secret place remained, desolate and small
The house of learning. She covered herself in the shade
And I was with her, together in her anguish.

And when my heart longed to the window, to the light,
And as the place under her wings narrowed for me,
She hid her face in my shoulder, and her tear,
On my Talmud page dropped.

Silently she wept on me and clung to me
And as if fencing me with her broken wing she said:
The wind has carried all of them, the light has swept all of
    them away,
And I am left alone, alone.

And like an ending of a very ancient lament
And like a prayer, a plea and a great fear
All these things my ear heard in that silent cry
And in that seething tear.

(Translated by Chani and Daniel Smith)

In this poem we find the Shekhinah in exile, deserted by her people. She is like an angel with a broken wing, trying to protect her last remaining child, and at the same time clinging to him, to the one for whom there is no room any more under her wings.

We are in exile, and the Shekhinah is in exile too. She is separated from her husband and her children – us – in many ways.

The Shekhinah calls us to return. In our story, it is the princess who advises the minister what steps to take. She knows the route to her salvation, and can direct us and give us inspiration, but we must not forget that she too is in the wilderness and needs our help.

One such route is turning to our heritage to look for the bits of the Shekhinah which got buried too deeply. We must not be afraid. Vera von der Heydt in a talk about modern myth says: 'Why is it that these stories are still important, and how do they

11

affect and concern us today? ... I believe it has to do with fear. It is difficult to bridge the gulf between yesterday and today, and it is frightening and maybe humiliating to experience and accept the past as belonging to the totality of one's life.' The Shekhinah is part of Jewish myth past and present. She is very human in her characteristics, which can help us see ourselves as mirrored in her.

The Shekhinah, being the last sphere, is the nearest to man and woman. Therefore she is the gate through which we might enter the divine world of the spheres. For many Jewish people finding the Shekhinah is a need. Rabbi Adin Steinsaltz, in his interpretation of the story of the lost princess, points out that our exile is not an external one, imposed on us by the almighty, as we often think. It is we who choose to go into exile in order to find the Shekhinah.

And when we find her and redeem her, we have found our soul.

NOTES

1 Translation by Howard Schwartz ('The lost princess') from *Elijah's Violin*, Penguin Books, England, 1983.

2 For further study of the term 'Shekhinah' in Biblical and early Rabbinic sources see E.E. Urbach, *The Sages*, Magnes Press, The Hebrew University, Jerusalem, 1987, ch. 3, pp. 37–65.

3 Mekhilta de Rav Ishmael, Massekhta de Piskha, XIV.

4 E.E. Urbach, op. cit. pp. 55ff.

5 G. Scholem, *On the Kabbalah and its Symbolism*, Schocken Books, New York, 1977, pp. 104–8, 138–51.

6 See G. Scholem, *Major Trends in Jewish Mysticism*, Schocken Books, New York, 1967, p. 232.

7 Zohar II, p. 24.

8 G. Scholem, *On the Kabbalah and its Symbolism*, op. cit., p. 107.

9 A. Steinsaltz, *Six Stories of Rabbi Nahman of Bratzlav* (Hebrew), Dvir, Tel Aviv, 1981, pp. 30–5.

10 Cf. G. Scholem, *Major Trends in Jewish Mysticism*, op. cit., p. 233, on the concept of Tikkun – the restoration of harmony in the world, above and below.

11 This formula was influenced by sixteenth-century Lurianic Kabbalah which placed the act of unifying God's fragmented sparks as the main purpose of all religious life.

12 H.N. Bialik (1873–1934), an outstanding Hebrew poet and writer; born in Russia and buried in Israel. Also known as co-author of Sefer Ha-Aggadah, a collection of Talmudic Midrashim.

13 See Meir Gertner, *An Anthology*, Furnival Press, London, 1978, pp. 64–8: 'Alone: a reflection from a psalm by H. N. Bialik' – a study of the relationship between the poem and psalm no. 91.

LILITH, THE POEM
Michelene Wandor

Lilith is not a reason
Lilith is not a cause
Lilith is not an inspiration
Lilith
is

When I was ten
we had a cat
and I called her Lilith
she was black
with white paws
a white ruff
and white strips running between
her two fore feet
and her two back feet

my mother told me later
that I had wanted to call her Lilith
she did not know why
I could not remember why

Lilith was cool
aloof
friendly only to me
she spat and scratched
but I would not let her be
and persuaded her
against all the world's odds
that I loved her
and in return
she loved me

14

she had two litters of kittens
that I remember
and all were given away
or disappeared

after the third litter she was
sad and slow
hiding with her kittens
behind a pile of sacking
only allowing me near her with food and milk
when the last kitten had gone
she walked away across the fields
she never came back

Lilith, the cat
the mother

many years later I began
writing poems
and Lilith sometimes
showed her face
I did not know why
I cannot remember why

many years later
I discovered I was allergic to cats
many years later
I became a mother

Lilith, the mother
the cat

and many years later
my mother died
and shortly after that
I began
re-reading the Good Book
and found that it felt as
familiar as a cat's fur
and as infuriating as a rash

and I began to answer back
late at night
when no one was awake
and two voices spoke
and one of them was kind

and caring and fed up
and the other was dark and glittering
and brave
and fed up

and when the reading was ended
after months
and the voices were sprawled
over pages
I gave the voices names
and they were called Eve and Lilith

and the one could not be without the other
the cat and the mother

Eve was the cornerstone of the Good Book
(for had she not 'sinned'
it would never have been written)
the world owes her everything

Lilith was never even a runner for the Good Book
having transgressed before sinning was a crime
Lilith, the cat, the mother
the female Lucifer

Eve's children people the world
Lilith is never allowed to keep her children

Eve cares about everyone
Lilith cares about art

Eve is never alone
Lilith cannot rely on anyone

Eve has never had the luxury
of a dark night of the soul
Lilith has never known her own hearth

the two women meet for the first time ever
in Gardens of Eden

where they cultivate new plants
and find there are alternatives
to being fed up

this is the story of Lilith
who cannot exist without Eve

Lilith is spiky
and can be as tall as Cruella de Ville
in Walt Disney's
'Hundred and One Dalmations'
Lilith is still black and white
Lilith can still spit and scratch
Lilith can look into your heart
and your soul
and release angels and demons
Lilith will love you
and frighten you
with her love

and when
in the warm limbo of night
Lilith curls alone
on a soft cloud
the vapour floats warm and steamy
round her
and she weeps
for she cannot understand
why her beauty
makes others fear her

Eve comforts her
from afar
with tea
and vodka
and brings the spark back to her eye

she sleeps
to wake another day

Eve finds tears
and Lilith finds a friend

a deal

say the women to each other

knowing that clouds drift in many shapes
a cat, a mother, a book

17

DREAMING UP
THE GODDESS
Howard Cooper

'A dream uninterpreted is like a letter left unopened.'
(Talmud)

I

I am writing these reflections on the 'goddess' as a rabbi and as
a psychotherapist: as a rabbi who found his own life so
incomprehensible and the life of the Jewish community he
worked with so painful, that he turned to therapy as a way of
understanding himself and others; as a therapist who earns his
living through his analytic work with individuals but who still
keeps the 'rabbi' (i.e. spiritual guide and teacher) alive within
his being and his ways of thinking and working.

As a therapist and a rabbi I am the heir to two traditions
which have always taken seriously dreams and those who
dream them. 'Do not interpretations belong to God?' says the
Biblical Joseph to Pharaoh's butler, 'so tell me ...' (Genesis 40:8).
In Pharaoh's dungeon an anxious and uncomprehending
Egyptian comes with a dream to a Hebrew fellow-prisoner. And
what does Joseph, the Bible's great dreamer, say to him? The
original text is subtle – revealing and concealing at the same
time. Literally, it reads: 'Are not interpretations of dreams
of/for/from *Elohim*?', that is – God; the gods/goddesses; the
divine realm; another part of our consciousness.

This confounds our expectations. It is not that the *dreams
themselves* come from somewhere else, but their interpretations.
The Bible does not question where dreams belong, or come
from. They are ours. But, says Joseph, the *interpretations* of
dreams come from another place of understanding – the divine.
It is, however, the divine in us. That is why he goes on to say,

18

'So tell *me* ...'. The dreamer must speak the dream s/he has had and understanding will come from the 'godly part' of the one who listens.

Joseph the dreamer is also Joseph the interpreter of dreams. Just as the therapist is also the spiritual guide; and the rabbi is also the healer, the one who is 'in attendance on the gods' – the primary meaning of *therapeia* .[1] Just as God (He) is also Goddess (She); and the 'Goddess' (Shekhinah/Lilith/Hochmah) is still 'God' (YHWH).

II

The dream of a young Jewish man, who dreamt for us all. This is what he dreamt:

> I am watching the marriage ceremony of a young Jewish couple. The Chief Rabbi is conducting the ceremony. In the middle of it the woman starts arguing with what is happening. The Chief Rabbi ignores her and continues the ceremony. This seems wrong to me. A certain traditional phrase is reached in the service, but instead of it being 'this great people' what I am surprised to hear is the phrase 'this dead people'.[2]

Is this shocking, or liberating? Perhaps it is both. It is shocking because it acknowledges what we all know but cannot bear to face. And it is liberating because it dares to speak the unspeakable.

A transformation has occurred. Something of our once great people, the Jewish people, has died. We know immediately what 'this dead people' alludes to: two-thirds of European Jewry, one in three of all the Jews that were alive in the world in 1939, were dead by 1945. But that is not the end. It is only the beginning. For when we look around us something else has gone for ever. What seems to have died in our times is the piety of old, the learning of the centuries, the idealism of generations, the passion for truth of countless men and women through the ages.

Instead there is a great emptiness, a vacuum of unacknowledged depression and despair – a living death. The dominant materialism does not fill this spiritual hole in the heart of the Jewish world.

These I recall and pour out my soul.
How the arrogant have devoured us!
This has happened to us, we tell it again and again.
We pour out our hearts full of grief.[3]

Has all of this really happened? We resist what we know. Or is the dream only a warning? Does it suggest that if we continue what we are doing – the outer ceremony of Jewish living, the set rituals of our lives – but ignore what is actually happening to the people involved, then our reputed greatness will be exposed as a hollow sham, a deadly lie?

In the dream the (male) religious leader of the community authoritatively pronounces the death of the people. But before he reaches these fateful words the woman starts arguing with what is happening. What is liberating here (and perhaps shocking for representatives of the patriarchal tradition) is to see that it is the woman who voices the life-affirming dissent: 'No, I cannot continue with this.'

For at least two millennia Jewish creativity has rested predominantly with men. They have argued with the old words and wrestled with them for new interpretations to fit changing times and different situations. Their genius has sustained us through time. But now the dream speaks of the woman breaking through the established ritual, the way things have to be done, the words we always repeat, the forms we have inherited.

The woman wishes to introduce a new consciousness into what is happening. She is involved and will not stand by passively. She realizes that it is a matter of life and death – not just for herself but for the whole people. She will be heard. She must insist on being heard.

I believe that Judaism and the Jewish world will be transformed when the Jewish woman finds her true voice, when she is able to speak the knowledge she possesses, can express fully the reality she experiences. We men, like the Chief Rabbi in the dream, would prefer to ignore her. It threatens us, makes us feel insecure: we might have to change if we listened to the voice of the woman.

At a certain point, Jewish men will have to develop a capacity for silence and within that attentive silence learn to hear (*Shema*) the voice of Jewish women. We will have to begin to take with full seriousness what one of our leading feminist thinkers has expressed as follows:

At the moment, in spite of what we share as Jews, to

speak of Jewish culture, Jewish tradition, Jewish religion
... is a serious misnomer, embodying a large and
unpassable scandal. I use that word in its original sense
of 'stumbling block'. We should, if only for the sake of
accuracy, speak of the culture, the tradition, the religion
of Jewish men, in which the creative share in, and the
participation of, women has been defined and
circumscribed by men.

Judaism can have no pretence to being a universal
religion, Jewish culture cannot think of itself as a truly
human culture, until they have opened themselves to,
and faced the challenge of, the individual and
communal self-understanding of women as women.
Both Judaism and Jewish culture will, sooner or later,
have to come to terms with the full weight and
complexity presented by the lives of women – our
particularity, our differences, the specificities of our
experience with each other, with God, and with men.
None of that can be articulated for us, understood for
us, judged for us, defined for us, or explained to us, by
men.[4]

III

The central statement of our monotheistic tradition is the
Biblical text, now a prayer, an invocation: 'Hear (*Shema*), O
Israel, the Eternal (YHWH) is our God, the Eternal (YHWH) is
One.' If God is 'One', how then is it possible to talk about a
'goddess'? Are we not creating a potentially damaging, even
blasphemous, split at the very heart of Judaism?

Cautiously, anxiously, provisionally, I would want to
respond by looking to the key word of Jewish tradition – the
untranslatable four-letter name of God: YHWH. We betray the
essence of the divine when we do translate this (as most of our
translations render it) with the masculine term 'Lord'. YHWH is
a Hebrew neologism: it is an amalgam of the past, present and
future tenses of the verb 'to be'. So YHWH means 'being', 'is-
ness', 'the eternal (One)' – we grasp after a way of expressing
the inexpressible.

The central statement of Jewish faith demands of the
community: 'Hear, O Israel, "that-which-was-and-is-and-will-
be" (YHWH) is our God, "being-and-becoming" (YHWH) is
One.' Formless and genderless is our God. 'That-which-is' is our
God. But of course it is hard for humanity to bear that much

reality. It proved difficult for humanity to stay in a personal relationship with the nameless Eternal One. That which is without name and form and sex acquired a thousand names, a diversity of identities and descriptions and designations. Many of these involved gender: father and king were two of the most common, one expressing intimacy, the other distance. Sometimes the words projected onto the divine One who resisted being named carried a feminine resonance, like the attribute *rachamim* (mercy) which comes from the Hebrew word for womb. Here God was seen as having the capacity to hold us and contain us and nurture us as we grew in our being, just as a mother carries a child.

Jewish tradition always recognized that the Eternal One contained duality, indeed multiplicity. God was a transcendent, dominating, all-powerful, angry and loving 'masculine' force. God was an immanent, playful, strong, angry and loving 'feminine' force. Just as our human 'being' contained multiplicity, the constant interaction of contradictory creative energies and impulses, so too did the divine 'Being'.

Here we press up against the inadequacies of our language. C.G. Jung hypothesized two 'intuitive concepts' in each one of us. 'Logos' – active, penetrative, objective interest; and 'Eros' – emotional; receptive; implying psychic relatedness. He suggested that both principles ('masculine' and 'feminine') exist within us all – men and women. Their harmonious (or disharmonious) interrelationship constitutes the drama of our psychological lives. Here Jung is using *symbolic* terms for psychological factors that are independent of anatomical sex.[5] And so it has to be when we talk of 'masculine' and 'feminine' in the divine.

To talk of the nameless One, Being itself, as God or Goddess, male or female, is always betraying the essence. A necessary betrayal perhaps, an inevitable betrayal – but a betrayal nevertheless. Once we confuse the symbols and metaphors which have evolved to describe the divine with the reality to which they point, we are lost, hopelessly.

As I struggle to move beyond what I find, ultimately, to be an unhelpful split into 'masculine' and 'feminine' attributes of the human 'being' and divine 'being', I return to what is for me, in my understanding of the Jewish tradition, the genderless essence of 'YHWH'. God is Oneness, a unity which holds the tension between manifold opposite energies and qualities. For me 'YHWH'/'God' is inclusive. My problem with 'Goddess' is that the language excludes.

Maybe we are at a stage of our history when 'Goddess' needs to find her own voice, to separate herself out and affirm her identity. But whether she likes it or not she is part of YHWH. The nameless One contains her. And – paradox – the nameless One is Her.

IV

Where does this leave us in relation to the young man's dream? The dream's significance has been rendered quite beautifully by Alix Pirani in her reflection that:

> If I see that young man's dream as a collective-unconscious dream for a renascent Jewish spiritual need for meaning, then I would say that the Goddess is in that dream: She comes in the shape of the arguing woman, the Queen who needs to be married to her partner the King, but feels it can't happen under the control of the patriarch, the Chief, who ignores Her voice and Her wisdom. And when she is ignored, the context continues to be that of a spiritually dead people. But 'dead people' is a phrase acquiesced in by the Chief, whose status is disturbingly linked with the holocaust of His chosen people. The Goddess is showing signs of life. And the dream, like most significant dreams, is telling us about dreaming itself, asking us to take it seriously as a message from the soul that is there to shift and question the controlling frameworks of conscious thought. That, for me, is the Shekhinah in action – Her way of being present for us as a mediator, soul, psyche.[6]

The Shekhinah is the divine energy which we all have the possibility of experiencing and which can lead us forward. This cosmic principle is, traditionally, manifest in each human soul. Its concern is our personal growth, our development, our change as human beings.

When I look around at the Jewish world I recognize how hard it is for Jewish men in particular – the men who by and large still lead the Jewish religious and secular institutions – to heed this inner voice, this inner guide, our intuitive helper. Yet the dream suggests that when we fail to hear her voice, or ignore her voice within us, we die. A living death. A little like many Jews experience their own identity – or lack of it.

But we can recognize too that the traditional domination of the Jewish world by 'Logos' unbalances us all – men and women alike. It is not just Jewish men who can be manipulative and egocentric, dominating and authoritarian. It is not just Jewish men whose intellects enjoy having answers, possessing truths, whose mind and will and logic can come to predominate in the personality. To be ambitious and greedy, to enjoy judging, owning, using, to have to be right, to want our own way, to be detached and aloof – these are not only 'masculine' qualities. We all know it well: our destructive capacities are enormous.

Let me finish by returning to the metaphor. The Shekhinah is still restless. She is wandering and in exile. The Shekhinah still weeps for the exile of the Jewish people – even in their homeland – but she weeps too for our exile from our own true home, our inner Jewish identity.

We are in exile as Jews from our real selves. Our redemption can come only from the reintegration of the assertive, organizing, 'halachic', and reflective, imaginative, 'aggadic' energies within us. Intellect and feeling, mind and soul – together in our bodies. This is our responsibility, individually and collectively. It is clear to me that the future of Judaism depends upon this work. When we lose the mystery, the wonder, the excitement, the pain of our own search to hear God's voice within us, then our identity becomes distorted, and eventually is lost.

Like God, we are One and yet are divided. To become as conscious as possible of the divine interplay between our own, for want of better words, 'masculine' and 'feminine' sides, is to recognize that within our essential individuality there is duality. In the end, the struggle to find our own Jewish identity becomes both a reflection of, and a part of, that eternal drama, the redemption of God: the reuniting of the Shekhinah, the Queen, with her partner *Avinu Malkenu*, our Father, our King.

May it come speedily, and in our days.

NOTES

1 See H. Cooper (ed.), *Soul Searching: Studies in Judaism and Psychotherapy*, SCM Press, 1988, pp. 167 and 203.
2 This dream was first recorded in the above volume (p. 230) in my essay 'Aspects of the Jewish Unconscious'.
3 These lines are at the centre of a commemorative section of

the Yom Kippur (Day of Atonement) prayers concerning Jewish martyrology. See *Forms of Prayer for Jewish Worship* (Volume III – Prayers for the High Holydays), Reform Synagogues of Great Britain, 1985, pp. 499ff.

4 Sheila Shulman, 'A Radical Feminist Perspective on Judaism', *European Judaism*, Vol. 21, No. 1, Summer 1987, p. 16.

5 For a discussion on the limitations of the traditional Jungian terminology of 'masculine' and 'feminine', see Andrew Samuels, 'Gender and Psyche: Developments in Analytical Psychology', in *British Journal of Psychotherapy*, 1:1 (autumn 1984), pp. 31–49; also chapter 7 of the same author's *Jung and the Post-Jungians* (Routledge & Kegan Paul, 1985).

6 Personal communication.

THE GODDESS IN JUDAISM – AN HISTORICAL PERSPECTIVE

Asphodel P. Long

All religions start with a cosmogony, a myth that tells the worshippers how the world was formed. The first verses of the Hebrew Bible conform to this pattern. They seem quite straightforward and have provided the basis of belief among Jews and Christians for several millennia, although the Christians recast the words of Genesis to conform to their own new ideas.

In the words of Genesis, Beraishit, 'in the beginning', God created the heavens and the earth. The latter was a formless void, there was darkness 'on the face of the deep', and God's spirit moved on the waters (Genesis 1:1-2). This seems quite straightforward and, given a religious cast of thought, easy to assimilate. But here we must pause.

There is another, quite scholastically respectable, way of translating the Hebrew words. The verses would read: 'In the beginning, a number of gods ("Elohim") began to give birth to the heavens and the earth. The earth still belonged to Tohu and Bohu (goddesses of formlessness and ultimate space), and darkness was on the face of the mother creator goddess Tiamat, and a huge wind flapped its wings over the face of the water.' This translation (which will be commented on in detail in the later section on 'Goddesses in the Hebrew background') is at least as indicative of what the original might have meant as are all the interpretations and translations that have been set out until now. As will be seen, references are made to goddesses and perceptions of creation by them that appeared to be present in Hebrew culture. How different would our attitude to religion and to society be if the above interpretation or a version of it had been accepted by both Jews and Christians as a reasonable understanding of the text.

Even if a standard explanation of the Hebrew word Elohim – the gods – could be accepted – that the one God encompasses the whole – yet the concept of female deities or female aspects of deity, of the birth-giving female being associated with the birth of the heavens and the earth, of ideas of chaos and formlessness being a symbol of the totality in which creation is possible – all this would have produced enormous changes in consciousness of the relationship of women and men and both to the divine.

But it was not the case. All biblical texts are androcentric. They are written, edited and expounded by men, men concerned about male status. When women's stories and words are given, they are interpreted and judged by men.

The new method of feminist interpretation of the Bible is to redress this uneven situation. The texts are reviewed again in the light of a search for the lost female; to find her story, her own words, to attempt to understand what was happening for her and to her, to reclaim and proclaim her. The female in the divine is to be understood in this search as well as the human woman. Feminist Bible scholars have outlined their methods and rationale. For example the theologian Elisabeth Schüssler Fiorenza writes:

> Androcentric texts and linguistic reality constructions must not be mistaken as trustworthy evidence of human culture, and religion ... the text may be the message, but the message is not co-terminal with human reality and history.[1]

Bernadette Brooten, who has surveyed Jewish Hellenistic inscriptions, suggests:

> Literature composed by men is the product of men's minds and not a simple mirror image of reality. As we begin to evaluate all the sources for Jewish women's history ... a much more differentiated picture will emerge. It will then be impossible to mistake male Jewish attitudes towards women for Jewish women's history.[2]

Feminist Judith Plaskow affirms that the

> deep resistance called forth by naming the Goddess in Judaism indicates the needs she answered are still with us ... for a God who does not include Her is an idol

made in man's image ... acknowledging the many aspects of the Goddess among the names of God becomes a measure of our ability to incorporate the feminine into a monotheistic religious framework.[3]

Where feminist views have been criticized by establishment academics as speculative or subjective, Carol Christ answers their objections:

Though the notion that scholarship is objective has been criticized in ... critical, hermeneutical and other theories, radical feminist scholarship continues to be dismissed as biased, polemical, limited or confessional. This may be especially true of religious studies ... let me state very clearly that I do not propose that we abandon historical research, philosophical reflection, literary analysis or any of the other scholarly methods we have inherited ...[4]

These quotations provide the context of the research I set out in this paper. I try and look beyond the androcentrism of biblical and related texts and for sources where I can find the female, divine and human. If challenged about the question of monotheism, I can, if necessary, envisage a monotheism that sees in the One the totality of the All. In human terms the All includes women; in divine terms, I see the All had for many millennia strong acceptance of the female as deity or as an important aspect of it. That perception changed, and the result was then its banishment from history, with the female divine and human so put down, degraded, patronized and derided, obscured and reviled that only now women are beginning to be able to attempt to redress the balance. This means seeking Her out, and reviewing all material in the light of Her banishment. Where is She? We have to ask this at all points. As we do so, we open up a new perspective in history. The landscape to which we are accustomed shifts; its familiar features are still there, but the whole has taken on a new meaning.

My brief is to set out an historical perspective for the Goddess in Judaism. This is of course immediately beset with many problems. How much of what is apparent is historical? I will deal with three questions here. What do we mean, in this context, by historical? When we refer to 'the Goddess' who or what are we referring to? And lastly, when we speak of Judaism what era or kind of Judaism are we dealing with? I will set out the parameters I have chosen, otherwise I might founder in those vastly chaotic waters which are our beginning.

1 HISTORICAL PERSPECTIVE

If by history we mean something provable, I am lost already. Nothing in this context is 'provable'. I have chosen a period whose early date is about 2000 BCE and end date at about 400 CE. The first centuries provide a background in which the Hebrew religion and ultimately Judaism were born. The later date sees the Jews dispersed, the Talmud and rabbinical commentaries well under way, and a homogeneous religion established, while at the same time the mainstream Christian Church has its creed and structure well in place, and is free to spread its doctrines throughout the world.

I have used information from the various disciplines that are concerned with Bible history: exegesis, archaeology, ancient history, etc. I have invented nothing and if I have had personal insights I record them as such.

Dates

I do believe, contrary to much modern accepted wisdom, that dates are a signpost to understanding events. The Bible progresses along a line of history, and it is useful to have some dates to guide us. For those who believe the Hebrew Bible was, directly, or indirectly through prophets and scribes, written by God, no mundane eras are necessary. The rest of us are presented with mountains of contradictory material – which is likely to change, as new scholarship is presented. Taking a middle line between the various controversies, I am placing the period of the compilation of the Law and the Prophets, and possibly some of the Writings of the Hebrew Bible at about the time of Ezra, say early 400s BCE, and the actual canonization of the texts, after which nothing could be added or taken away, at about five hundred years later. This was undertaken by the rabbis at Jamnia (Javneh) who set up their religious stronghold there after the destruction of Jerusalem and its temple in 70 CE.

The events in the Bible may be dated to about 1800 BCE for the time of Abraham, 1300 for Moses and from about 900 for David and Solomon. The Assyrians conquered the northern kingdom of Israel in 721 BCE and dispersed the Israelites living there. (The riddle of what happened to them has intrigued generations and unlikely answers such as their identification with the Khasis of Russia or the British Israelites of the United Kingdom continue to be asserted.)

The southern kingdom of Judah continued under its kings until the arrival of Nebuchadnezzer of Babylon who destroyed the temple in 587 BCE and took the royal and upper classes into Exile. About thirty years later Cyrus King of Persia conquered the Babylonians and allowed the Hebrews back home.

2 THE GODDESS

It will be useful to outline some of the meanings this word holds, since it is used indiscriminately and there is no set definition. I will then give my own understanding of it:

(i) For many, the Goddess is god with an -ess. That is, She is the Supreme Being, the Ultimate, the Creator and Sustainer of the universe. Most of the attributes of God belong to Her although on the whole, despite some texts to the contrary, she is not considered warlike. She may also be felt as a personal deity, available for support and prayer.

(ii) In much modern pagan and wiccan thought and practice, the Goddess is teamed with the God. She is 'prima inter pares'. Both are worshipped together but she is held to be foremost. Goddesses and gods from the mythology of the world are called upon; often the deities associated with one's own country are particularly to be invoked. Such deities are intimately associated with nature and the round of the seasons.

(iii) In feminist spirituality 'the Goddess' is often used to mean the idea of female deity. Sometimes, it may introduce the idea into monotheism as the female aspect of God. On the other hand it may mean any goddess from religion or mythology or any number of goddesses. The classical description of Her as 'many-named' sits well here. She is all or any of the Goddesses of the past or the current polytheisms as well as a reclaimed goddess of today. She is not only a transcendent creating deity, but also immanent and part of Nature and the world. In fact, for many, she is Nature. Women are her representatives because of her birth-giving ability, but that is not all. The words of Isis inscribed on the temple at Sais in ancient Egypt sum her up for today's followers: 'I am all that is, was or ever will be.' (It is quite possible, date-wise, that Moses was familiar with this inscription, which appears in similar form concerning Jahweh in Exodus 3:14, 'I am that I am,' and becomes the holy unspeakable name of God.) In general understanding the trajectory is

31

perceived firstly of a creator mother who conceives a son autonomously; this son becomes her lover and eventually steals her power and overcomes her. Then as this happens a concept of domination in society and over nature takes the place of a previous concept of participation and egalitarianism. This leads to a position of male supremacy and the downgrading of the female in every aspect.

In my own opinion researching and reclaiming information and developing insight concerning goddesses assists women (and possibly men if they are willing) to overthrow their conditioning. Women begin to feel stronger and inspired to overcome their feelings of guilt and inferiority. They feel better about themselves and can demand and take a more satisfactory place in the world, at the same time renewing and being refreshed by spiritual wholeness.

Because I come from an Orthodox Jewish background (though never in adult life being 'observant'), I choose to research the goddesses in the background of my own culture. If I refer to 'the goddess' without a particular name attached it will refer to the idea of a female aspect of deity, a facet of the whole.

Religious practices concerning the goddess today include celebration of seasonal and calendar festivals. Classical and area myths and rituals are 're-invented' in the light of today's needs.

3 JUDAISM

Since I am dealing with so vast a period, I have chosen to call 'Hebrew' the period before the rebuilding of the second temple (i.e. pre 400 BCE) and Jewish or to do with Judaism what came after it. I am aware this is open to challenge, but it is as good a working definition as any I know.

Finally in this section, it is important to say I shall not at any time use the phrase 'Judaeo-Christian'. Although it appears to be convenient, in fact there is now growing acceptance of the understanding that it is both inaccurate and imperialistic. Inaccurate because Christianity owes a great debt to Hellenistic cultures as well as to Judaism, and imperialistic because it implies a progression from Judaism to Christianity with the latter taking over from the former. This is not the case. Thus I shall refer to the 'Hebrew Bible' rather than the 'Old Testament'. The New Testament seems to be self-descriptive and as far as I know quite acceptable.

The Hebrew Bible is composed of material from different dates and sources. Some were ancient when they were written down and preserved through an oral tradition, or through more ancient documents; these are usually narratives, hymns, poems and oracles. They may owe a good deal to the background cultures. On the other hand, laws, commandments, strictures and a system of reward and punishment and above all the covenant between God and His people appear to be written by the later authors and editors, whose main concern was to impose male supremacy through their version of monotheism. These editors are often called the Deuteronomists. It is their struggle against the influence of the Goddess in the popular religion that forms much of their Biblical material.

But however hard they tried to banish Her, they were not successful. The concept of a goddess or goddesses in Israel runs through the whole of the Hebrew Bible. We will try and trace it, starting with the background female deities of the ancient Near Eastern people, through the concept of a Goddess as wife or consort to God (Jahweh), then the ambivalence of the wisdom figure (Hochma/Sophia), to the Hellenistic Gnostic world and the birth of Christianity.

There, first subsumed into Jesus Christ, she emerges sometimes as the Holy Spirit within the Trinity and then as the Church, which is totally male-directed.

Finally in much popular understanding she may become identified with the Virgin Mary. It is this long journey of the Goddess that we are beginning to travel now.

GODDESSES IN THE HEBREW BACKGROUND

The Patriarch Abraham is said to have lived in 'Ur of the Chaldees'. It is from there he is called by God to leave his birthplace and travel to the land of Canaan, and it is he with whom God made his covenant. It is clear, therefore, that before this call Abraham and Abraham's parents worshipped the deities of their land, and certainly his father is quoted as so doing (Joshua 24:2). Who were these gods and goddesses? Perhaps they bear some relationship to those that Rachel, his grandson Jacob's wife, hid beneath her when she left her father's home (Genesis 31:19, 34-5).

We are able to gain some idea about them and to make informed guesses. In the last century or so archaeologists have discovered substantial material concerning the religions of the ancient Near East, and have provided the basis of research for scholars of many other disciplines. Raphael Patai is among those who have researched and commented widely on the female deities who entered the consciousness of the Hebrew people.[5] Here I will only draw attention to the main primary sources of information. These are the Babylonian epics of about 1800–1500 BCE; the Ras Shamra texts from ancient Ugarit, c. 1500 BCE; and a mass of Egyptian papyri which date from the second millennium until the first years of the Christian centuries. In all of them we meet goddesses who bear a very close relationship to female divinities mentioned – usually in a hostile way in the Bible, although one may not always recognize them at first sight.

(i) Babylonian epics

Variously called Babylonia, Chaldea and Mesopotamia, this is the 'country between the rivers' – the Tigris and Euphrates – fertile land on which it was easy to live and on which great civilizations had been built. The Laws of Hammurabi and the work of Chaldean astronomers and astrologers are typical examples, and in particular there are a number of long poems, epics, written on clay in the cuneiform script, which record the cosmogony and the religious mythology of the people there.

Two of these poems are the Epic of Creation and the Epic of Gilgamesh. It is from the former that the figure of Tiamat is drawn. Here are its first lines:

> When on high were not raised the heavens
> And also below on earth a plant had not grown up
> The abyss had not broken its boundaries
> The chaos Tiamat was the producing mother of all of them.

George Smith, the original translator of the cuneiform tablets, believed that Tiamat was the living principle of the sea and chaos.[6] She is depicted on reliefs and in drawings as a vast dragon, and is shown rearing herself on two legs, when she confronts Marduk, her grandson who kills her. The epic recounts: 'She raised herself to her full height and planted her feet firmly on the ground.' Another depiction of her shows enormous wings. She is thus the primaeval dragon, living under water, able to walk on land, able to fly and possibly to breathe fire. The formlessness with which we are confronted symbolizes, for me, a wholeness of totality, of land, sea, air and fire, the four elements of creation. It includes all there is waiting to be born, whether the material or the inspirational.

Tiamat is also referred to as a sea serpent who, in the course of the struggle with Marduk who wants to gain from her the Tablets of Destiny which she holds, creates out of herself all sorts of monsters, mixtures of animal and human and extraordinary shapes of creatures.

The epic goes on to relate how Marduk with the help of his friends blows her belly apart with a mighty wind, and then cuts her into pieces. Each part of her body becomes a different part of the cosmos and is ruled over by Marduk and the other gods. This defeat is proclaimed as the triumph of order and beginning of creation.

Tiamat's name is recalled in Genesis 1:2 where the Hebrew 'Tehom' is usually translated as 'the deep'; it will be recalled that Tiamat is the sea goddess living in the deep. It was her home and in it life itself was waiting to be born.

In addition to the Genesis resonance, there are many passages in the Bible where God celebrates his victory over the dragon, the sea monster and the abyss.[7] Indeed, there is a school of thought which believes that the Babylonian New Year Festival which celebrated Marduk's triumph over Tiamat was the origin of the Hebrew and then Jewish New Year Festival where God in the liturgy for the occasion still celebrates his victory over chaos.

And what was meant by chaos? It is extraordinary that today the notion of chaos, so long condemned, is coming into the foreground of many branches of science as a positive description of basic natural forces. It seems to have an affinity with the 'chaos' of the ancients, then presented as a birth-giving female with all the necessities of creation within her. There also seems to be an appreciation of the relationship of creation to vast emptiness. For a long time the debate about the Genesis creation story included questions as to whether God created the universe *ex nihilo* – from nothing – or put into order something that was already there. The mentions of Tohu and Bohu (Genesis 1:2), usually translated as 'void and without form', indicate there might be a reference to these goddesses of formlessness and ultimate space; it has been throught that Bohu at least may be identified with the great Mesopotamian goddess Bau, another creating mother of the universe, and one who is linked to the 'Mother of the Physicians', Gula. In this association we may see an idea not only of creation but of maintenance and sustenance. Gula's temples in Mesopotamia were arranged as hospitals, and it was part of religious practice in her honour to study medicine and heal the sick. She is the source of medical knowledge. I see a connection between Gula and Wisdom, also the source of understanding and a teacher to humanity. Many texts refer to Gula-Bau as well as to each alone.

Tiamat's form as a dragon needs further comment. Dragons and serpents are interchangeable in ancient literature as well as more modern folklore. The Epic of Creation is an early example of a young male person killing an older dragon monster, which conventional wisdom presents as evil. Even today who is a 'dragon' but a powerful older woman whom younger men would like to be rid of? In the dragon and serpent as the symbol of evil we are naturally reinforced by the story of Eve and the serpent in the Garden of Eden. When we meet the serpent she is coiled on the Tree of Knowledge of Good and Evil which has been forbidden to the first couple. The serpent can be seen as knowing all the mysteries; for a long time they have presented an ambivalent problem to commentators. Serpents have remained depositories of knowledge of medicine and have symbolized long life and even immortality as well as indicating temptation and evil. In the Eden story I suggest the serpent is a form of Tiamat who is offering Eve knowledge, good and evil as it might be used; the knowledge that is her inheritance which she can share with her partner if she wishes. It is the power which this gives that is denied, and the outcome is a double defeat. Not only is Eve deprived of the ancient powers that are hers by inheritance, but God puts enmity between her and the serpent: a clear example of the patriarchal policy of dividing women from each other, particularly the young from the old, and causing them to depend on their male partner rather than on female support. We can see in this story a paradigm for the situation where male 'specialists' have deprived human female wisdom of any authority.

To return to Genesis 1:2. Who is it that 'flaps its wings like a bird' over the face of Tiamat? The Hebrew word for this action is *merachepet*. It is variously translated as 'move', or 'hover', the later being more accurate as it gives the impression of vast wings.

Who has wings? The very first name to come to mind is Lilith. There is a statue of her dated to about 1500 BCE where she is a naked woman with spreading wings, she has the feet of a bird and is attended by owls. This is contemporary with a story about her in Mesopotamian literature,[8] in which she is a 'dark maid' who flies off on her wings to the desert.

But in the Genesis account Lilith is not mentioned, although much later the rabbis revealed a story about her in the same time and place, perhaps based on ancient material, that has found much resonance, and which we shall reach in a short while. In Genesis 1:2 it is *ruach elohim*, translated as the 'spirit of God' or alternatively as 'mighty wind', which hovers or moves over the waters. But what is *ruach*? *Ruach* is the Hebrew word for spirit or wind, and like the Latin *anima* or the Greek *pneuma* it can be used for either. Now, whose name tells us that she is also spirit or wind? None other than Lilith. The word Lilith is connected with two root words – Layil, the Hebrew for night, and Lil, Sumerian (*c.* 3000 BCE) 'wind' or 'breath' or 'spirit'. Traditionally, until the information from Sumer came to light, Lilith was always associated with night and darkness. There is only one mention of her name as such in the Hebrew Bible. It is Isaiah 34:8–14. The prophet declares:

> *The land shall become burning pitch*
> *Thorns shall grow over its strongholds*
> *It shall be the haunt of jackals*
> *Yea the night hag shall there alight*
> *and find for herself a resting place.*

(RSV)

Very few translations provide the word Lilith itself. 'Night hag' in the RSV replaces the older 'screech owl' in the King James version. The New English Bible gives 'night-jar', RV of 1881 suggests 'night monster'. The Latin vulgate of the fourth century CE from which most Christian translations stem says Lamia – these are the Greek 'dirty goddesses'. The Moffat translation uses 'vampires' (plural). French Lilith is 'le spectre de la nuit' and German Lutheran translates her as *der Kobold* (masculine), a spirit or goblin. The Jerusalem Bible is to be commended for actually using her name.

Apart from the last, all these translations have relied on the concept of Lilith as to do with night. But if one accepts the other meaning then Lilith is spirit or air or mighty wind and it is she who hovers over the face of Mother Tiamat, perhaps in her form as a woman and bird. So much has been written about her. She is the ultimate demon of Jewish tradition, most particularly to women in childbirth and a danger to their new-born infants. People have been taught to fear her. She also became Queen of the Witches in Christian tradition.

But I believe her to be the Lady of the air and wind and the spirit, the living breath of life. She has all knowledge. The rabbinic eleventh-century tale of her in the Genesis story is that during sexual intercourse with Adam – for she was, it seems, his first wife – she refused the 'missionary' position saying, 'I am made of the same earth as you' (and here there may even be a reference to female Adamah, Hebrew for earth, and possibly a lost Mother Earth Goddess). She called on the magic and holy name of God, freed herself from Adam and flew off – yes, flew – into the desert. How did Lilith know the powerful name of God when Adam could only ask God to help him? I suggest it is because it is she who is the Wisdom figure, the spirit.

The presence of Lilith, named or otherwise, in the creation story links her with Hochma who will be discussed below. Patriarchy has turned her into queen of the demons, killer of children, particularly to be feared by mothers in childbirth. And that sums it up; instead of the creatrix she has been made the destroyer. The symbol of women's wisdom and power, she has become a source of evil to be feared most particularly by women. She represents to us our innermost herstory. In reclaiming Her, we women throw off and pour away for ever the poison about ourselves, our so-called inferiority, our evil inner selves, our guilt. On reclaiming Lilith we reclaim the breath of life that emerges as we give birth to our children, to our works of all kind; we reclaim our wisdom, our knowledge, our power, our autonomy.[9]

Back to the Garden of Eden and the Babylonian epics. In the Epic of Gilgamesh the eponymous hero sets out to seek eternal life. He reaches the Paradise Garden which he is allowed to enter because of the divine blood inherited from his mother Ninsun. He meets in the garden the Goddess Siduri-Sabatu, who is able to provide the 'gift of life'.

The Paradise Garden is of 'dazzling beauty'. The Goddess is sitting by a vine which is the garden's centrepiece, and she is also 'by the throne of the sea'. She is addressed as 'Goddess of Wisdom, Genius of Life'. She is referred to as 'Keeper of the fruit of life'.[10]

Obviously the connections with the Garden of Eden are very clear. We have a goddess, actually keeper of the fruit of life, sitting by a throne of the sea, in the garden. Even the vine is a strong symbol which is repeated many times in both Hebrew Bible and New Testament (Jesus says, 'I am the true vine'), often also indicating God's strength or God's people. The association with the sea is reminiscent of Tiamat and also bears a close relation to the goddesses to be found in the next group of texts we shall discuss.

(ii) Ras Shamra texts

In 1929 a body of texts was found at a place called Ras Shamra in northern Syria, the site of ancient Ugarit, home of the Hittites. Dated to about 1500 BCE, they are composed of descriptions of the life and religion of the Canaanites, including legends, myths and religious invocations, hymns, etc.[11]

Ras Shamra religious texts are usually interpreted as myths which control creation, and whose enactment ritually helps keep creation in being. The proper round of the seasons, the arrival of rain, the changing of light to dark and back again, the unending miracle of new life and its nurture, all these are enacted in such ritual myths. The battle with the sea is a major theme.

In these myths we meet major figures who previously were known to us almost entirely from their appearances in the Hebrew Bible. The supreme Deity is named El, a word which until the time of the discovery had been thought merely to indicate 'God'. One of the major deities is his wife the Lady Asherah. This is the Asherah who appears continuously in Bible narrative. Until Ras Shamra there was a good deal of controversy as to whether she was a goddess as such or either the symbol of a goddess in the form of a tree or pole or wooden statue or else merely one of these which the 'heathen' worshipped without its actually representing a deity in her own right. Now it is clear that she was an ancient goddess, mother of the Lord Baal and the Lady Anat, and chief of a pantheon of enormously powerful female divinities. It is to them that Baal must turn for help in conducting his everyday business. He cannot obtain a house to live in without his mother's assistance. More importantly, when he is killed by the figure of Death it is his sister Anat who brings him to life again. Another goddess, Shaqat, restores a dead child to life. It is the goddesses who have this power, not the gods.

The controversy concerning the Asherim as trees or poles seems to be resolved easily. That these represented her can be in no doubt. It is even possible that the May Pole has links with the Asherim. The tree is widely known to be a symbol of life and a source of and shelter for life. The Bible records the destruction of a large number of trees and groves sacred to her, in an effort to drive out her worship. Thus Asherah was both the goddess and the tree or bough representing her. There was no need for the prophets to call for the destruction of trees in a desert land where every tree was important, unless they believed that with the trees they were exterminating the goddess.

The Ras Shamra stories and the Biblical texts have many similarities and have been analysed widely. Certainly the hostility in the Bible to the goddesses is reflected in the prominent position they held in the Canaanite pantheon. However, it is also clear that they became as much divinities of the Hebrews as of the earlier people. Baal, Lord of the weather in the Ras Shamra myths, is found in the Bible often as the god in opposition to Jahweh.

Asherah's particular powers can be deduced from another well known Bible story, that of the contest between the prophet Elijah and the 'four hundred priests of Baal and four hundred priests of Asherah' (1 Kings 18:19). Elijah is successful at producing the magic that Baal's priests cannot, and they are killed by the people around. Nothing is said about the fate of Asherah's priests. Why not? Several suggestions come to mind. Perhaps that while the people did not mind killing Baal's servants, those of Asherah were too holy and could not be touched; or that Asherah was too well loved to be offended. Some scholars suggest that the introduction of Asherah's priests to the story is a later interpolation, and the editors forgot to say what happened to them. The suggested reason for the interpolation is that the editors wanted to make Elijah's victory all the more conclusive of the power of Jahweh. But the latter idea seems to me to be unsatisfactory, and I prefer the earlier ones, since they would explain why Asherah's priests not only were spared but why there was silence about it – since the Bible editors would not want to draw attention to Asherah's power with the people.

Moreover, my feeling is that she may provide an answer to the much-asked query concerning the choice of knowledge of good and evil as the forbidden tree in the Garden of Eden. Can there be a connection with Asherah, was she the mother of all and source of wisdom, that tree whose fruit which above all was not to be eaten? It has to be mentioned here that Biblical authors often used Ashtaroth instead of Asherah, a word which incorporates the word 'shame', and she is also often referred to as 'abomination'. The hostility which was heaped upon her by these religious leaders is balanced by the persistence of her worshippers who refused to allow her to be dismissed from their religion.

The position of the Lady Anat within the Ras Shamra texts is a very powerful one, and has been analysed widely. Cassuto's book provides a sense of the dimension of strength and longevity, the passion and the inspiration, the death-dealing and the cleansing powers of this goddess, whom we will meet again in a later setting. Among the many deities among the Canaanites who are reflected in some way in the Hebrew Bible, I also draw attention to Paghat, goddess of the sun. It is often thought that if there were goddesses, then they were associated with the moon, and the sun represented the masculine deity. However, the Hittites have left us many artefacts indicating that the sun is seen by them as a goddess. In today's Turkey there are numerous depictions of her while their ancient literature is full of her praise. Here is one such verse in praise of Paghat which has later resonances:

> She rises early in the morning
> She sweeps the dew from the grasses
> She carries the clouds on her shoulders
> She instructs the course of the stars.[12]

Who else rises early in the morning? We are reminded of the panegyric concerning a good wife in the well known chapter of Proverbs 31. This good woman rises while it is yet dark to prepare food for her household. There, the goddess has become demythologized: she is now an ordinary woman – but is she so ordinary? In the Proverbs passage we find signs of unusual strength and power. In addition to providing food and working with textiles, she is able to go out and buy a field, plant a vineyard. She 'girds her loins with strength and makes her arms strong.' Above all, 'She opens her mouth with Wisdom.'

The good woman still has some aura of goddesses about her, from Paghat to Hochma – whom we meet shortly and where we will also discuss the heritage from Egypt. In the meantime we will follow Asherah from her Canaanite to her Hebrew domain.

(iii) Jahweh and his consort

The publication in 1979 of a paper entitled 'Did Jahweh have a Consort?'[13] by Israeli archaeologist Ze'ev Meshel brought to a head long-standing disputes by scholars on this subject and opened up to the informed public a changing vista of Jewish religious history and tradition.

Conventionally, Judaism is identified with an absolute monotheism which was to a large extent inherited also by Christianity. Such monotheism is centred on God, Jahweh

(Jehovah) who is always referred to in the masculine gender. How *could* God have a consort? Such an idea must surely be totally pagan and be dismissed out of hand. But no. Current opinion has it that the ancient goddess Asherah was worshipped not only in the setting of the Canaanite religion as wife of El and mother of Baal and Anat, but quite disparately, as the consort of Jahweh. This would have been part of what is called the 'popular religion' of the Hebrews and it is the one that the Deuteronomists and their successors were trying so hard and so unsuccessfully to stamp out.

Because this appears to be such a revolutionary idea it will be helpful to outline some of the material associated with it.

Meshel's excavations took place in 1975 and 1976 at Kuntillet Ajrud, which he describes as a 'remote desert station in the wilderness of North Sinai'. At a crossroads he found the remains of a large building which he believes was used for religious purposes, possibly by travellers on country routes, and was inhabited and kept in order by guardians of the shrine who lived a religious life there. The major find was a collection of ancient Hebrew and Phoenician inscriptions on walls and stone vessels, and there were also spectacular drawings on two large storage jars (*pithoi*). It was assumed that the community was able to survive in this desert region because of the proximity of wells in the vicinity. Meshel remarks that the modern Arabic name means 'solitary hill of the wells'. The site was dated to about the eighth century BCE.

The inscriptions that caused the explosion of interest were found in the bench room and two adjoining side rooms. Including both the name El and the name Jahweh, some of the inscriptions were written on the jamb of the entrance – recalling possibly the instruction in Deuteronomy 6:9 ('you shall write them on the doorposts of your house', which also has become the basis of the *mezuzah* in Judaism). They blessed Jahweh and asked to be protected by him and – this the key surprise – by 'Asherato', mostly translated as 'his Asherah'. Some scholars contend that the word can be translated as naming Asherah in her own right. Beneath the words are drawings of a tree and of a cow with a calf. Nearby are other drawings, particularly one very clear 'tree of life' flanked by two ibexes. Again, 'May you be blessed by Jahweh and Asherato' is inscribed on a jar nearby.

Just as scholars were getting down to an analysis of these finds and their possible meanings, a similar inscription was published from another source. This was a site called Khirbet-el-Qom which has been identified as the Biblical Makkedah.

Following earlier communications by various scholars, it was only in 1979 that J. Naveh published the inscriptions and in 1984 that Z. Zevit expressed an opinion on their meaning. The inscription indicates that it was written by Uriyahu (the name includes a reference to God) who calls for a blessing from 'Jahweh my guardian and his Asherah'. The date is similar to that of Kuntillet Ajrud.

A great deal of research from many disciplines is trying to establish the meaning and implications of these finds and others like them. The linguistic and epigraphic problems of the inscriptions, the cultic or other meaning of the drawings, the symbols that they express, all are a matter of growing discussion which now tends to look outwards and backwards to relevant previous material that was not understood. Traditionalists may want to argue that 'his Asherah' may still be a 'cultic symbol'. Previously an 'Asherah' was identified with a tree or pole, but when one sees the blossoming tree of life, and also considers that the cow and calf together are always a symbol of the mother goddess in the ancient Near East, it is difficult to avoid the conclusion that the presence of the goddess Asherah is conveyed, and that she and Jahweh are worshipped together and seen as complementary to each other. Even the name Uriyahu would show that the writer was a practising Hebrew, and the supposition that the shrine was inhabited by a group of guardians would indicate that it was supported by enough people to keep it viable.

From Jahweh and his Asherah we turn back to a Biblical married couple, Hosea and his unfaithful wife (Hosea 2). This narrative appears to be a tale of a kind husband who forgives his erring wife, but who turns into God speaking to Israel. There is an obvious parallel but in fact the symbols in the story indicate strongly that the wife is Asherah the goddess, whom God will forgive only when she has yielded her divine powers to him.

This narrative, which starts as a moral tale about the prophet and his apparently unfaithful wife, alters to the relationship of God and his people, who conventionally in Deuteronomic terms are husband and wife. When husband Hosea suddenly turns into God, are we not entitled to conclude that God is speaking to his 'erring' wife, Asherah? She is after all addressed as a 'harlot', the term used by the Deuteronomists to describe a goddess. Her fig trees and vines, well known symbols of the mother goddess, are to be laid waste; her way of life in celebrating nature and seasons owes much to her ancient background.

Another account of Jahweh with a female partner or consort is contained in a set of papyri from Egypt, from a town called Elephantine and dated at about 400 BCE. A Jewish colony lived there which paid its dues to the temple in Jerusalem – this indicates it was accepted as part of the mainstream Jewish community. The surprise is the name of the temple which is recorded as having sent the money – Anat/Jaho. Jaho is a form of Jahweh and Anat the goddess is known to us from the Hittite Ras Shamra texts and elsewhere. What is not in doubt is that the temple of Anat/Jaho was a Jewish temple. It links Jahweh with a goddess, they are complementary and worshipped together and it is reasonable to suggest that they are partners or consorts. This view is strengthened by the records of other temples in that area. They are referred to as those of Anat Bethel and Asham Bethel.

Bethel is familiar to us. The Hebrew words mean House of God, and we first meet a Bethel in the Bible when Jacob the Patriarch has spoken with God and anoints the stone on which he had slept when God visited him (Genesis 28:19, 22; 35:14–15). The stone is holy because God had been present in it or on it. However, a 'Bethel' is not confined to this, the God of the Bible. The Greek *baetyl* – a similar word – is a meteorite or black stone which falls from heaven, having within it the essence of the goddess, the queen of Heaven. The temples of Elephantine appear to be worshipping her as well as Jaho/Anat; and this is not surprising in view of the Queen of Heaven story in the book of Jeremiah (44:15–19; 7:17–18). Who is the Queen of Heaven? When we meet her the prophet denounces the people for worshipping her. He tells them that their wickedness is responsible for their current disaster. Both women and men reply that when they burned incense and baked cakes for the Queen of Heaven no such trouble fell upon them. They recall that when they lived in Jerusalem the 'children gathered sticks, the men lit fires and the women made the cakes' for the Queen of Heaven.

For me this cameo shows that it was not only the women but the whole family and whole communities who joined in Her worship, and it is important to emphasize that these were Hebrews and not Canaanites or other 'heathen'.

The Queen of Heaven is unnamed and it has often been suggested that she is naturally the consort of the 'king of heaven' as well as being a major deity in her own right. Certainly her longevity is remarkable and is worth noting in our story.

A ritual of baking cakes for the Queen of Heaven, there named as Ishtar (Astarte), is available to us from Babylonian records of about 2000 BCE. A hymn to Ishtar includes the lines:

O Ishtar I have made a preparation of milk, cake, grilled bread and salt, hear me and be kind.[14]

Another hymn to Ishtar prays:

O Ishtar I look on your face, and I make an offering of pure milk with a baked cake.[15]

A similar sacred practice is recorded again from a Phoenician settlement in North Africa. A list has been found which sets out the wages to be paid to various work people, on it is inscribed: 'wages to the bakers of cakes for the Queen of Heaven'.[16] In Tunisia today there is a site which still contains a temple to the Queen of Heaven and there are stones there with inscriptions to her.

Such inscriptions may be of a very much later date, since well into the Christian era Bishop Augustine of Hippo, in North Africa – the same Augustine who 'invented' the idea of original sin – thundered against women whom he described as going out with filthy dancing to the Queen of Heaven.

This title eventually became attached to the Virgin Mary, who interestingly enough was worshipped in the early centuries by a Christian sect denounced as heretical, who baked cakes in her honour. They were called the Collyridians, a name based on the Greek word *collyridos*, which means a small cake or bread roll.

This is a long continuum of cakes for the Queen of Heaven from the wayside desert shrine at Kuntillet Ajrud. In Meshel's description of the settlement there he observed that there were two large ovens for whose size he could see no real reason. In the course of an interview he kindly gave this writer, he agreed that they certainly could have been used to bake ritual cakes.

Although the path we have followed has been one of jumps and crevasses, yet there seems to be a very strong connecting path. The Lady Asherah, a Canaanite goddess, became part of the religion of the Hebrews and appears to have been worshipped as the partner or consort of Jahweh. She is not one particular goddess figure but rather a female deity who can be identified by various names, including that of Queen of Heaven. Her worship continued over several millennia, always condemned by the leadership and always retained by the popular will. That God did have a consort or, understood another way, that the one God included the female with the male and could be approached as either or both was a tenacious belief of the Hebrews. It seems also that while the Hebrew leadership denied Asherah and her sisters, they were open to a female concept of deity in a form more satisfying, yet more perplexing and they had to find new ways of solving the problem for them of the female in the divine.

THE WISDOM GODDESS

Hochma

Throughout the Biblical period and then far beyond it a divine female presence has been continually present in Hebrew and Jewish consciousness. This is Hochma, Wisdom.

Everything to do with her is mysterious and paradoxical. In the Bible she is always female. The rabbinic Kabbalists a thousand years later turned her into a male *sephira* on the Tree of Life. She is continually being sought and found, lost and found; she ascends and descends; she finds her place in Israel, she can find no place in Israel. She is the divine female companion of God eternal with him before creation, and is herself involved in the cosmos as creator, nurturer, teacher and artificer. She acts as intermediary between God and humans and is willing to share herself with them and with the world. She may be married to God, or to selected men, and she may be the mother of the created world. Human beings must follow her rules if they are to succeed in this life, and also possibly to partake in an afterlife with God. It was she who helped God to create the universe and she knows all its secrets. She moves through it and orders it well.[17]

All these descriptions of Wisdom are to be found in the Bible or in the Apocrypha. At the same time, she is also portrayed as a woman whom men must seek to marry, she has sex appeal, she can behave like a spurned woman, and she has a sister or counterpart named Folly who boasts that she has knowledge better than Wisdom can offer. She has been described by commentators as a bonus for upper-class men and there is no doubt that she has been subject in the Bible to a great deal of sexist description.

Jewish writers found a solution to the problem of her female divinity and to some of the contradictions by identifying her with the Torah, and this became the normative view in Judaism.

I will take a few only of these Wisdom themes to try and establish a picture of her. Her precedence over creation is found, for example, in Proverbs 3:19, Psalm 104:24. The Lord founded the earth by means of Hochma; he needed to search her out and discover her ways, and he made all his works through Hochma. She is the pre-existent cosmic order that is the source of the world and sustains it. If the casual reader feels that all that is being said is that the Lord used Hochma – or Wisdom – for his creative work, then turn to the famous passage of Proverbs 8:22–30. She is, firstly, created by God, 'the first of his acts of old'. Yet she is there 'from the beginning' before the world is made, and what is more – she was beside him and was daily his delight.

In what capacity was she beside him? The Hebrew is *amon* and reputations have been built and lost on interpretation of this word. Major English language translations give different versions 'as one brought up with him' (AV), 'master workman' (RSV).

Various interpreters have added 'nurseling' or even 'nurse' and finally 'connecting post'. The latter is not as remarkable as it may first appear, since Christianity relies on Paul's description of Jesus as one who has taken on the whole of Wisdom and is a connecting link between all creation and the divine (Collossians 1:17).

This set of meanings gives an indication of how extraordinary the description of Hochma actually is. She is a transcendent – or the transcendent cosmic force of the universe – yet she may be a little child. The meaning 'master craftsman' was used by the Greek translators of the Hebrew Bible in the second century BCE – the septuagint, known as LXX, where they used the Greek word *technites* to describe one of Wisdom's characteristics. It will be remembered that in Proverbs 9:1 Hochma 'builds her house with seven pillars', although one Israeli modern commentator says that she did not, that it was done by the wise men of Babylon.[18]

Religious thinkers concerned to expunge all ideas of female divinity from the Jewish religion solved the problem by making Hochma the Torah. Even then her effect could not altogether be dismissed. The Torah itself became identified with Hochma. The written texts of the Law, the first five books of the Bible, took on a sacral character, even a mystic relationship with God. The Talmud tells us that the Torah 'existed before the creation of the world' although prior to the creation of time it is a creation of God. The Torah is the 'eternal now', it existed before time and is not encompassed by time and is the eternal present for those who fear God. It is above history and the action of God in history. The Torah is older than creation and was originally written in black letters of flame on a white ground of fire. God held counsel with it at the creation of the world 'since it was wisdom itself'. This Wisdom is safely, for the pious, banished into the Torah and yet she illumines it with her own divine presence.

Hochma, then, in this religious system which became normative Judaism, is what is left when the divine is taken from her. She is a woman, and one who is viewed with much ambivalence, yet she retains something of the divine which men (that is male human beings) want to use for their own purposes.

This trajectory of thought becomes very clear in the Book of Wisdom of Solomon (BWS), part of the Apocrypha and written in Greek. The author is assumed to be a first-century Jew in Alexandria, centre of the Hellenistic world, where over one million Jews are said to have been living at the time. There they are exposed to all the temptations and attractions of Hellenism, and the author seeks to bring them back to their traditional faith and to demonstrate that their rich cultural heritage has much in common with that of the Greeks. The Wisdom of BWS is now Sophia, Greek translation of Hochma, and it is the Hochma of the Hebrew Bible who is being described in the book.

The Sophia of BWS is either identical with God, is the Spirit of God or is an autonomous divine figure who herself 'protected the first formed father of the world' and led the children of Israel out of Egypt and who at once was responsible for the salvation of the Hebrew and Jewish people. She is the source of all learning and understanding. She taught the author, the Sage (pseudo-Solomon):

> to know the structure of the world and the activity of the
>   elements ...
> the cycles of the years and the constellations of the stars ...
> the nature of animals and the tempers of wild beasts ...
> the varieties of plants and the virtues of roots.
>
> (BWS 7:17–22)

She instructs him in 'what is secret and what is manifest' and she is described as the fashioner (*technites*) of all things – the last word linking her with the *amon*, the master craftsman of Proverbs 8:30 (see p. 47). It indicates she was the co-fashioner, with God, of the universe. In the same passage Sophia is

described in a series of adjectives which emphasize that all that is good is within her.

She is intelligent, but holy, all powerful, overseeing all, beneficent, humane, she pervades and penetrates all things. She is a reflection of eternal light and 'though she is but one, she can do all things, and while remaining in herself she can renew all things ... she reaches mightily from one end of the world to the other, and she orders all things well' (BWS 7: 21–8:1).

In this description we have, perhaps for the only time openly in Judaism, a laudation of the female divinity who is part of the essence of the religion. She is an initiate in the knowledge of God and an associate with his works (8:4), she is praised as identical with God or even as God Herself. She springs out of a Hebrew context; she is described in detail and she is there for the Jews to worship and to follow her ways.

At the same time, the Book of Wisdom of Solomon is shot through with contradictions about her. Sophia suddenly changes. The Sage

> 'determined to take her to live with me ...
> Because of her I shall have glory among the multitudes ...
> Because of her ... I shall govern peoples and nations shall be
> subject to me
> Dread monarchs will be afraid of me ... I shall show myself
> capable and courageous in war.'
>
> (BWS 8:9–15)

He has introduced the theme of greed leading to self-aggrandizement, domination, hierarchy and war that has been a keynote of Western civilization. At the time of BWS it is only one thread of a many-layered skein. My own feeling is that this thread became so dominant later because the female had been devalued and the male overvalued, in concepts of divinity and thence of humanity. In BWS, by the end of the book, Hochma/Sophia has vanished entirely. It is as if she had never been there. Before following her on her journey into Gnosticism and then into Christianity it is helpful to place her in her Hellenistic context, since this had enormous influence.

There is some speculation that part at least of BWS may have been written by women. The Jewish philosopher Philo, who lived a little earlier than the author of BWS, wrote about a community, mixed men and women and all Jewish, who lived on the shores of the Dead Sea and were called the Therapeutae. They reached into the lives of the communities around them,

preached Sabbath services, and were an influential source of
religious instruction. Philo described how women interpreted
scripture and led ritual. It has been suggested that possibly BWS
may have been their work, or at least those parts of it in praise
of Sophia, and that the other parts were put in by opponents
who wanted a more establishment-style monotheism. The
Therapeutae are among the numerous Jewish sects who existed
until the time of the Roman destruction in the first century CE
and who perished: the Sadducees, Essenes and others of whom
little is known. The Jews remaining were the Pharisees, strict
followers of Ezra and the Deuteronomists, who were able to set
up their school at Jamnia and establish the religion of Judaism
now believed to be normative. In this Sophia is not mentioned,
and Hochma is the Torah.

In the Hellenistic world which was the matrix of the birth of
Christianity, Jewish religion was held to be of great influence
and antiquity, but it was one only – and a one relatively small in
numbers among a great many widespread religions. Perhaps the
most influential was that of the goddess Isis of Egypt which had
spread throughout the 'known world', continuing for something
like three millennia and ending only when destroyed by about
500 CE. Wisdom, whether Hochma or Sophia, has frequently
been compared with Isis and her sister goddess Ma'at. Isis of
Egypt is the great goddess. She has described herself in a well
known aretalogy (self-praise) which is available to us. Here are
some lines from it:

> *I am Isis, I am she who is called goddess by women*
> *I gave and ordained laws for humans which no one is able to*
> *change*
> *I divided the earth from the heavens*
> *I ordered the course of the sun and the moon*
> *I appointed to women to bring their infants to birth in the*
> *tenth month*
> *I made the beautiful and the shameful to be distinguished by*
> *nature*
> *I established punishment for those who practise injustice*
> *I am Queen of rivers and winds and sea*
> *I am in the rays of the sun*
> *Fate hearkens to me*
> *Hail Egypt that nourishes me.*[19]

Here we see the goddess who is divine and creative, queen of
nature who also points out the best ways of living for human

beings in whose world she takes part. There is an ethical side to her. The complete hymn, of over fifty lines, balances descriptions of her transcendence with her very real concern for the everyday world of human beings. She punishes injustice, she 'causes the trickster to be caught by his own tricks', she is concerned with women and birth-giving and with the relationships of parents and children. She is very much to be compared with the Hochma of Proverbs in this respect.

Alongside her is Ma'at, goddess of truth, right and justice. This name actually describes a measure of land, and it is on this concept of exactitude and rightness that order and justice depends. Such earthy mundane order is duplicated by the order of the eternal: Ma'at becomes goddess of the underworld where she judges human souls. In this capacity she also exercises mercy, and again there are strong resonances in her judgments and in what she expects from human beings with those of Wisdom in Proverbs. Here is part of a confession the soul is called upon to make before Ma'at. It is called a 'Negative Confession':

> *I have not committed iniquity ...*
> *I have not oppressed the poor ...*
> *I have not defaulted ...*
> *I have not in aught diminished the supplies to the temples ...*
> *I have not murdered ...*
> *I have not made any to weep ...*
> *I have not falsified the beam of the balance ...*[20]

It is noticeable that in addition to setting out what the Egyptians considered proper for human behaviour, in the manner of Proverbs, the ideals of human justice usually associated with the Hebrew prophets or even the Ten Commandments are there. But there is also a very human, and one might even say a very female compassion – 'I have not made any to weep' – and also particular exactness and precision in everyday dealings. Ma'at is the cosmic order of the world, like Hochma, which is itself built on order and precision, and in this respect heaven and earth are linked.

Isis and Ma'at have been identified in much of the description of Hochma and Sophia and have also been described as figuring largely in the New Testament understanding of Jesus as Logos in the opening chapter of the Fourth Gospel.

That the masculine Logos is closely connected with Hochma and Sophia is not in doubt. Wisdom is there, but from now on as

Christianity develops it is Jesus Christ and becomes a part of him. He is described often with her words and there are statements that all wisdom is in Him.[21] Much of her journey is duplicated in His. Where the Jews encapsulated Wisdom in sacred texts, the Christians subsumed her in the Saviour and then in various ways and times into the Holy Spirit and often into the Virgin Mary. But before that transformation revealed itself, there was a period when Sophia, who had herself changed her character, appeared and was venerated. It is in this Sophia, successor to Hochma in the intertestamental and early Christian world, that we can begin to see another account of fall of the female aspect of divinity.

THE GNOSTIC DIMENSION

Gnosticism is becoming a powerful influence in feminist research into the overthrow of the female in the divine. The discovery in 1945 of a substantial number of documents in the sand of Egypt at Nag Hammadi brought fresh light to our knowledge of a religious system which previously had been only available through the hostile polemics of some of the early Christian Fathers. These Nag Hammadi texts, now available in translation,[22] cover a period of four hundred years, which span the two centuries before the common era and the following two centuries. Composed of between fifty and sixty separate 'books' or tractates, they are firmly placed in Judaic and Christian or pre-Christian modes of thought. The documents fall into various groups, based mainly on their dating and the schools which produced them.

Common to many of them, and taking a major part in several, are divine female figures, named Sophia, Epinoia, Protennoia or Barbelo. The first three are all words to do with Wisdom. Sophia herself, although related to Hochma, in fact stands for the Wisdom of the Gnosis. This is the knowledge of the divine mysteries: where we came from, where we are going, the nature of heaven, the divinity within us.

While it is impossible to give an account here of the different religious systems entailed, it is important that there were vast differences between the various schools of thought, and there is no one interpretation of Gnosticism or Gnosis. The only theme that may be common to all is the insistence that divine Wisdom is available to those who, despising the world, seek their spiritual salvation in her; or, in the more Christianized texts, in the Saviour. The earlier Gnostic writers showed Sophia and her divine sisters to be joined with God, creator figures in themselves, or in unison with God. They are available to humans, and in themselves reflect the comprehensive differences in humanity – in fact, they represent the whole and all its inter-connecting parts. One quotation will illustrate this:

> I am Protennoia, the Thought that dwells in the Light.
> I am the movement that dwells in the All, she in whom the All takes its stand, the first born as among those who came to exist.
> I am invisible within the thought of the Invisible One.
> I am revealed in the immeasurable, ineffable.
> I am the head of the All, since I exist in everyone.[23]

She is the invisible essence, yet she is also the first-born of All who came to exist; that is she is immanence and transcendence. In this she reminds us of Hochma. She is the female principle in deity. Protennoia goes on to declare:

> I am perception and knowledge, uttering a voice by means of thought
> I am the real Voice. I cry out in everyone.[24]

For me, these words are extremely moving. Here is the acknowledged and venerated female divine being, who lives in me and who calls out in me.

But for how long has our female voice been silenced, for how long our perception and knowledge dismissed as worthless, for how long have we women been silenced? Protennoia calls on us to break our silence, to cry out, to speak out. She assures us she is there within us – and has been there from the beginning.

Another female divinity who calls to women and assures us of our dignity and our power is the otherwise un-named Thunder Perfect Mind. She appears to be everywhere and encompasses everything:

> I am the first and the last
> I am the honoured one and the scorned one
> I am the whore and the holy one
> I am the wife and the virgin
> I am the mother and the daughter
> I am the members of my mother
> I am the barren one and many are her sons
> I am the one who has been hated everywhere and who has been loved everywhere

I am the one whom they call Life and you have called Death.[25]

She is everything and everybody and its opposite. She is female and within her there is the whole range of female life from birth to death, from the mundane woman in the world to the divine Wisdom of Heaven. She shows for me that there is no disunity between something and its opposite. A totality includes all aspects. Linear and dualistic divisions do not exist. So many times we, women in the world, are aware that we are something and we are not something; or we are called names that put us down, and we are punished for being who we are. In Thunder Perfect Mind we can rejoice in a revelation of a goddess who is both outside us and within us, and we can be reminded of that same goddess figure who is the first and the last, who is called life and you – the others – have called Death. Asherah and Ashertaroth were called whore, abomination and death, by those who hated them. Hochma, their sister and descendant, was called the tree of life (Proverbs) before she was divested of her female form. I see in the 'Thunder' the vision of a goddess human and divine who speaks again. Her words are taken over by the newer male-oriented religions. 'I am the first and the last' is a description of God and of Christ (Rev 21:6; 22:13); it not only recalls 'Thunder' but also Egyptian Isis.

The differences in the Christianized and pre-Christian texts in their attitudes to Sophia have been analysed in detail by Rose Arthur. She points to the contrast between the early female Gnostic divinities and the 'fallen Sophia' of the Christians. She remarks that in the Jewish documents Sophia is not a personage in need of male redemption; this idea comes in the Christian texts.

In particular Sophia's fall from divinity is traced in the story of the birth of her child. I will quote part of it from the Apocryphon of John:

> And the Sophia of the Epinnoia, being an aeon, conceived a thought from herself with the reflection of the invisible Spirit and foreknowledge. She wanted to bring forth a likeness out of herself without the consent of the Spirit – he had not approved – and without her consort and without his consideration. And though the personage of her maleness had not approved, and she had not found her agreement, and she had thought without the consent of the Spirit and the knowledge of her agreement, (yet) she brought forth. And because of

the invincible power that is in her, her thought did not remain idle and a thing came out of her which was imperfect and different from her appearance, because she had created it without her consort. And it was dissimilar to the likeness of its mother for it has another form. She cast it away from her, outside the place, that no one of the immortal ones might see it, for she had created it in ignorance. And she surrounded it with a luminous cloud, and she placed a throne in the middle of the cloud that no one might see it except the holy Spirit who is called the mother of the living and she called his name Yaltabaoth.[26]

Here is a summation of the travels of the goddess. She has invincible power within her, she is able to create without the male principle and does so because she wishes to do so. In this she is behaving in the same way as a long line of ancient mother goddesses, but by now, in the second centuries after Christ, this has to be condemned as a fault, a fault so grievous that her child is imperfect; and this imperfect being then becomes the creator of a faulty and imperfect world. Whose fault is this? Sophia's. Why? Because she does not ask for male approval.

From then on Sophia's only way open is repentance, and this means she is constantly weeping. Eventually, fully penitent, she is allowed to return to the lowest place in the spiritual world, well away from her former glory. Where the author of the Book of Wisdom of Solomon moved to wanting to possess Sophia for his own aggrandizement, the later Gnostic books have gone far further. Now she is to bear the guilt for all the world's shortcomings. Much was made of her relationship to the 'fallen' Eve of Genesis 3.[27]

There is little doubt that the female divine Hochma and Sophia of earlier Gnostics was never forgotten. Vestiges of that philosophy were carried steadily in an underground stream throughout European history. Sometimes they bubbled up strongly, as for example in the Hermetic Philosophy of the Renaissance, as Frances Yates has shown. They continually nourished 'unofficial' movements and sects within the mainstream religions, sometimes openly, sometimes disguised. Where the later Gnostic view of Sophia's disobedience and fault was planted firmly on to all women by the Church, yet many Christians found in Mary the Virgin, and often the Black Virgin, a vision of the earlier goddess. In the Jewish world the establishment religion was satisfied with Hochma as Torah, the law, thus effectively denying the presence of the female in the divine.

This view was challenged by the influence of the mystical sect of Kabbalists who saw in the Shekhinah the female presence of God and venerated her accordingly. But since women themselves were denied access to or knowledge of the Kabbalah for most of its history the idea of a Jewish acknowledgment of the female deity was a closely guarded secret among men who treated it as a hidden doctrine and did not allow any of its consequences to pass into the community.

It is only today that Christian women may understand that Mary might be God the Mother as well as Mother of God; and that Sophia may be the unacknowledged female aspect of Jesus and possibly of the Holy Spirit. Jewish women in the present time may at last enter into their heritage of the divine female, for them in the guise of the Shekhinah, the female indwelling presence of God. The living waters which have bubbled underground for so long are now rising up and pouring out their revivifying streams.

SHEKHINAH CONSCIOUSNESS

The idea of the Shekhinah is full of contradictions and yet of inspiration.[28] It is used to denote the presence of God and is derived from the Hebrew word to dwell. In Biblical texts it denoted the presence of God at some particular place – e.g. at Bethel, where Jacob met God, in the Meeting Tent with Moses in the desert, in the temple of Solomon at Jerusalem, and even as the deity as a resting place or refuge for humans. The Hebrew word is feminine in gender but for mainstream Talmudic and rabbinical thought it was not used to denote any female essence or element within God. It was, for them, synonymous with His presence, His glory, sometimes with His Holy Spirit (*ruach-ha kodesh*). Sometimes called the Face of God, the glory associated with the Shekhinah shone, for example, on Moses' face when he came down from the mountain. In a comprehensive work of reference on the indwelling of God in the world according to rabbinical literature, a writer early this century was able to provide copious detailed information about the Shekhinah without ever mentioning a feminine aspect.[29]

However, in the alternative and mystical tradition of Judaism known as Kabbalah, the Shekhinah, while keeping her characteristic of 'dwelling', became more and more personified as both divine and female. The Kabbalah literature may be taken to begin in the first four centuries of our era and itself related to an earlier mystical trend associated with the Merkabah (chariot) visions in the Book of Ezekiel, and it had certain affinities with some Gnostic material. From the early rabbinic years, the Kabbalah developed widely, rising to a peak during the Middle Ages, and again was renewed in later Judaism by the Hassidic sects of Eastern Europe.

We meet the Shekhinah on the Tree of Life, yet we also meet her as the 'community of Israel'. In the latter case, she is re-mythologized to become the marital partner of God, reflecting the Biblical tradition of God the husband, Israel the wife. She is addressed as 'Queen, Daughter, Bride' of God. A good deal of sexual imagery is used, in the tradition of that used in the Book of Proverbs about Hochma. Yet at the same time, some sects within the Kabbalists took the Shekhinah right out of this relationship to make her into what Patai has called 'an independent divine female entity, a direct heir to ancient Hebrew goddesses'. This point is also made strongly by Scholem, who compares the Shekhinah within the Kabbalah to the goddesses of the past, yet stresses that it is only for the Kabbalists that she has this character. For everyday and mainstream Jews, the Shekhinah must always be comprehended as God's presence or, at the utmost, the community of Israel.

It is clear that while the Jewish mystics pursued a comprehensive study of female divinity, yet no human female was allowed to take part in this activity or indeed to know anything at all about it. It was totally androcentric in concept and performance. The male students and teachers glorified the female but placed her in relation to themselves, and did not allow her divinity to enter into the lives of the general Jewish community, or into their worship. It has been emphasized that the study of the Kabbalah was 'not for the rabble'. It was for an élite, which in any case must necessarily be male.

Within this restriction, veneration of the Shekhinah was unbounded. It was emphasized that her glory is God's glory. She is described as a garden full of fruit and nuts, the latter being to do with riddles, puzzles and problems and, at a deeper level, the mysteries of alchemy and magic. Modern students of magic often look to the Kabbalistic writings as a primary source of material.

The Shekhinah has been compared to Lilith and to Hochma. As for Lilith, by the time the Kabbalists were writing she had long been turned into a ferocious demon, although there are a few positive references to her in the literature. Hochma they transformed into a male, equating the creative activity and direct knowledge of the world with the masculine, leaving the more passive aspects of perception and understanding to the female. There is also another fundamental difference between Hochma and the Shekhinah. The latter belongs to Judaism and is identified with the trials and hopes of the Jewish people, whom she comforted in their exile, and mourned within their trials. She was the essence of *tikkun* – the return to harmony of the world. She stands as a female aspect of divinity within Judaism to which Jewish people and especially women can now relate. By contrast, Hochma, Wisdom, was always universal. She called on all to enter her home and eat her food; all could learn from her the secrets of the universe; all could benefit from her instruction and learn to order their lives well. She reached from one end of the world to the other. She was not attached to any one group or people or religion. (Although some writers spoke of her making her home in Israel, this was never pursued widely.) She was co-existent with the universe, the mediator between all within it and deity which she shares.

Just as it is true that Hochma, like Shekhinah, became submerged in male culture, so both can be reclaimed in their free, powerful feminine forms. Now is the time they are both emerging from their long imprisonment.

THE GODDESS TODAY

A transformation concerning woman's place in both heavenly and earthly society has taken place in the last decade. The underground streams have become torrents. They have led to concern, even crisis, within traditional religions. While during the last hundred years or more women have spoken out strongly against Biblical-based subordination, it is only now that their numbers are large enough and the ideas are propagated widely enough to secure actual changes – many of which are still strongly resisted. Ursula King [30] in her survey of women's spirituality today has listed seven categories of voices: of protest and anger; of challenge; of experience; of spiritual power; of a new spirituality; of a new theology; of prophecy and integration. These come from disparate places, traditions, languages, cultures. They all join into one voice, that of a new women's spirituality. From that list I move on.

All, if we look at any of the categories, must start with anger – at the androcentrism of society and, within religion and theology, of the biblical and religious texts which have formed our culture. What next? It is to seek methods by which the subsumed, the forgotten half of humanity, the underclass of women, the no-no of humanity and of divinity, may be raised up and proclaimed. There is no consensus as to method – far from it – nor as to belief. There are many distinctions and some conflicts. But serving as a framework for all is the knowledge of past injustice and the will to put matters right.

Within the new theology, a network of methods of re-interpretation has been under construction for some years. Christian women research both the Hebrew Bible and the New Testament, concentrating strongly on demythologizing the stories of sin and on remaking woman in the image of God – both themes in Genesis. Many include such subjects as the immanence of goddess or god in our lives, a new view of salvation that depends on wholeness and connectedness rather than reward and punishment. Areas of research deal, for example, with Mary the Virgin, or with Jesus–Sophia; with sexuality and religion, and with Jesus' position in the background of his times. Some scholars are researching the divinity of Wisdom.

Women within the Jewish tradition are, among much else, reclaiming the Kabbalah, and finding that the Shekhinah, God's female presence, is as much for them as for the men who previously appropriated it. They are able to copy early rituals, such as the blessing of the new moon, that was biblically the province of women, and in their academic studies are able to see and discuss rabbinical rituals outside the mainstream that in fact do not deny women's equality with men. They are taking a hard look at Bible texts and extra-biblical material and finding the forgotten and the overlooked female within them. There is an international growing network of feminist theological dissent.

The Bible has for over a hundred years been subject to various methods of interpretation and exegesis; today the feminist method is followed by more and more scholars. Elisabeth Schüssler Fiorenza and Rosemary Ruether, both American Catholic feminist theologians, have been pioneering academic methods of demonstrating the received androcentric views and reconstructing a Christianity based on a wholism, indeed a love, that is traditionally purported to be its root. Theories of egalitarianism are suggested in different ways by these authors, who both fully realize women's previous subordination in their religion and who endeavour to see a way out within it. Women in theological research in Europe have formed an organization which centres on exchange of ideas and

60

research in feminist theology. The subjects are of vast dimension: whether of a maligned woman in the Bible – such as Jezebel – or a new understanding of the meaning of the female *ruach* (spirit) in the Hebrew Bible; a discussion of the violence against women in the Bible, and the possibility of a women's liberation theology; a discussion of Mariology and its effect on women – positive or otherwise; a vision of Jesus as liberator of women (although this has serious drawbacks); and, above all, many views of the image of God – referring to Genesis 1:26 – and of reversing the Christian concept of women as vehicles of sin. All these were matters for discussion at a recent conference, as was a new one: within the 'Image of God' concept came the image of justice. The participants at a conference in Germany in 1989 took up the Christian roots of anti-Judaism. Judith Plaskow, in a paper entitled 'Feminist anti-Judaism and the Christian God', warned against the easy way that Christian feminists might follow by taking Jesus out of context to deliver women from their apparent oppressors, thus taking an anti-Jewish theme for granted.[31] She pointed out that the theme of connectedness within Christianity is also present within Judaism and both religions can be called upon by women for a vision of totality and community.

Those who remain in the traditional religions try and work them through to establish a base for egalitarianism and wholism. Others have left them, finding that effort or dream impossible. Daphne Hampson, a British feminist theologian, has put Christianity behind her. She does not, she says, need Christianity for connectedness. She sees a vision of the whole, within a transformation of the meaning of God.[32]

An identification of one's woman-self with God is taken further by many women who move right away from their background religion. Those who turn back to older roots, pick up the myths and stories of the ancient goddesses, take them into sacred activities for themselves today. Again, there is no doctrine or homogeneity: some belong to a wiccan tradition, or faerie; some believe they have inherited secrets through grandmother to grandmother; some take up the cause and the practice of the ancient women healers; some seek goddesses from various cultures and defend and renew them. There are many others. Common to most is the assertion that the divine is not only 'out there' but is in ourselves, most particularly that the goddess is in us women and we in her. Others, myself among them, will state quite definitely that the goddesses who were despised, rejected, tortured, overthrown and continuously kept

out of sight by ongoing ferocious brutality are a paradigm of what has happened to women and women's spirituality. In reclaiming them we reclaim ourselves; in reclaiming ourselves, we reclaim them.

Common to all – those in traditional religions who are re-working them; those who have left them behind but still stay clear of goddesses; those who attach themselves to goddesses whether inside or outside their 'home' religion; those who re-evaluate and reconstruct texts without a religious drive – is a sisterhood of understanding and endeavour. Whatever the method used, whatever the actual religious faith or lack of it, whatever charge of intensity is to be found in the work, there is no doubt that all involved with feminist theology – or thealogy as many of us would have it – are struggling to bring justice and truth to religion, especially as it affects women, and thence to the community in which they live. Such justice and truth are not words nor mirages, but affect the everyday lives of women – and men – everywhere.

Throughout the long journey at which we have taken passing glances, there has never been a point that did not contain a female aspect of God. From the goddesses of the ancient Near East who became transformed into the consort of God, and then demonized; from the acknowledgment of Hochma as both cosmic Wisdom and immediacy in the world, to the Torah; from Sophia, identical with the supreme divine power and instructor and guide to human beings, her sisterhood with other female divinities in other surrounding cultures, to her fallen state and her disappearance within the Trinity, and then her re-appearance in another form as the Virgin Mary – the goddess has been there. The unfortunate part of the whole matter is that she has been disguised and dismissed. When we look at her history we understand how immense was her defeat.

What do we mean by this? Who was defeated? There is only one answer. We were defeated. And who are we? Well, first we are women, who have undergone defeat after defeat but somehow, like the goddess, on the whole we manage to survive through continuous catastrophes, crippled. Also defeated are men, who have paraded and gloried in their 'godliness' to bring the world to the brink of extinction and themselves to a place of nowhere in particular. The Bible, Hebrew and New Testament, both in their different ways chronicle the godhead of the female and its overthrow. The results of such male supremacy in religion have been and are horrific.

To heal and revive our world and all the people in it, we need to look again at the older religious traditions that sought and followed a concept of a female God, or within God, or aspect of God. The Divine She, the Mother Earth and Queen of Heaven, the She of the underworld, all express a concept that has been swept from the patriarchal thought and tradition. The kernel of the She within the divine was her association with earth as well as heaven, participation with humankind, a bridge between the transcendent and the mundane, making all of it sacred. Can we re-learn her lessons? Of Wisdom it was written: 'She shall be a Tree of Life to you.' Do we not have to face the flaming sword that the androcentric writers placed in front of her and deny it, so that we may again recognize Her and revenerate Her? Only in this way can our women's 'thirteenth hour' help humanity survive the crisis which male imbalance has brought upon the created world.

NOTES

1 Fiorenza, Elisabeth Schüssler, *In Memory of Her*, Crossroad, New York, 1983, p. 29, and others by this author.
2 Brootten, Bernadette J., *Women Leaders in the Ancient Synagogue*, Scholars Press, CA, 1982, p. 150.
3 Plaskow, Judith, 'The Right Question is Theological', in Heschel, S. (ed.), *On Being a Jewish Feminist*, Schocken, NY, 1983, p. 230.
4 Christ, Carol P., *The Laughter of Aphrodite*, Harper & Row, CA, 1987.
5 Patai, Raphael, *The Hebrew Goddess*, (new enlarged edition, Wayne State University Press, Detroit, 1990).
6 Quoted in Durdin-Robertson, L., *The Goddesses of Chaldea, Syria and Egypt*, Cesara Publications, Eire, 1975, p. 2.
7 E.g. Isaiah 27:1, Psalm 74:13, Psalm 89:10.
8 Wolkstein, Diane and Kramer, Samuel Noah, *Inanna*, Harper, New York, 1983, p. 7.
9 Long, Asphodel P., in *Arachne*, No. 2, MRRN, London, 1985, pp. 26–30.
10 Albright, W.F., *Hebraica* 36, 1919–20, pp. 258–9.
11 Driver, G.R., *Canaanite Myths and Legends*, 1956.
12 Gray, John, *The Canaanites*, Thames & Hudson, London, 1964.
13 Meshel, Z. 'Did Jahweh have a Consort?' in *Biblical Archaeological Review*, March 1979.
14 Delcor, M., in *Von Kanaan bis Kerala*, ed. Delsman, Verlag Butzon & Berckerkevelaer, 1982, pp. 101–22.

15 Ibid.

16 Ibid.

17 E.g. Proverbs 3:18–19, 8:22–30; Book of Wisdom of Solomon 7:8, 8:1; Ecclesiasticus (The Book of Sirach) 24; The Book of Enoch 42:1–2.

18 Greenfield, J.C. 'The Seven Pillars of Wisdom. A Mistranslation', in *Jewish Quarterly Review*, LXXVI, No. 1, 1985, pp. 13–20.

19 Engelsman, Joan C., *The Feminine Dimension of the Divine*, Westminster Press, PA, 1979.

20 Durdin-Robertson, L., *The Goddesses of Chaldea, Syria and Egypt*, Cesara Publications, Eire, 1975, pp. 324–5.

21 E.g. 1 Corinthians 1:24.

22 Robinson, James R., *The Nag Hammadi Library*, E.J. Brill, Leiden, 1977.

23 Robinson, J.R., 1977, op. cit., pp. 461–70.

24 Ibid.

25 Ibid., pp. 271–7.

26 Arthur, Rose H., *The Wisdom Goddess*, University Press of America, 1984.

27 Robinson, J.R., 1977 op. cit., pp. 103–4.

28 For historical information on Shekhinah see Scholem, Gershon, *The Kabbalah and its Symbolism*, Schocken, New York, 1969 and Scholem, Gershon, *Kabbalah*, Keter, Jerusalem, 1974; also Patai, Raphael, 1967 (1990), op. cit.

29 Abelson, Joshua, *The Immanence of God*, London, 1912.

30 King, Ursula, *Women and Spirituality*, Macmillan, London, 1989.

31 European Society of Women in Theological Research, Arnoldshain, Germany, 1989.

32 Hampson, Daphne, *Theology and Feminism*, Basil Blackwell, Oxford, 1990.

EXULT!
Jean Head

Elijah on Mount Carmel
(flames consume his sacrifice)
contended for his God,
routed the prophets of Baal,
slaughtered his falsity.
Did he not know
four hundred prophets of Asherah
were gathered there?
Did he ignore,
unable to bear their power?

Goddess:
I have lived long
not knowing,
not seeing.
You were hidden.
You were not.

Surprised:
I look
I see
I discover.
Psyche leaps
Mind erupts
Heart opens:
Recognition.
You live
Goddess.

THE PSYCHOLOGICAL STATUS OF GOD AND GODDESS
Ruth Barnett

In this essay I propose to compare the development of the human race to that of the human infant. My hypothesis is that just as the infant invests its parents with magical power, so the infant human race could not survive without belief in an external protective power. Goddesses, gods and religion have to be invented as symbolic possessions, the way the human child often uses a cuddly toy. I follow this through by speculating on the parallel we might draw between the human child's relationship to its parents and the human race's experience of God, as both develop into adulthood.

The essence of life is change. Being is always becoming. Yet we strive to hold life static by taking photographs, building monuments and clinging to traditions to create for ourselves the illusion that we have stability. The reality of our infinitessimal minuteness within the vastness of the universe is unbearable if even thinkable – so we create the world we need and want around us. Then we imagine it to be reality. As a species, the human race is young and still naive. We know very little of our origin and what we are. Somehow we each arise from a state of being undifferentiated from the matrix of the environment around us. A psychoanalyst, Michael Balint, called this state of the baby being unseparated from its mother 'harmonious interpenetrating mix-up'.[1] Another way of looking at it is that we start undifferentiated from God; God is all and we are God in our beginning.

Another psychoanalyst, Donald Winnicott, said that there is no such thing as a baby, only a mother-baby unit. He coined the term 'good-enough mother' to describe the mother who anticipates her baby's needs.[2] In this way the baby is protected from too quick and drastic disillusionment in its belief that it is

God. With good-enough parenting the environment will not fail the infant too much or too soon, as fail it surely must, to obey the infant's omnipotent commands. The baby then experiences God as sometimes inside and sometimes outside in the breast that provides food, warmth and everything. In hunger the baby hallucinates the breast and when it then appears the baby feels like God. When the breast is not immediately there but can be summoned by screaming, the infant still experiences some power in itself, but also some in the breast. First the baby becomes bonded with the mother in a symbiotic relationship and then develops a two-person relationship with her. If all goes well a three-person relationship emerges by including the father. Some power is still experienced in itself as the infant finds ways of getting the parents to meet its needs. Sometimes charm is used, at other times cunning manipulation. But most of the power is invested in the parents. They are huge God-like beings: to be challenged but not too much, to be manipulated if possible but to be appeased and pleased at all costs. Sometimes they are benevolent, generous Gods and sometimes harsh, cruel tyrants but always they are Gods to the baby who becomes ever more aware of its vulnerability and defencelessness without them.

But the parents can't always be there. When they cannot be seen or heard, the baby experiences them as gone for ever. The feelings of being abandoned and totally vulnerable are unbearable, so it clings onto something, a cuddly toy or cloth, that can be a symbol for them in their absence. Winnicott called such things transitional objects.[3] Perhaps the first human beings were at one with God – in the Garden of Eden. At some point in the human race's infancy the growing awareness of the terrors of the real world became intolerable – the result of eating the mythical apple of the tree of knowledge. Once the awareness dawned of our appalling vulnerability the human race might not have survived psychologically without inventing goddesses and gods as transitional objects.

Every baby experiences its mother first, simply due to the fact that babies grow in the mother's womb. So it would make sense for the first deities to be goddesses. The history of goddess cultures suggests that the Primordial Goddess, and then lesser goddesses, were invented before male gods. Perhaps male envy of the womb eventually ousted the Goddess from her throne. Or perhaps it was more to do with female power being abused. A multitude of squabbling and warring goddesses and gods were created. No single god or goddess could be relied upon as a secure transitional object. Monotheism seemed a better proposition. So Man created monotheism and the male God Jehovah or Allah. Women, the Womb-men, were relegated 'on earth as it is in heaven' to second place and not included in the decision-making groups that designed and controlled male monotheism. God the Father threw out Lilith the mother of all. Bit by bit the Shekhinah, the feminine aspects of god, were discarded to leave a very fierce punitive vengeful male God 'up in the sky', a mirror image of the ideal macho man down on earth; an ideal that most men could not live up to.

It is interesting to speculate on how the three-person relationship of infancy (mother, father and child) is dealt with in the Christian religion by the Holy Trinity: Father God with a ghostly partner and messianic son? Father God hasn't quite been able to get rid of Lilith; her 'ghost' remains as the Holy Ghost or presence of God like the Shekhinah, and her femininity as woman, represented by Mary, is split in half. The Virgin Mary is worshipped as the mother of God but denied deity while Mary Magdalen is despised as the whore, the symbol of sinfulness that has tainted mankind. And only the son, Jesus, has a place in the religious order of things; not so for the daughter. Is this a punishment for the powerlessness each man once felt when his mother had total domination over him in his infancy?

Religion seems to have been losing credibility and power in many Western countries during the second half of this century. One way of viewing this might be that the human race is no longer an infant but perhaps an adolescent. By the onset of adolescence children have usually long discarded their transitional objects, quite often to be stored away somewhere 'just in case'. Similarly many people today keep in nominal contact with their religion while no longer being devoted, while for others it still provides a source of comfort and structure for their lives. Father God, like all parents, has failed us with glaring flaws in his omnipotence. His way of running the world has become unacceptably unjust to our adolescent way of looking at things. The meek and righteous are not getting their due reward as they should and the promise of an after-life is beginning to sound like a 'con trick' to fool us into accepting our plight. Furthermore, the female half of the race is simply not standing for the appropriation of all the power and privileges by the males. The cry of 'move over darling – it's my turn now' is becoming deafening (BBC Television series in March 1990 for International Women's Day). And what is Father God going to do about it? Perhaps we can do better ourselves without him. That is what we seem to be trying to do.

Some adolescents become very destructive in their efforts to separate from their parents and become adults in their own right. Usually the more controlling and authoritarian the parents the harder it is for the adolescent to pluck up courage to dare to break away. But when they do, all the more violent and abrupt a rift may occur. Father God of Judaism, Christianity and Islam is an exceedingly mighty, jealous and punitive God. Perhaps this is why the adolescent human race has come so near to destroying the Earth with weapons of war and pollution of the environment. Is this an attack on the Garden of Eden, the womb that expelled us and won't let us back, the parental bedchamber from which we were excluded and in which Father God is still making more babies, new species that might oust us from our place as God's favourite and heir? How much more damage are we going to do before we come to our senses? Do we have to annihilate the whole Earth and ourselves with it to wreak vengeance on our disappointing Father God? Has Father God abdicated? Or has he gone to look for Lilith in a hope for reconciliation that might turn the tide? And what can Lilith do? Is she willing to come back? Can she heal her wounded daughter? Can she mend the split between 'madonna' and 'whore' that patriarchy has inflicted on womankind?[4]

The future is female. Not to go back to women in power, but to reinstate the female attributes that were denigrated and cast out. Macho male strength was at a premium in the industrial society that has long passed its peak and is on the way out in the West. Hierarchies of domination are everywhere breaking down. People refuse to be ruled in an autocratic way. We are in a changeover period of seeming chaos because the new post-industrial society has not settled down yet from the ferment. Female ways of doing things are coming into their own – nurturing, relating and interconnecting in networks – not possessed by females alone but by women and men in partnership. Hopefully, like the adolescent offspring of the 'good-enough' parents, the human race will eventually 'grow up'. We can speculate further what might become of God. What could the adult relationship of the human race with God-the-parents be like? The human adult, if development has been 'good-enough', usually relates to the parents as equals (but perhaps never quite totally equal). And this relationship is internalized so that it continues, after the death of the parents, in the person's mind. Perhaps the human race will experience the death of organized religion and gods as 'outside' while developing god or religious consciousness within the human mind. Naomi Goldenberg suggests that 'religious sensibility turns inwards when father-gods fall' and sums up the situation, I think, very aptly: 'The location of a God in the mind may be the most effective place that she, he or it can be in an age of post-Oedipal culture.'[5]

REFERENCES

1 Balint, M., *The Basic Fault*, Tavistock Publications, London, 1968.
2 Winnicott, D.W., *Collected Papers: Through Paediatrics to Psychoanalysis*, Tavistock Publications, London, 1958.
3 Winnicott, D.W., *Playing and Reality*, Penguin, London, 1971.
4 Welldon E.V., *Mother, Madonna, Whore: The Idealization and Denigration of Motherhood*, Free Association Books, 1988.
5 Goldenberg, N.R., *Changing of the Gods*, Beacon Press, Boston, 1979.

EPIPHANY 1990
Jean Head

A girl child was born.
Grew up, dominated, isolated, asking no questions.
> *Village chapel on Sundays with mother,*
> *met afterwards by dog-walking father.*
What absence, what presence,
> *in that confused childhood, long ago?*
In home: absent father offered no safety from
> *all-pervading mother, negative, destructive.*
In church: pews for women, passively accepting
> *powerful elevated men in pulpit*
> *(cassocked clerics suppressing sexuality).*
> *Centuries, millennia of men,*
> *priests, rabbis, theologians,*
> *forcing subservience;*
> *teaching God as king, lord,*
> > *omnipotent, omnipresent, omniscient,*
> > *warring, judgmental, separate;*
> *language exclusive, male;*
> *denigrating, denying alternatives;*
> *dogmatic, hurling stones not offering bread.*
> *Absent mother, harsh father.*

Girl child lingered as woman aged,
Damaged, so nearly destroyed.

Woman's hair greyed:
Life came.
In struggle, hurt flowed,
Eyes opening, began to see, through healing tears.

Women, rare men of sensitivity,
*   patient, gentle; gave space, time, holding.*
Slow inner transformation, new patterns of being.
Surprises, amazement, excitement;
Dreams, story, music, trees liberate truth.
Away from rigid church,
Models of God as mother, lover, friend;
Goddess glimpsed, quietly waiting in Judaeo-Christianity,
Stretching hand to ancient Goddesses
*   stepping from museum shelves;*
Earth rites, stone circles, Silbury hill, womb waters, landscape breasts;
Fertile, creative, generative, eternally cyclic.

*   Not ousting tradition,*
*   Not usurping God by Goddess,*
*   Not replacing He with She,*
*   Not either–or.*
For wholeness,
Both–and, including, embracing,
Feminine joining masculine,
Honouring, encouraging the other,
Freely, fearlessly.
Mother and father together
Parenting new life:
Showing forth
Mystery:
The Divine beyond all images.

MIRIAM: WILDERNESS LEADER, PRIESTESS ANCESTOR OF MARY
Mhairi MacMillan

When I was asked if I'd like to contribute to this book on 'the absent mother', I didn't think of my own mother but of the name which she gave me and which was her name and the name of my grandmother. Mary. Mairi or Mhairi as it is in Gaelic. Recently the story of Exodus has meant a lot to me in terms of the freedom attained by the individual after the time 'in the desert'. But one important figure was mentioned in that story only to disappear. This was Miriam, whose name I also carry.

In my Presbyterian Sunday School, I liked the story of Miriam's clever plan to save her baby brother. She seemed very real to me, brave and resourceful, a 'role model' we might say nowadays (but not then). As for the other Mary, mother of Jesus, she was not given any special place, no more than any ordinary mother. But my growing acquaintance with the first Miriam has awakened my interest in the second and in the light of the coming back to consciousness of the feminine and of the Goddess herself I have been able to begin to give them the attention they deserve.

INTRODUCTION

I brought you up from Egypt
I ransomed you from the land of slavery
I sent Moses and Aaron and Miriam to lead you.

(Micah 6:4; New English Bible)

In these words, the Lord reminds Israel of his great mercy towards her. Three leaders were sent to lead the Hebrew people to freedom; one of these leaders was Miriam. We can read a great deal about Moses and Aaron in the Bible, but hardly anything about Miriam.

Yet her stature was such, we are told, that she died by the Kiss of the Shekhinah, because the Angel of Death had no power over her.[1] Only six people merited this death: the others were Abraham, Isaac, Jacob, Moses and Aaron. Miriam is the sole woman.

It is time now for Miriam to be brought out of the shadows so that she may take her rightful place in our spiritual heritage.

MIRIAM'S EARLY LIFE

Miriam is not named in the Biblical account (Exodus 2:1–10) of how the infant Moses was saved from death by setting him adrift on the waters. However, the Aggadah (the sections of the Talmud dealing with homily, legend, folklore and maxim) leaves us in no doubt that it was Miriam who engineered Moses's survival and adoption by Pharaoh's daughter. Not only that, she also arranged that their own mother, Jochabed, would be his wet nurse. Miriam had already been instrumental in Moses being born.[2] Before his birth, because Pharaoh had ordered the death of all male Hebrew babies, Miriam's father, Amram, decreed that all Hebrew men, including himself, would separate themselves from their wives so that no male children would be born. Miriam reprimanded her father. Amram, she said, was more wicked than Pharaoh thus to prevent the birth of *any* children. Did he not have sufficient trust in the Lord to protect His people?

Amram accepted Miriam's rebuke and remarried his wife, and the other men followed suit. Miriam then had a prophetic dream that a son would be born to her parents who would be the saviour of Israel. Thereafter Miriam was called a prophetess.

Another legend identified Miriam and Jochabed, her mother, with Puah and Shiprah, the Hebrew midwives reported in Exodus 1:15–22 who courageously saved Hebrew infants in defiance of Pharaoh. Puah (i.e. Miriam) upbraided Pharaoh to his face for his cruelty and wickedness.

The young Miriam fully justified her description as 'fearless in her rebukes';[3] nor did her fearlessness desert her later.

MIRIAM IN THE BIBLICAL TEXTS

I am indebted, for much of this section, to Rita J. Burns's engrossing study of the Biblical portrait of Miriam.[4]

Miriam is first named in a Biblical text when, with timbrel in hand, she led the women of Israel in celebrating the victory over the Egyptians and the safe passage of the Israelites through the Red Sea (Exodus 15:20–21). It was the role of women to lead such victory celebrations and the oldest versions of the text confirm that Miriam, not Moses, took this part.

Miriam is next mentioned in Numbers 12:1–15. At a later stage during the Israelite community's journey in the wilderness, Miriam challenged the unique position of Moses as the spokesman of the Lord, Yahweh. She asked (rhetorically, it seems): 'Has the Lord indeed spoken only through Moses?' In response, the Lord summoned Miriam, Aaron and Moses to the Tent of the Presence where he made it clear that Moses was not merely an ecstatic prophet, receiving God's message through dreams and visions, but one with whom God spoke face to face.

Miriam became stricken with leprosy and her skin turned 'white as snow'. Aaron, who (in what Burns believes is a later version of the story) was associated with Miriam's challenge but was not punished, pleaded for Miriam to be forgiven, as did Moses. The Lord declared that Miriam had to remain outside the camp for seven days, then she was pronounced cured.

On the face of it, Miriam had been punished and put in her place. Miriam's leprosy is taken to indicate that she was in a state of ritual uncleanness. However, 'white as snow' is used in other contexts to designate purity. Burns cites a suggestion that Miriam's ordeal may have been some kind of initiation.

Because she was designated a prophetess the incident is usually interpreted as Miriam claiming equality with Moses.[5] The Biblical texts do not, however, offer evidence of her prophetic activity. Alternatively, therefore, she can be seen as not so much claiming to be Moses' equal but rather asserting that there were other, equally valid ways of conveying the divine message. That is, that Miriam had *her* way, which we may assume to be somehow the women's or feminine way. We are not told explicitly what that way was, but may infer something about it.

Miriam is known as the sister of Aaron and Moses, and the three of them are seen as constituting a prophetic family of Levite descent. The designation of 'sister' also indicates parity of status; Miriam is shown as being on a par with Moses and

Aaron in the leadership of the wilderness community.

Burns draws clear conclusions from the biblical portrait of Miriam. A 'mediator of God's word', Miriam was connected with the religious cult of the Israelite people at that early time. In effect, she fulfilled a priestly function. Thus the term 'priestess' would seem more appropriate than 'prophetess' to describe her position.

Let us now return to the Aggadic material.

MIRIAM'S WELL

A most deeply symbolic legend is that of Miriam's Well.[6] This miraculous well accompanied the Hebrew community on their wanderings through the desert. It was a gift from God 'for the merits of the prophetess Miriam'. Water bubbled out from a special porous rock whenever the elders of the community spoke or sang to it. This rock appeared whenever the people made camp; finally, it settled opposite the Tabernacle. When Miriam died at Kadesh, the well disappeared.

Water supply is of vital importance in the desert; it is the difference between life and death. It is notable that there was a critical difference in the gentle and reliable way in which the water came forth from Miriam's well and the more violent means whereby Moses drew water from the rock. We are told that the well first appeared after the incident at Rephidim (Exodus 17:3–7) in which Moses, acting on the Lord's instructions, *struck* the rock with his staff to bring forth water. Thereafter water was not lacking until after Miriam's death (Numbers 20:1) when the well disappeared and the people again called angrily on Moses to supply water. This time, the Lord instructed Moses to speak to the rock but Moses *struck* the rock with his staff and had to repeat this action before water came forth. For this sin, of not having faith in the Lord and wilfully striking the rock for his own aggrandizement, Moses was barred from entering the Promised Land.

Dorothy Zeligs, in a psychoanalytic study,[7] points out that Moses' aggressive, sinful act followed directly on the death of Miriam, his older sister, who had been like a mother to him from infancy. Moreover Miriam had been 'the group mother and source of nurturance' to the wilderness community and her loss to them was likely to have been followed by deep distress and anger. Zeligs suggests these feelings were unacknowledged and uncontained and may have led to Moses' aggressive acting-out, in anger against the Lord.

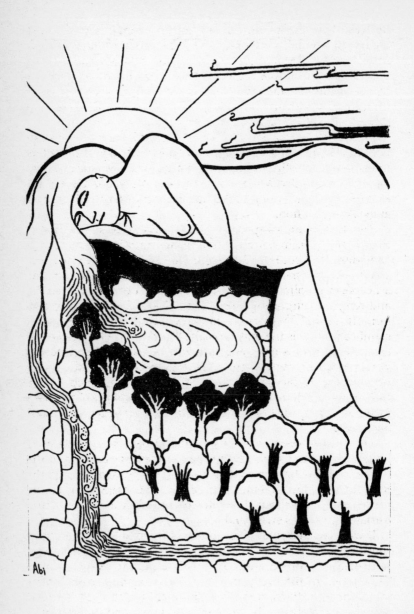

THE OTHER MIRIAM – MARY, MOTHER OF JESUS

By New Testament times, many Jewish women were named Miriam in honour of their remembered forebear.[8] One Miriam is more familiar as Mary, whose son was Jesus the Messiah.

Tradition has it that the first Miriam was the direct ancestor of the second.[9] The royal house of David descended from Miriam through her marriage with Caleb and Mary is a descendant of the house of David.[10]

Many further comparisons have been made, notably by early Christian writers, between Miriam and Mary.[11,12] Some went so far as to hint at Miriam being a prior existence of Mary, others merely commended Miriam as a 'type' of Mary, comparing, for example, Miriam's Song at the Red Sea with Mary's Magnificat at the Annunciation.

Two themes are of special symbolic interest here. The first is that of *virginity*. In contradiction of the tradition, Miriam was considered by some to have remained a virgin because her marriage is not mentioned in the Bible. Virginity, however, has a deeper symbolic meaning than this literal one. A woman is, and remains, 'virgin' by being 'one-in-herself' or 'belonging to herself alone'.[13] Miriam is very much one-in-herself; significantly she is the only woman named in the Old Testament genealogies who is not someone's wife or mother. Mary, too, is very much her own woman, as is evident when one looks beneath the surface of her story.[14] This is recognized by the linking of Mary to the Matronit of the Kabbalah[15,16] who includes in her attributes both sexual lover (of men and God) and virgin.

The second theme is that of *water*. The image of water is widely associated with Miriam. She placed her brother in the waters and saw him drawn forth safely; she passed through the Red Sea with the Israelites to freedom. Her name may derive from *marim*, bitter; but the water provided in the desert from Miriam's Well was sweet and life-giving.

It was said that rivers flowed from Miriam's Well, so large at times that the people needed a vessel to cross over from one part of the camp to another.[17] This fantastic description is reminiscent of the imagery in the Zohar relating to the rivers which come forth from the Sefirah Binah, which itself is called Marah the Great Sea, the Mother of all living and the Matronit. Mary's association with the Matronit has already been mentioned.

Mary, whose name in Latin, Maria, also means 'seas', was known as *stilla maris*, i.e. a drop of the sea, and is venerated as Queen of the Sea. Her tears, representing purity, were said to have special powers of healing.

Miriam and Mary, both, are representative of the profound mystery of the Deep, the reservoir and source of life, those waters which 'precede every form and sustain every creation'.[18]

CONCLUSION

'Seldom mentioned, but never forgotten',[19] Miriam continued to appear in traditions and legends down through the ages. In medieval times, she was identified with Maria Prophetissa, the greatest woman alchemist,[20] echoing the Islamic tradition that when Caleb married Miriam he learned from her the secret of alchemy.[21] Although it seems that Miriam acted in a priestly capacity, she is not acknowledged as a 'priestess' in the texts. Indications are that the priesthood had to be presented as, and subsequently maintained as, exclusively male. Barker[22] points out that the priesthood, from the time of Miriam to most of the Christian priesthood today, *had* to exclude women because it had taken over, symbolically, those functions (such as giving life, providing nourishment and healing) otherwise performed by the feminine archetype. In her words: 'Without a monopoly of the creative, feminine role, there would be no power left to them. Now, as then, it is a corruption.'

Behind Miriam stands the feminine archetype, the infinite depths of the waters, the Great Mother, the well of living water. She was a woman complete in herself and fearless in her rebukes. The pattern is repeated with her namesake who is called Mother of God.

Miriam, priestess leader of the Israelites in the wilderness, should now take her place as one of the mothers of our Judaeo-Christian heritage; through whom, indeed, God also spoke.

REFERENCES

1 Ginzberg, L., *The Legends of the Jews*, Vol. 2, Jewish Publication Society of America, 1909–38.
2 Ginzberg, op. cit., Vol. 2.
3 *Encyclopaedia Judaica:* Miriam
4 Burns, R.J., *Has the Lord Indeed Spoken only Through Moses?*, SBL Dissertation Series 84, Scholars Press, Atlanta, Georgia, 1987.

5 Halevi, Z., *Kabbalah and Exodus*, Rider, 1988.

6 Ginzberg, op. cit., Vol. 3.

7 Zeligs, D., 'Why did Moses Strike the Rock?', in Sauna, V. (ed.), *Fields of Offerings: Studies in Honour of Raphael Patai*, Associated University Presses, 1983.

8 Ashe, G., *The Virgin: Mary's Cult and the Re-emergence of the Goddess*, Arkana, 1988.

9 Le Déaut, R., 'Miryam, soeur de Moïse et Marie, mère de Messie', *Biblica*, Vol. 45, 1964.

10 Ashe, op. cit.

11 Le Déaut, op. cit.

12 Ashe, op. cit.

13 Harding, M.E., *Woman's Mysteries*, Rider, 1955/1982.

14 Warner, M., *Alone of all her Sex: the Myth and Cult of the Virgin Mary*, Weidenfeld & Nicolson, 1976.

15 Patai, R., *The Hebrew Goddess*, new edn, Wayne State University Press, 1990.

16 Fortune, D., *The Mystical Qabalah*, Ernest Benn, 1935/1979.

17 Ginzberg, op. cit.

18 Eliade, M., *Images and Symbols: Studies in Religious Symbolism*, New York, 1969.

19 Burns, op. cit.

20 Begg, E., *The Cult of the Black Virgin*, Arkana, 1985.

21 *Encyclopaedia Judaica*: Miriam.

22 Barker, M., *The Lost Prophet*, SPCK, 1988.

LILITH LISTENS TO THE WIVES OF THE SCRIBES OF THE LEVITES
Valerie Sinason

We come from the sickbed
long time lying
long time lying

We give you the crippled mother
inside the crippled mother
inside the crippled mother

We give you grandmother/nanna
the hollow household idle
on the pyrrh of her piles
on the incense-itivity
of her vast incontinence

We give you the women warping
through their unsealed envelopes of flesh
leaking through the braille bones of corsets
Between their prayer fingers – air –
Between their lips the chatter of false teeth
biting on false letters
trying to lose roots

Everyday their souls spill
out of saucepans and soup, household scrubbing,
from tiny holy leaks
plants and children sometimes grow.

Worn by the weight of Buddhas in sickbeds
the children ask for words.

But it is the fathers who have words
and the ritual comforts of prayer shawls
Where hands have failed to hold them
God sticks them down
in His Self-addressed envelopes

And God shrugs His shoulders
upturns His hands
Around His fingers
the lack of a wedding ring burns circles

'Mary Mary, how does your garden grow?'
He cries to the desert wilderness.
He has tablets of stone to draw on.
Once He had a son.

Lilith grins blackly from her
lone desert wheelchair,

Her children have gone to the devil.

Once she had man and babe, soul and words

Once she said 'No' like an angel.

MARY – RECEPTIVE WOMAN
Vera von der Heydt

When I was fourteen I was asked to write an essay: 'How do the heroes in Schiller's Ballads conduct themselves in the light of the philosophy of Kant and Schiller, particularly with reference to the concept of the beautiful soul?' At that time I lifted up my finger and my voice and said: 'Herr Professor, I am sorry I can't write about that, I am too stupid.' We were eight girls between the age of fourteen and sixteen in my class; we had read all Schiller's plays and ballads, one a week, and we had had one hour on the concept of the beautiful soul. It may seem odd that such an essay had been suggested and expected from us, but thinking back, it made us aware that beautiful souls exist in reality as well as being an abstract principle. In English it sounds peculiar to speak about 'beautiful souls', in German it does not.

A little while ago I was asked to speak about soul, anima, receptive consciousness, receptive woman. Some of the feelings I had when I was fourteen invaded me then. What did these words mean? What was behind them? Are these words of importance today? Suddenly I saw them moving around in a circle and in the centre there was the Virgin Mary sitting next to Her Son. The Virgin Mary: the Eternal Feminine who guides men and women through Hell and Purgatory to Paradise, into the experience of forgetting and forgiving, helping sinful women and men find repentance and redemption: standing behind Beatrice, and protecting Gretchen and Faust: 'Our Lady of the Way'. These thoughts went through my mind; I looked again; the centre of the circle was empty.

In the second half of the nineteenth century the soul got lost; scientists declared that it was nothing but a childish illusion, unreal as it could not be touched. Men's attitude to women became more and more condescending, their expectations more stereotyped: she had to be sexually attractive, able to get children (only her fault if this did not happen), and a good housekeeper; her brain was supposed to be like that of a hen. Contempt for woman: contempt for the soul.

Then, in the 1920s, Jung the psychiatrist re-introduced the soul as a reality in psychology – though not in the accepted Christian theological sense.[1] He asserted that the search for one's soul, one's own neglected soul, was the key to the healing of the collective and individual neurosis of our time. In religion, 'To have pity on one's soul is pleasing unto the Lord.'

Loss of the soul is serious; primitive people believed that the soul then goes into the land of the dead; this means psychologically that the soul withdraws into the collective unconscious. The land of the dead is the land of the ancestors who have left unanswered questions, unresolved problems; the unredeemed past emerges clamouring for answers. When, if, a soul returns from these dark regions, it will be stronger than before; sometimes, however, the pull and the desire to remain in the dark is too great. This is the lure of the unconscious and its destructive power, the devouring mother. In some languages there is only one word for soul and shadow: there is the terrible temptation and sin of selling one's soul to the devil. The soul in the hands of, possessed by the devil: the ugly soul. Have we sold our souls? Or have we lost them?

Soul, Seele, anima, psyche are feminine in gender. In Jung's definition, the soul is the organ through which an individual relates to inner processes, to the unconscious, to life in its totality. Eros, relatedness, is woman's basic principle. Man is now searching for Eros, for the feminine within himself, and for woman's reality, by becoming more aware of the anima, the image of femininity in his psyche, attempting to discover what he feels about woman, for woman – without sentimentality and idealizations of a positive or negative kind. A man meets the anima in various guises in his dreams, in fantasy, and his moods – dominating, disturbing, possibly even destroying him. When he can face her in the inner world without fear, ask her questions, say yes or no to her demands, and realize her insinuations and plottings, she will be his muse, his inspiration.

Jung called the anima Eve, Helen of Troy, Mary, Sophia, to indicate her various aspects, the roles she can play in a man's life and the images he projects onto woman.[2] However, modern man has not yet understood what the Greeks knew: women do not only play different roles, they are different in kind.

The strongest, most powerful figure is still that of the mother; not only because of the need for containment and warmth, but also for another reason which has not been much discussed: namely, man's breast- and womb-envy. Once upon a time this was dealt with in initiation rites; not so long ago there was the couvade and there were men who took to their beds with a 'real' illness when labour was imminent or had started, in order to draw attention to themselves, it was said. Today a man is expected to assist his woman when she is giving birth and perhaps the vicarious pains he suffers are a substitute for the physical sufferings that were inflicted on him by the ritual subincision.

For a long time women carried and conformed to anima projections; they colluded with them, hid their own feelings not only because of physical fear of male violence, but also from emotional fear of being abandoned and because of social and financial implications. So they pretended, flattered, lied, treated men like little boys, forever mother, great mother, the Great Mother. Now no more. Justifiably proud of their achievements, women are very conscious of their capacities, and they are fighting with courage and indignation for independence and the right to be what, who they really are, without feeling guilty. This is a wonderful example for the positive masculine spirit alive in them: logos, discriminating, active, thinking: the animus. The animus corresponds to the anima in so far as he is the personified male figure in the woman's psyche; but he is her spirit, not her soul.

The animus has a very destructive side; as women have become intoxicated with their power, many are ignoring their essential womanhood and are denying 'choice' to their sisters. Identified with the animus, they are possessed by the negative male spirit: opinionated, intolerant, greedy, inflated. The strident compulsiveness with which their demands are made points to a deeper grievance behind the obsession with equality in the sense of sameness, or with a power-drive, a grievance which is profoundly unconscious. The Church has treated women badly, we all know that. Not only woman, but the feminine principle – instinct, the body, nature – had always been suspect, but during the Reformation the figure of the Virgin Mary, woman's cherished light aspect, was removed and banished by Reformers and Protesters, and human nature was declared to be wholly evil. Woman is closer to nature than man; therefore woman is more evil than man. Is she? By being 'more like a man' does she become less evil? Or perhaps since man is discovering his femininity has he become more evil?

In all this turmoil on the physical material plane, is a spiritual battle being fought? For the time being there is a split between woman's ego-consciousness and the value and meaning of her essential being: to be receptive, to be a vessel, is considered an insult. In the I Ching the 'Receptive' is vessel, and the expression for the feminine. To be receptive is thought of as being like the dark, yielding power of the earth; earth which gives birth and nourishes reality, carries all things, good and bad, without exception gives beauty and splendour. The image for earth is the mare who combines strength and swiftness with the gentleness and devotion of the cow. The feminine Receptive co-exists with masculine Creativity; they are the two worlds of power which complete one another.

Receptive consciousness is the feminine attitude to thinking. It is a kind of totality of knowing through inner experience in which the heart is involved as well as the mind. It is a 'knowing' in which the intellect plays hardly any part: knowing by feeling and intuition. Receptive consciousness is an expression of a feminine attitude to life, in other words, it is soul.

The embodiment, the model for this attitude in the Christian culture is the Virgin Mary. Men and women, Catholics and non-Catholics alike have difficulties in relating to this ideal figure, who is also an actual woman. Negative feelings have been aroused against her by the way she has been portrayed – dressed in white and blue, roses on her feet, looking up to heaven, unaware of sin, temptation and its pain – and the commercial razzamatazz around her in places where she has appeared. All this feeds prejudice and enviousness. In a way it is not surprising that there is so much resistance, hostility and ignorance with regard to her. She represents so much of that which we do not want to know: the feminine, the soul, goodness. We cannot 'take' that she is 'only light', ever virgin, ever fruitful, and that she is pure, not innocent. She knows, but her feeling is not contaminated with thinking.

Born without Original Sin: being before time, like Eve, free to choose, like Eve. Eve chose to be disloyal to the Spirit, Mary chose to be loyal to the Spirit and to her body, experiencing it as a channel through which spirit is born into the world.

She received the Word and conceived in Faith – 'Fiat Mihi secundum Verbum Tuum', 'may it be done unto Me according to Thy Word' – and in Joy – 'Magnificat anima mea Dominum', 'my soul shall magnify the Lord ... because He has regarded the humility of His handmaid'. It has been said of her that she was filled with the presence of God, that she was filled with the Holy Spirit, and that the Word Made Flesh dwelt in her womb: the Holy Trinity in Woman.

Where was her darkness? There was darkness in her blood. Three women are mentioned by name in her ancestry, and a fourth is alluded to: Rahab, disguised as a prostitute, seduced her father-in-law; another Rahab was a prostitute, but saved the Israelite army; Ruth was a foreigner, a Moabite woman; the fourth was Bathsheba so greatly desired by King David that he sent her husband to his death. There was her loneliness and her grief and her anxiety. Her Son's words she did not understand though she moved them in her heart. Only once he gave her the name of 'Mother', from the Cross: not personal mother, but mother of us all, inner mother of men and women who all can give birth to the Christ, to the Messiah, ever anew.

Since the end of the nineteenth century many more appearances of the Virgin have been recorded than ever before. The most impressive vision was that of Bernadette Soubirous at Lourdes. Our Lady appeared to the girl when she was standing near a grove said to be haunted by evil spirits. She indicated a place where the girl was to dig the earth with her bare hands to release a spring of healing water. When Bernadette asked her 'beautiful Lady' who she was, she got the answer: 'I am the Immaculate Conception.' She linked herself to being before time was, anything was, when she played before 'Him' and was 'His' delight. Eve, her younger sister? Symbolizing consciousness and Ego? Mary, the Eternal Feminine, Healer of the split between Ego and the Self? Mary, holding the key to healing through water, living water? The miracle of finding, discovering a new attitude to one's infirmity, to one's own illness, dis-ease becoming meaningful. Sometimes the miracle of physical healing also happens in Lourdes. Lourdes is a numinous place and many people who go there have a numinous experience; in spite of the vulgarity, ugliness and noise connected with it? No, curiously enough because of it, because of the shadow which belongs to soul, to the totality of life.

Mary was a strong steadfast Jewish woman. She fell asleep according to tradition when she was sixty-three years old. Angels took her soul and carried it to heaven where her Son and King received her. There are many pictures of this event. But the Dogma of the Assumption was declared only in 1950. In the official document,[3] the Apostolic Constitution says, 'that the Immaculate Mother of God, Mary ever Virgin, when the course of her earthly life was finished, was taken up body and soul into the Glory of Heaven.' In another passage it is stated: 'It is moreover reasonable and fitting that as a man's so also a woman's body should have attained ever-lasting glory in heaven.' A wrong has been righted: woman, and with her the feminine principle, has been given her rightful place; in fact, the Virgin has joined the Trinity. Jung called it the greatest event in the Church since the Reformation:[4] Mary the woman who embodies soul, the feminine principle, has been recognized collectively. Individually one has to find one's own soul.

For Alchemists the Assumption of Our Lady was the completion of the process, the ultimate reconciliation of the complementary opposites, feminine–masculine which symbolize the *unus mundus*. This is the great mystery we have to live but cannot solve as if it were a problem. Jung was an Alchemist; he knew about transformation and the mysterious transformation which takes place in a woman when she has received and conceived. I am grateful that I was born a woman.

REFERENCES

1 C.G. Jung, *Modern Man in Search of a Soul*, London, Routledge & Kegan Paul, 1933.
2 C.G. Jung, *Collected Works*, Volume 9, Part 1, 'Concerning the Archetypes, with Special Reference to the Anima Concept', London, Routledge & Kegan Paul, 1968 (1933).
3 Pius XII, *Munificentissimus Deus*, 1950.
4 C.G. Jung, *Collected Works*, Volume 11, 'Answer to Job', London, Routledge & Kegan Paul, 1969.

QUIETLY WAITING
Jean Head

GODDESS: Why did I glimpse you so late?
Why hidden so long?
You: quietly waiting
till eyes open, ears unstop.
Now, touch of finding.

Power of patriarchy,
iron – gripped
the male God
imprisons and hides you.
Tradition turns you invisible,
blinds, deafens, those who follow.

Now; stirrings;
many explorers, many discoverers.
How different You are, Goddess,
quietly waiting.
You, She;
earth, cave, stone, water, tree,
moonshine opens dark potency,
greets unknown new life, unafraid,
welcome of a parent
glad as life unfolds.
You do not have to know all things,
can wait for seeing, quietly.

How different from
You, He God;
sky bound,
distantly creating,

expecting good,
spying wrongdoing of children of men,
needing knowledge, power, obedience.
You God, He;
distorted by minds of men,
men's supremacy, men's emphases,
turned You fearful, destructive,
overweighted,
Godhead burdened.

Godhead longing:
relaxing strong grasp
forged by male exegesis,
moving towards Hochma, Shekhinah.
Finding new wisdom, new glory,
new grace,
quietly waiting.

SEX, SYMBOLS AND THE UNITY OF GOD
Jenny Goodman

INTRODUCTION

There is an incompleteness. In ourselves and in our Jewish history and practice, we sense the absence of the suppressed feminine half. We need 'the Goddess' now because she illuminates aspects of Divinity which are left out of patriarchal Judaism. But the incompleteness we seek to rectify as we reinstate the Goddess is in our culture and our language, not in the Divine. The female half is not missing from God; it is missing from our picture of God.

Throughout this essay I attempt to distinguish between the nature of the Divine, about which we can hardly speak, and the nature of the symbols – words and myths – which give us our access to the Divine and our way of communicating about the Divine. Symbols are vehicles; they convey – or distort – the truth that cannot be expressed directly.

Gender is a characteristic of human beings, of words and pictures, and often of the great archetypes of myth. But it is not, I suggest, a characteristic of God.

LANGUAGE: THE POWER OF NAMING AND THE PROBLEM OF THE PRONOUN

There is a difficulty: we need to use words to refer to that which transcends words. On the one hand, Jewish belief states that God, being One, indivisible and beyond physicality, is beyond gender. On the other hand, Jewish texts and liturgy convey an inescapable impression of the maleness of God. Such is the power of the pronoun.

Hebrew has no neutral pronoun, only 'He' or 'She'. Whatever

our beliefs, the almost constant use of 'He' in relation to the Divine is likely to block or distort our spiritual experience and expression. No amount of reassurance from rabbis that 'He' really includes both female and male will alter what we hear – we hear five thousand years of 'God' made in the image of man, by men.

What happens when we say 'She' instead? The first thing to happen is that everyone sits up and takes notice. They notice that you've changed the gender, so they proceed to notice that there *is* a gender routinely attached to God. For some men (and, it must be admitted, for some women), the new pronoun 'gets in the way', precisely because it makes them *conscious* of the act of attributing gender to God. That act was also going on with 'He', of course, but familiarity rendered it unconscious.

Moving from pronouns to nouns, what happens when we say 'Goddess'? The word 'Goddess' exists inevitably in relation to the word 'God', as does 'Jewess' in relation to 'Jew'. When we say 'Goddess', which is clearly female, we leave 'God', with all its long-embedded resonance of power, with the masculine gender. Thus we are actually reinforcing the idea of a powerful male deity. So I find the best way for me is to use the noun 'God' with the pronoun 'She', which at least makes quite clear that God is not male, and thus begins to correct the imbalance. Perhaps eventually our languages will evolve an animate, transgender pronoun – or we will manage to do without the pronouns altogether.

There are two problems associated with the use of 'He' for God; one is sexism and the other is anthropomorphism. Changing to 'She' (or 'You') may improve the situation vis-à-vis sexism, but leaves the problem of anthropomorphism intact. Our language seems to force us to speak of God as a person. And the English neuter pronoun 'it' is of no help, because it would force us to speak of God as a 'thing', an object, so instead of anthropomorphizing we reify God. Any noun, even the impersonal 'deity', implies an entity, a being within the world, whereas God is that in which all entities – people, objects and worlds – exist and have their being. Nouns create limitation; God is limitless.

Goddess names like Shechina, Matronit, Lilith, Hochma and so on, much as the masculine god-names, suffer from this linguistic problem. Their resonance of 'Mother' may meet a deep emotional need, and/or re-establish historical continuity, and these are valid enough reasons for their use. But like any name they also carry the risk that we may mistake the name –

the symbol – for that which is symbolized. In the case of the Shechina, or Hochma, whose names represent deeply significant aspects of the Divine, the risk is that we mistake the part for the whole. She and all her names may be vital symbols for us at this point in our history, but I want to keep remembering that symbols are only gateways. 'She' may be an open gate to God and 'He' a closed gate at this moment, but neither 'She' nor 'He' is really God.

MYTH: TORAH, TRUTH AND STORIES

The Kabbalists made a distinction between the core or true essence of the Torah – Her meaning – and Her outer garments, which are the stories of Torah. I would like to make this same distinction.

Taken as mythical narrative (to borrow Raphael Patai's term), the Torah seems to be documenting the often violent transition to patriarchy in Israel. And the tale is distorted because it is told by the victors.

Taken as mystical symbolism, however, Torah can be seen as profound truth in code, as one of humanity's greatest sacred texts, like the Tao Te Ching or the Bhagavad Gita.

The *core* of the Torah is an insight, attributed to Abraham, about the unity of the Divine. Not that trees and mountains are not sacred, but that no tree or mountain is the whole of sacredness. Not that the goddesses and gods of grove and hill and rock and river, sun and moon and sky are not real – in fact these polytheistic figures all have their place in the Kabbalistic scheme of the Divine – but that each one is just a *part*. Idolatry, to me, means mistaking the part for the whole, and worshipping the part. God has many names in Judaism, many aspects, but is still One; God *is* the interconnectedness of all the parts.

But profound insight rarely remains pure and simple. Truth comes encased in layers of language, and language carries culture. The Torah is mediated to us by the cultural context of the men who wrote it down, and by the male scholars who have commented on it, interpreted, extrapolated and 'decoded' it over twenty-five centuries. It has been filtered through patriarchal consciousness, and distorted by patriarchy's ideas of good and evil, higher and lower, female and male. It is told through their symbols and seen through their eyes. All truth is open to corruption, and the more profound the truth, the more devastating the effects of its corruption. So we read in the Torah stories of a holy war against the Goddess – and the woman in us screams in pain.

How do we live with this tension, this paradox? My answer – very Jewishly – is: *we grapple with it*. We grapple with the fact that the God who is One and all-inclusive was quickly turned into just another male Canaanite deity battling for supremacy against other local gods; we grapple with the knowledge that a moment of profound illumination about the nature of creation degenerated, in mens' hands, into a 'Jihad' against the women. And we remember that this process (seeing the Light ⟶ describing, distorting and selling the light ⟶ forcible conversion) is, sadly, universal in human history. Vision turning into its own opposite can be seen happening around us today.

It is true that my heart sinks when I read the Biblical prophets yelling against the Goddess Asherah, and hear the latter-day prophets similarly yelling against women's participation in Jewish ritual. But vital as it is for me to raise my voice against their misogyny and speak out for women and the Goddess, it is equally vital for me to hold onto Abraham's insight – if his it was – which started the whole thing off.

As we reclaim the Goddess and concomitantly disown much of what is patriarchal in Judaism, I ask that we continue to distinguish carefully between the essence and the garment of Jewish teaching, and not throw out the baby (the essence, the mystical truth) with the bathwater (the garments, the patriarchal myths).

UNITY, DUALITY AND GENDER: A KABBALISTIC VIEW

The idea of divine Unity is at the centre of Kabbalah, as of all mystical traditions. God is seen as both immanent and transcendent, filling and surrounding the earth, sea and sky, yet simultaneously unknowable and 'beyond'. There is nothing which is outside God.

Yet within Unity, there is Duality.

The Kabbalistic Tree of Life, which is nothing less than a map of the whole of creation, has two outer pillars. The right-hand 'active' pillar is about expansiveness and mercy; the left-hand 'receptive' pillar is about constraint and justice. This kind of polarity – between love and discipline, revelation and reason, art and science, right-brain and left-brain, yang and yin – exists on many levels in creation, and is described in the mystical systems of many cultures. (And in the Kabbalistic Tree, the harmony or balance between the two poles is represented by the middle pillar.) How far does this polarity relate to gender, the

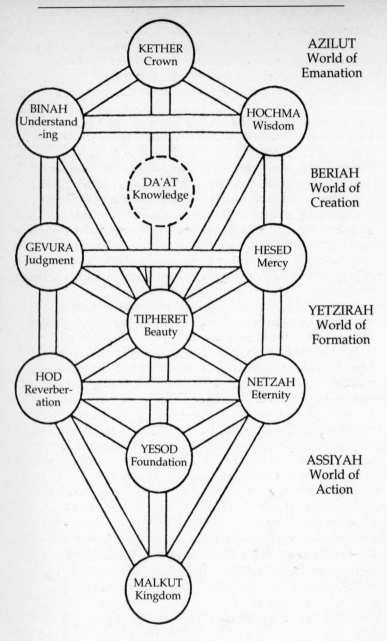

Tree of Life

polarity of male and female?

Gender is a feature of the lower two realms of the Kabbalistic world – the physical and the emotional – but not of the upper two realms – the intellectual and the spiritual.

I believe that it was one of patriarchy's errors to equate directly the obvious earthly polarity of male and female with the dimly perceived celestial duality reflected in the upper levels of the Tree of Life. Such a simplistic equation is dangerous but also tempting, because we tend to want direct analogies – like anthropomorphism – for what seems abstract and remote.

Having said that, however, there is a Kabbalistic maxim, 'As above, so below.' We seek such analogies precisely because we are reaching towards this truth, towards a pattern. In fact, analogy is no mere linguistic device; analogy is built into the fabric of creation. Any resemblance between earthly sexuality and 'heavenly' duality, while needing cautious interpretation, cannot be total coincidence. I *do* see a parallel, tentatively, between the left-hand pillar of receptivity and inward containment and certain physical aspects of female sexuality, and similarly between the right-hand pillar of active outward expansiveness and male sexuality.

But we are far more than our physical gender. Just because aspects of sexuality may be a metaphor for spiritual levels of polarity, this *doesn't* mean – as patriarchy has assumed – that the corresponding emotional, intellectual and spiritual attributes are accordingly distributed between women and men. We are a mirror of the Divine ('made in Her image') on all our levels – and the mirror is crudest on the physical plane, and increasingly subtle as we ascend the Tree. Each of us, in the Kabbalistic view, is a miniature complete Tree of Life, containing the whole – with its potentially perfect balance – within ouselves.

The Goddess as Hochma (Wisdom) and as Shechina/ Matronit has a central place in the Kabbalistic scheme of things. But 'She' is by no means confined to one side of the Tree (in fact, Hochma is situated at the top of the right-hand, active pillar) and no more should we, as women, be confined to one side of creation.

AUTHENTICITY AND TRANSFORMATION

Hinduism is not short of Goddess-figures, but men still dominate its practice. Reclaiming the Goddess may be an important part of 'depatriarchalizing' Judaism, but it is only one part of the process. A Judaism for our era requires changes not only in the focus of worship but also in its structures; from hierarchy to participatory democracy, from dogma to tolerance of diversity, from institutional formality to ... but that is another book in itself. In any transformation there arises the issue of authenticity: 'if we change it, is it still Judaism?'

Firstly, if our transforming of Judaism is to be authentic, I believe we must start where Judaism is now, not from Biblical times. There is a tendency in Goddess-circles to take interpretations and implications direct from the Bible as through the Talmud hadn't happened. The fact is that Jewish thought and practice today is removed from the Bible by many layers of interpretation, legend, law-making and custom.

Secondly, how do we define what is authentic Jewish practice? Is it what the rabbis say, or is it what the people do? The prophet Jeremiah scolded the people for 'baking cakes to the Queen of Heaven', but clearly this is what the people did. Jewish practice could be defined simply as what Jews practise. If I do it in good faith and from my heart, it is authentic.

Thirdly, Judaism has always evolved; in fact it has only survived as a spiritual tradition by moving with the 'Zeitgeist'. The history of Jewish literature and practice is the history of changes, some gradual, many cataclysmic. Those who resisted the major transformations of Jewish culture largely disappeared from Jewish history; those who flowed with the changes created the Judaism of their times. It has been suggested that Judaism is approaching a transformation now of a magnitude comparable to that which followed the destruction of the second Temple. The change then was from sacrificial worship and agricultural festivals in a central Temple in one land, to verbal worship and learning in local synagogues in towns and villages scattered all over the world. The transformation today – following the unspeakable Destruction of our own century – may need to be equally deep and equally drastic. Will it still be Judaism? That depends on us. If we are serious about Judaism and we are serious about feminism, we have a formidable intellectual task. A genuine integration of these two strands of our lives will take us many decades of dreaming, studying and talking together.

In my dream, it will still be Judaism when the Mechitzas (the physical barriers separating men and women in synagogue) have all been swept away, when the menstrual taboos have sunk and died, when women's voices raised in song and women's dances on the face of the earth form part of our sacred ritual, when professional rabbis no longer exist and gay and lesbian marriage is part of our ceremonial life, when prayer involves body and heart and soul as well as mouth and prayerbook, when nobody sits in rows of chairs and no Jew tells another what is and is not permitted, when a synagogue can be a seashore or a wooded mountainside – it will still be Judaism.

A heartfelt 'Thank you' to Stuart Linke for many hours of patient typing, and for many more hours of exciting debate, challenging criticism and loving encouragement.

THE DIVINE WOMAN IN CHRISTIANITY
Roger Horrocks

And a great portent appeared in heaven,
a woman clothed with the sun, with the
moon under her feet, and on her head a
crown of twelve stars; she was with child
and she cried out in her pangs of birth,
in anguish for delivery.

Revelation 12:1–2 [1]

In the early 1980s my perceptions of the Virgin Mary altered drastically in two ways. First, while I was on holiday in France, apparently fortuitously I kept coming across churches which contained statues of Black Virgins, which are quite common there. I found these statues to be very powerful images, radiating majesty and authority. Some of them were quite primitive, almost like African statues. They were totally unlike the rather saccharine, simpering statues of Mary I had seen in England. Here was no symbol of feminine submissiveness and piety. They were stripped down, archaic, fierce. In places like Chartres and Rocamadour, I was also amazed at the popular devotion to the Black Virgin. There was a tremendous aura round the statue – people knelt, prayed, contemplated. A deep silence pervaded everything, and filled my own mind. What did that black face, which seemed to come out of ancient time, signify? Why did it move me so much? What did it offer? What did I need from it? These questions haunted me afterwards. I had studied theology within a Protestant tradition, so Mary had been a blank spot for me, and my own spontaneous response was shocking to me, because it was non-intellectual, it was visceral.

At roughly the same time, something else had been happening that surprised me. In my work as a psychotherapist several of my clients – both men and women – had dreams or visions of the Virgin Mary. A forty-year-old man, who had been doing a lot of bodywork therapy in connection with his need for touch, had an almost overpowering vision of Mary holding him, and he communicated very poignantly the great tranquillity and trust that filled him. A fifty-year-old woman had a dream of Mary enveloping her, sustaining her, like some elemental force field. I had also started to come across women who had powerful experiences of *being* the Virgin Mary.

These people were usually indifferent or hostile to Christianity, and yet the images of Mary were evidently of the greatest importance to them. One could say in some cases that they were life-transforming symbols. Interestingly, they had all had fairly negative mothers in their own childhood, and the images of Mary seemed to offer them internally some kind of motherly love and care that they had lacked externally.

My own experiences of the Black Virgin, and my clients' experiences, were non-cerebral, non-theological. They were personal, intuitive, emotional responses. It was as if we had been addressed in a language that was not made up of words, but spoke to the heart and opened it up.

These experiences set me off on a trail of exploration of Mary, who she was, where she had come from, and what she meant.

GODDESS?

Christian theology has always been careful to stress that Mary is not a deity in her own right. She is the 'handmaid of the Lord' (Luke 1:38), subordinate to Father, Son and Spirit. Hence when one prays to Mary, this can only be seen as prayer to God through Mary.

The early Church was evidently concerned about an excessive veneration of Mary:

> God came down from heaven, the Word clothed Himself with flesh from a holy Virgin, not, assuredly, that the Virgin should be adored, nor to make her god, nor that we should offer sacrifice to her name, nor that, now after so many generations, women should once again be appointed priests. . . . Let no one adore Mary.[2]

This citation is taken from the fourth century *Heresies* of

Epiphanius, and illustrates the explicit fear of the return of the goddess-cult ('after so many generations') and its priestesses. It also refers to that split between flesh and spirit that dominates Christianity for two thousand years. Mary is needed to give her flesh to the Word, but in the theological hierarchy, flesh must rank below spirit. From this polarity flows so much of the hatred of the woman and the body that is found in Christianity.

And the theological downgrading of the feminine can still be found in twentieth-century Mariology expressed with unabated vigour:

> The essence of woman was already defined in Eve: to be the complement that exists entirely in its derivation from the other. . . . Here [in Mary] this essence reaches its acme: pure derivation from God.[3]

This passage from Ratzinger's book *Daughter Zion* appears quite imperturbable in the face of the modern claims of women for social and spiritual equality, but in fact Cardinal Ratzinger is merely distilling the traditional view of Mary (and of woman): that she is a pure *response* to God, and can be no more. In this kind of theology, the central thesis of Marian celebration is the *fiat mihi*: 'Behold, I am the handmaid of the Lord; Let it be to me according to your word' (Luke 1:38).

But theology is the conscious rational articulation of spirituality. There is a deeper non-rational level of spiritual expression where a different picture of Mary is found, for example in this eighth-century liturgy from the Ethiopic Church:

> *O Mary, immensity of heaven,*
> *foundation of the earth,*
> *depth of the seas, light of the sun,*
> *beauty of the moon,*
> *splendour of the stars in heaven .*[4]

In such texts, characteristic of the Eastern Church, we see a different vision of Mary – cosmic, all-embracing, theophanous. And a similar response to Mary is found in certain paintings of her. An amazing example is Leonardo's cartoon for the Virgin and Child with St Anne and St John, a sublime image of feminine mystery, creativity, infinity. It was only recently that I realized that in this cartoon, Mary is sitting in her mother's lap, forming an extraordinary symbol: womb to womb, a matrilineal descent (or ascent) through the Goddess.

In Leonardo's *The Virgin of the Rocks*, we find a Mary set against a background of tremendous natural energy that almost threatens to become chaotic. Huge crags tower over the figures, seemingly menacing them, but Mary's hands reach out protectively, as if protecting humanity itself.

Both these great images by Leonardo show Mary as a powerful force of lovingness. She is love, not in a sentimental or tawdry way, but love as a world-principle, as a universal energy. As such she cannot be contained or defined doctrinally – she is immense, she is limitless. But Leonardo seems to say that this is the force of love within us – it is not some theological abstraction. Mary represents our own capability for profound human love, that goes out to another person, holds them, feels infinite pity, tenderness, melting compassion, yet does not obliterate them. She is non-narcissistic love, love that holds you without swamping you or choking you.

In some mystical way, these images of Mary reveal love as the structure of the universe, the principle of order itself. This is the greatness of Leonardo's perception – working before the huge splits caused in the Renaissance between science and religion, between knowledge and love, he was able to synthesize in her image the love that exists in the natural world, in the physical world, and in the human heart, which is itself a home of the divine. In *The Virgin of the Rocks* physics and psyche – so long opposed to each other in the modern world – can still be reconciled, brought together as a cosmic yet natural ordering.

One can only imagine also that these great works came out of Leonardo's great love – his love for Mary, for life, for the creation, for himself.

Christianity has often said that God is love, but this has often remained an abstraction, a moral precept. In Leonardo's Mary we see the divine, living, love, not as a far-off impossibility or a moral imperative, but as something alive and spontaneous in the human heart, and revealed *in bodies*, which are painted in a fully fleshly way, yet held in great stillness and peace in Mary's presence.

Thus the human response to, treatment of, Mary has been highly stratified. The emotional response to her has been quite at odds with the rational delineation of her role in theology. And this is something we might have predicted, if we assume that the Goddess figure exists in the unconscious as an archetypal image, often unassimilable, rejected by the patriarchal intellect, but capable of being directly apprehended by the imagination and the emotions. In fact, ironically, a similar split can be seen in relation to God. Theologically God has no gender, but people have always treated him as male since, theology notwithstanding, the Christian God is experienced as an expression of the archetypal masculine deity.

But even in certain areas of theology, we find statements that take Mary closer to the godhead. Again in the Orthodox Church Mary can be described as follows: 'the very heart of the Church, one of her most secret mysteries, her mystical centre, her perfection already realized in a human person fully united with God.'[5]

Here we seem to approach closely to the acceptance of Mary as divine. Jesus and Mary are seen as two aspects of the human/divine relationship. In Jesus we see the divine spirit become flesh; in Mary the flesh becomes deified, is lifted up. Thus the Dogma of the Assumption into Heaven (which states that Mary was taken up body and soul into heaven), is symbolically a perfect summation of this elevation. Jung was full of praise for this dogma, since he saw it as the acceptance of the feminine into the godhead.[6] *Consciously*, this is certainly not so, and any devout Catholic would be outraged to hear Mary spoken of as Goddess. But of course the unconscious speaks quite a different language from the conscious, and Jung saw dogma as an expression of the unconscious: 'Dogma is like a dream, reflecting the spontaneous and autonomous activity of the objective psyche, the unconscious.'[7]

In a sense theologians assent to this when they insist that the truths described in dogma are pre-existing, are not concocted by theology itself. Thus in the great arguments that have gone on between Catholics and Protestants over Mary, the Catholics have taken the side of the unconscious archetype; the Protestants have taken a more rational conscious attitude.

But the great dogmas themselves are given a very ambivalent exegesis. For example, doctrinally Mary is Mother of God. On the one hand the Church has stressed the passive, auxiliary nature of divine maternity: 'Mary can only be understood when seen in the perspective of Christ.'[8] In this view, Mary is purely the channel for God to become flesh.

But the ancient and archetypal image of divine motherhood brings out the sense of Mother as origin and source. The 'Great Mother' is the *matrix* of everything, that is, the home, womb, destiny, and point of return for all life. 'In her benign aspect, the Great Mother is therefore life, as it comes to be and burgeons.'[9]

Thus poets and painters have instinctively responded to this symbolism of Mary and child, and have represented her primal role as Mother-of-all. In one of his poems the poet G.M. Hopkins calls her the 'world-mothering air'.[10]

The Magna Mater image even finds Biblical expression – in the great image in Revelation that I have already used as an epigraph:

> And a great portent appeared in heaven, a woman clothed with the sun, with the moon under her feet, and on her head a crown of twelve stars; she was with child and she cried out in pangs of birth, in anguish for delivery.
>
> (Revelation 12:1)

Later in the same chapter a 'great red dragon' appears, to wage war on the woman and her offspring, but 'the earth came to the help of the woman, and the earth opened its mouth and swallowed the river which the dragon had poured from his mouth' (Revelation 12:16). This material is distinctly non-Christian in its imagery, but it is of great interest that the woman has been identified with Mary, for the woman of Revelation is cosmic, a Goddess of the earth, battling with supernatural evil. She is surrounded by the great astronomical – and astrological – bodies; she gives birth to a son who is to 'rule all the nations with a rod of iron' (Revelation 12:5).

To discover the true significance of Mary for ordinary worshippers, we would have to penetrate into the devotions of those who pray to her, or contemplate her being. This is difficult to do, but I have reported the spontaneous visions of her by people in therapy, and here there is little doubt that the archetypal 'Great Mother' has appeared in the image of Mary. We also have accounts by writers that suggest a relationship with her that is profound and loving, as in this comment by the Irish Jesuit, William Johnston: 'Mary is now the atmosphere in which I walk, a feminine atmosphere, a protecting atmosphere, a guiding atmosphere, a loving atmosphere.'[11]

Thus one can express the contradiction of Mary as follows: although theologically she is not a deity, existentially, psychologically, symbolically, she *is* a Goddess, an image of feminine sublimity and transcendence.

If we accept that Mary is a partial or incomplete manifestation of a primal underlying Goddess, who shows many faces, many facets, then where does this being exist? For the theologian and the devout Catholic, Mary inhabits heaven.

For the sceptic, Mary, and the whole notion of the Goddess, is a fabrication or a compensatory fantasy, reducible to personal neurosis.

For me, the latter, positivist, approach is as unsatisfactory as the theological. Those people I have met who experienced an image or vision of Mary experienced something real, something life-enhancing. My own experiences with the Black Virgin felt as if a contact was being made with something in myself that urgently needed to contact me. In other words, the external image – whether in liturgy, or painting, or a statue – connects with an inner image.

Thus in a psychology that posits the autonomous world of the unconscious, it is not shocking or surprising to suggest that the divine being or beings exist *objectively* in that real if invisible world. 'The pre-conditions for myth-formation must be present within the structure of the psyche itself.'[12]

This formulation does not rule out the extra-psychic existence of the Goddess as a possibility. But here we can only draw back before the ultimate *mysterium*: the nature of the divine. I would only suggest that the psyche itself is the product of natural evolution, i.e. that it is not separate from nature as a whole. I therefore find it intuitively plausible that the divine beings exist outside the psyche, as some kind of inherent structure or energy in the physical world, or in a world whose dimensions we cannot grasp. The image of Mary in the twentieth century – in visions, in dreams – is surely therefore some kind of warning about the present threat to the natural world, and links with the contemporary recrudescence of paganist and pantheistic thought, which again is significant of our rupture with nature and the need for healing of that split.

But certainly I believe it to be a crucial premise in the study of Mary, that the Goddess within us recreates herself in the world of time and space, in order to exist, in order to pass from immanence to incarnation. But this coming into being, this eternal becoming, is not a complete or full revelation, since the masculine deity or numinous image has been dominant in the psyche for thousands of years, and has obscured, mutilated, even at times obliterated, the image of the divine woman.

Thus it can be said that the articulation of dogma, the growth of legend, the phenomenon of visions, which surround the figure of Mary, delineate precisely and spontaneously a psychic element, and constitute a psychic revelation. The Goddess exists independently of human consciousness; she is not 'man-made', or woman-made for that matter. She is not the property of women, nor of men. We experience her in subjective ways, but her being is objective and beyond us all.

DEATH FROM EVE, LIFE FROM MARY

The title of this section is a well known medieval tag,[13] and indicates the dualistic view of the feminine in the Church. It is expressed more vividly in the definition given by the fifth-century writer Theodotus: 'In place of the virgin Eve, mediatrix of death, a virgin has been filled with God's grace, to be the minister of life.'[14]

This ancient polarization of Eve and Mary has been used as a slur on the figure of Eve, since after all, the bringing of consciousness, the dispelling of innocence and unconsciousness, is a necessary development for human beings, both individually and as a species. Thus the clash between Eve and Adam, the conflict with God, and Eve's refusal to obey both, can be seen positively as a symbol of the conflicts within the individual, and within society, that lead to increased consciousness. In a patriarchal system the feminine is intrinsically the necessary opposition to the masculine that produces creative tension. But the Church has consistently feared, resented and maligned the feminine, precisely because it is 'the other'.

But the Eve/Mary split also reveals that division between the destructive and creative Goddess which is found in all cultures. The Goddess figure seems to bifurcate spontaneously into light and dark aspects, as does the male God. Esther Harding refers to this duality in her discussion of the Moon Goddess: 'The Moon Goddess is, in literal fact, the mother of all living things, and yet, strange though it seems, not only is she the life-giver, but also the destroyer.'[15]

We find Goddess figures who combine both these aspects – such a one is Isis – and also twin Goddesses who have split into positive and negative figures. Thus Mary herself is seen in her normal 'white' form, and as the chthonic Black Virgin. And Mary as Virgin is also counter-balanced by the ex-whore Mary Magdalen.

The Biblical references to Mary Magdalen are complex and confused, but as with the Virgin Mary, a tremendous superstructure of legend grew around the original references to her. British people probably do not appreciate the enormous popularity of Mary Magdalen in Continental Catholicism. She has often been portrayed as the intimate friend of Jesus; legend has it she fled to France escaping from persecution, and therefore she became quite a 'Europeanized' saint; and her role in the resurrection as first witness to the risen Christ gives her special prominence.

Mary Magdalen can easily be seen as another emblem of womanhood for a misogynist church – she renounces sexuality and becomes a saint. And there is no doubt that the whore/madonna polarity, exemplified in the two Maries, remains a potent and seductive representation of woman in our culture. But as with the Virgin's virginity and sinlessness, it is likely that the whore-saint is psychologically a deeper symbol that that. Many religions and mythologies have contained the figure of the holy harlot, or the temple-whore, who brought the devotee to God through erotic transcendence, through matter itself. Is there a suggestion of this in Mary Magdalen? It is particularly interesting that in our century there have been a number of books and films suggesting a sexual relationship between her and Jesus (e.g. *The Holy Blood and the Holy Grail*), provoking outrage in the devout, but giving an echo of the link between the erotic and the spiritual that has usually been eschewed in Christianity. But eroticism does leak into Christianity continually – are not some of the paintings of the Virgin Mary ambiguous in this respect? – and with Mary Magdalen it can be allowed in openly, if in a penitent form.

Thus these dichotomies are not merely a patriarchal dismemberment of the feminine, although the negative feminine aspect, in the shape of Eve in particular, has been used in a propagandist and pejorative way. The whore-Goddess, the black Goddess, the Goddess of death, are ancient symbols, and point to a profound sense of the interpenetration of life and death, good and evil, and even the necessity for death and evil.

In relation to the masculine deity, Jung argues, in his *Answer to Job*, that Satan is necessary to God's handiwork, to provide the necessary resistance, the disharmony in the harmony, the grit in the oyster that could produce a pearl.[16] Job's bewilderment is understandable: the same God that made the wonder of the Pleiades, the God that is the creator of time – he is Job's tormentor. This requires of the human being an ability to accept the light and dark aspects of the divine – and of the human – simultaneously. Christianity has found this impossible.

From the psychological point of view, all human beings have to face both their own dark side, the shadow, the aspects they would rather suppress completely, and the dark side of the divine. Within the feminine aspect of both men and women, one must confront and bring to consciousness the potentially destructive/vicious/amoral element (Lilith), as well as the loving/creative side: 'Eve and Mary are our two mothers. Like sisters, they are each other's opposite side. Together they are for our Western civilization the archetype of the Magna Mater, matter, earth.'[17]

But in relation to the Eve/Mary polarity, the Christian Church – and the society in which it existed – was unable to hold such a relativist view of light and dark. The figure of Eve has been used to castigate the inherent flaw in women: they are rebellious, sources of evil, death, corruption. This has been one of the great problems for Christianity – that it has been unable to accept the necessary dark side of life, and of the divine, and has therefore *acted out* its own dark side, in religious wars, persecutions, acts of genocide, attitudes of patronizing contempt to other religions, all of which has been breathtakingly brutal and 'unChristian'. Christianity became a murderous force, precisely because it clung too fiercely to 'the good'.

Thus the cult of Mary is the obverse of the suppression of the dark feminine. Mary is idealized and rendered ethereal; along with this goes a harsh refusal to accept women in themselves, a vengeful and murderous assault on women in the form of 'witches', and an unpreparedness for the internal psychic assault of the Dark Goddess. This is a dangerously schizoid fantasy about the feminine.

Mary is idealized in order to suppress the feminine shadow, and therefore ordinary women, confronted with Mary, can easily feel failures. Marina Warner makes the comment: 'I hold fast to my intimation that in the very celebration of the perfect human woman, both humanity and women were subtly denigrated.'[18]

The Church has also *literalized* the figure of Mary, and has preached that women should try to be like her. But from the symbolic point of view, this is nonsense, since Mary represents an *internal* force for both men and women, and the various attributes of Mary – virginity, sinlessness, obedience, reception into heaven – can be understood as values of the feminine element in the psyche. For example, virginity, which has been taken usually in its literal physical sense, and used to denigrate sexuality, can be seen at the psychic level as denoting completeness, wholeness, self-sufficiency, the marriage of human and divine. The virgin is like the virgin forest or virgin territory – untouched by human hand, but fertile, fruitful, perfect. Our modern sense of ecology has begun to teach us again that the virgin must be preserved – for example, the virgin rain-forest. Its virginity is a fountain of life, and human penetration has often come to despoil and wreck it.

The understanding of Mary as an internal dynamic force in human personality has been largely ignored in the promulgation of the external drama of the 'mother of Jesus', just as the life of Jesus has been understood in an over-literal sense. This is not to deny the need of people to do this – for example, to see Jesus and Mary as real people living in Palestine – but the Church has usually ignored the more symbolic levels of meaning. This has led to the current controversies over the Virgin Birth, where great fury is aroused when theologians question the literal truth of the Virgin Birth and point to its mythological status. But this debate is strangely sterile, and perhaps shows that as mythological truths, the great Marian symbols are decaying. When a great myth grips the collective psyche, it is always seen as literally true. The great modern myths of scientific objectivity and scientific methodology have gripped us for the past few centuries, and only now are we beginning to question them, as the myth loses its grip.

We arrive at the notion of Mary as an image of great ambivalence, Janus-faced. On the one hand, the Church, in its patriarchal misogyny, has exploited the popular devotion to Mary as propaganda for women to remain within the ambit of 'Kinder, Kirche, Küche'. A crude version of the propaganda would go as follows: 'Mary didn't have sex because she was pure, and she was the necessary antidote to Eve, who was disobedient when it is the duty of a woman to be obedient. All women are cursed through Eve, but Mary offers some solace.'

At a more profound level, the idealization of Mary reflects the ancient ambivalence about the relationship between the body and the spirit. Women were feared and loathed by many medieval churchmen since they had periods, they had babies and breast-fed them, and were obviously bearers of life in a very physical sense. This couldn't be spiritualized out of existence, but it could be painted black and evil, and persecuted. To the Church, women represented *matter* itself, that aspect of life which was corruptible, and therefore corrupt. Western civilization has been haunted by this rejection of the earth, which has led to the ecological disasters that confront us today: the masculine spirit/intellect has raped the soul/earth.

Mary therefore partly represents an etherealized, safer, version of woman, flesh, the earth. She is a masculinized, bowdlerized Goddess.

111

But we cannot just portray Mary as the emblem of misogyny. She also appears as a magnificent manifestation of the Goddess, Mother of the world, Mother of all people, Mother of the Divine itself. Many of the doctrinal attributes ascribed to her have profound symbolic meanings. The pregnant virgin is replete with life. She is an entire world. She contains the entire world within her: 'initiated into womanhood without losing virginity, the pregnant virgin gives birth to herself, to the man, and to all creation.'[19]

Mary is therefore fantastically complex, multi-faceted, multi-layered. She can be related to at many levels, from the faith of the Italian or Spanish peasant, often wrongly and patronizingly termed 'simple', to the theological complexity found in Mariology, or the personal vision or dream of the non-Christian, to the hermeneutics of psychology! She is related to in ways that are mutually contradictory, yet all of which are valid. In fact such great numinous symbols are always full of contradiction, since they express the deepest clash and unity of opposites at the heart of life. Life and death, love and hate, good and evil, feminine and masculine, female and male – these great, mysterious and incomprehensible facts of life confront human beings throughout their stay on earth. They cannot be rationally analysed or comprehended, and thus it is that such great symbols as the divine pregnant virgin mother arise to express them.

Below the level of theology lurks the emotionalism and intensity of popular devotion. And this folk-worship reflects the pressure of the archetypal image of the Goddess in the impersonal unconscious, the pressure to be expressed, recognized, worshipped. Thus the fantastic elaborations about Mary's life, which are clearly often legendary, the numerous visions which have occurred, particularly in this century, the extreme devotion that has been aroused in Europe and South America – all point to her as a *spontaneous* living product of the psyche. Therefore Marian symbolism is akin to dream symbolism – it arises naturally and freely as the self-expression of the deepest level of the unconscious. The Goddess – so much rejected in the last two thousand years in the West – has had to remain an unconscious figure, but sending forth this incomplete yet still numinous image of herself. The blackness of the Black Virgin partly suggests this unconsciousness: hidden from the light, long buried, full of dark mystery and magic.

A JEWISH MARY?

In very early Christianity the cult of Mary was negligible. In the Gospel of John, which is usually dated *c.* AD 100, and in Paul's letters from the first century, there is little reference to her. In his book *Christian Origins*, which is an account of the origins of Christianity as the 'most important Messianic Sect of Judaism', Rowlands does not refer to Mary once in four hundred pages, and in fact refers to women only four times.[20] Thus if Christianity is seen in its early period as celebrating the 'Jesus of Nazareth who preached an essentially Jewish message about God and his kingdom',[21] then in that message, Mary has no place. And Biblically speaking, this is correct. Jesus does not give a Marian teaching at all in the four gospels, and neither does Paul, the greatest of the interpreters of Jesus. One of the great weapons used by the Reformers in the sixteenth century was that the medieval Church had built up the magnificent edifice of Marian dogma and devotion with hardly any Biblical foundations to it.

But Catholic theologians have been at pains to point out the parallels between the Biblical Mary and Jewish women in the Old Testament. Thus Mary's song, the *Magnificat* (Luke 1: 46–55), has obvious parallels with the song of Hannah (1 Samuel 2: 1–10). The theme of the barren woman, personification of Israel (Isaiah 54), is found in the New Testament in the figure of Elizabeth, who gives birth to John the Baptist and who makes to Mary the acclamation which was to become part of the 'Hail Mary' – 'Blessed art thou among women, and blessed is the fruit of thy womb' (Luke 1: 42).

Ratzinger is led to conclude that 'the image of Mary in the New Testament is woven entirely of Old Testament threads.'[22] In a sense this is a little specious, since the story of the life of Jesus is also woven from such threads. His great cry from the cross, 'Eli, Eli, lama, sabachthani' ('My God, my God, why hast thou forsaken me?') (Matthew 27: 46), is a direct citation from Psalm 22.

One can argue that the four gospels, and indeed the New Testament as a whole, are made up of threads from the Old Testament. In relation to Jesus, the very early writers and editors of the gospels were concerned to place his story, including his birth to Mary, within the traditions of Judaism, and to see Jesus as fulfilment of the longed-for Messiah. Paul in particular is obsessed with the relationship between Judaism and the new Way – understandably, as the former arch-persecutor of Christians: 'Is God the God of Jews only? Is he not the God of Gentiles? Yes, of Gentiles also, since God is one; and he will justify the circumcised on the ground of their faith and the uncircumcised through their faith' (Romans 3: 29–30).

Modern scholarship within Christian theology has reasserted the Jewishness of Jesus, and of early Christianity: 'Jesus did not envisage a religious system independent of Judaism.'[23]

Unfortunately this fascinating and complex enquiry into the relationship between Judaism and Christianity, initiated by Paul, became among some sections of the Church a suggestion – more than a suggestion – that Judaism is 'incomplete' and that Christianity is its climax and its *supersession*. Ratzinger suggests this in relation to the figure of the 'daughter of Zion' in the Old Testament: 'this line of development in the Old Testament ... acquires its definitive meaning for the first time in the New Testament.'[24]

I feel we must reject such culture-bound, chauvinist, triumphalist, and indeed offensive pronouncements. Although Christianity has its roots in Judaism, this does not mean that Judaism is rendered obsolete by it. In addition, although Christianity obviously has many characteristics from Judaism it is also heavily influenced by Greek thought. In relation to Mary, the notion of the virgin birth is not particularly a Jewish idea, whereas it is rife in classical mythology.

But neither can we – from a Jewish chauvinist position – claim that Mary is only an extension of the Jewish maiden motif, or of the Shekhinah. This is to deny Mary her own independent development.

In this connection, there is a fundamental point to be made about the 'Biblical Mary' and the 'Mary of faith'. The Mary shown in the New Testament may indeed be a composite of Jewish themes, e.g. the barren/fruitful woman antithesis, but *the Mary who is found in later centuries is not that New Testament Mary!* She has become something quite different, richer, more elaborated, closer to divinity. In one sense the Protestant critique of this lack of Biblical basis to the growth of Marian devotion is quite correct – but misses the point that this in fact demonstrates the genuineness of Mary as an independent spiritual manifestation.

Here the Catholic theologians are correct, from the point of view of our understanding of the psyche, when they assert that the revelation of the divine is not fixed nor finite, but ongoing. The Biblical corpus describes an extraordinary series of manifestations or symbols of the divine being(s), but this is not the end. People continue to work on these symbols, to extract more and more from them. The psyche continues to elaborate on the existing symbols, and sometimes produces new ones. For example, the Christian Church itself does not feature in the teachings of Jesus – does this invalidate it? Our life as a whole can be seen as an ever-present self-revelation of the divine – how can this be pinned down to any written text, or any denominational orthodoxy? The Goddess figure in particular is a cyclical figure – and when the one-off fixed Creation of the male God comes to seem intolerable, as periodically it must do, then the Goddess inevitably reappears as the harbinger of new birth.

Thus the true continuity between Mary and other Goddess-cults is not demonstrable purely historically, culturally or archaeologically, but through psychological comparison. For example, although it is quite likely that the Marian cult was influenced by the classical tradition of Isis,[25] this does not *explain* the flowering of Marian devotion from the fourth century onwards. The gap between very early Christianity and the growth of the cult of Mary reveals the latter as a spontaneous development, responding to people's need for the divine woman to be represented and worshipped.

Extraordinary similarities can exist between mythologies that are separated by time and space. The similarities are often due not to cultural influence but to a common source in an archetypal image. Patai, in his book *The Hebrew Goddess*, makes an interesting comment on this in relation to the affinities between ancient Near Eastern love-goddesses, the Kabbalistic divinity, the Matronit, and the Virgin Mary:

> whether or not the Matronit (and Mary) goes ultimately back to Inanna, her coming to life in new and very greatly changed religious environments shows that she answered a psychological need in medieval Askhenazi or Sephardi Jewry as she had in 3rd millennium BC Sumer.[26]

And Patai shows the numerous parallels between the medieval Matronit and Mary: both are chaste, motherly, warlike (Mary's standard was frequently carried into battle). Both are considered to be the spouse of God, and the mediator between men and God.[27] It is possible that one influenced the other in such respects – but these traits are found in many Goddess cults from widely different epochs and cultures.

Undoubtedly there are other cultural influences on the figure of Mary. In his study of the Black Virgin, Begg shows how certain Black Virgin sites are ancient sites for the worship of Isis, and even suggests that some statues of the Black Virgin are actually 'converted' statues of Isis.[28] But this would not be surprising – Christianity was always adept at taking over the pagan symbols and festivals, e.g. Christmas. After all, the heart of Christian worship – the eating of the flesh and blood of the man-God – is highly suggestive of ancient pre-Christian sacrifice.

In a sense such cultural ancestry tells us nothing. The deeper question is: *why* did Mary, in her black form, take over some of the functions of Isis? Those functions – 'the ancient wisdom of Isis-Ma'at, the secret of eternal life that is the gold at the heart of the alchemical process, as well as the initial blackness'[29] – respond to inescapable and profound human needs, not created by culture, but creating culture itself.

One might, provocatively, ask the question: is Mary a *Christian* Mary? The answer is yes, in so far as the Church subordinates her to Christ, but we might also say no, in so far as she persistently escapes from the Church's clutches, and becomes an independent *Marian* Mary. In the great paintings of her, is she subordinate to the infant God? Or is she the over-arching horizon, the earth, the universe itself? I am reminded of the medieval statues of the *Vierge Ouvrante*, a statue of Mary which opens up to reveal Jesus concealed in her womb – and in some versions, the Trinity itself is hidden there. This is a heterodox but popular image of Mary, source and container of the divine.

And in many personal dreams and visions she stands *sui generis*. When Bernadette Soubirous asks her at Lourdes who she is, she replies, 'I am the Immaculate Conception.' In a way, this is a very naive reply (as if Bernadette thought this is what the Church wanted to hear), but in another way, it is cosmic, a great feminine 'I-am'.

There can be little doubt that the psychological need for the divine woman has existed in all human cultures. From the ancient fertility statues of prehistoric times, to the great Mother worship of Asia Minor, the Egyptian Isis and Hathor, the Hebrew Goddesses, the classical pantheon – Hera, Athene, Artemis, Aphrodite, Hestia – even the great 'goddesses' of the modern cinema – is this not inescapable evidence as to the

ubiquity of the need, and its satisfaction in Goddess-cults? And in current political life, the adulation and obloquy paid to the Queen and the former female Prime Minister in British society is quite striking, as if they represent secularized, degenerate forms of the Goddess.

But in relation to the Marian cult, one can point to more specific archetypal structures. The divine mother and sacrificed son figure in many mythologies – Ishtar and her son Tammuz, Isis and her sons/lovers Osiris and Horus, Cybele and her son Attis. The union of a woman with a god is also a universal motif: 'every religion, from the most primitive to the highest, is pervaded with the idea that union with a god, a *hieros gamos*, or "Holy Matrimony", is a necessity to every woman.'[30]

Mary is remarkable, therefore, not for the localized and culture-bound nature of her symbolism, but for its universality and timelessness. She is a recincarnation of the one true Goddess.

MOTHER AND SON

The mother–son dyad is a recurrent motif in mythology and religion. For example, Isis is shown in Egyptian paintings and sculpture holding her dead brother-husband-son Osiris in her arms. But she revives him, and conceives a child by means of an image of his phallus, which is missing from his body. Thus she is also a kind of virgin mother.

The evolution of the relation between Isis and Osiris is very complex. Originally brother and sister, they get married, but in later periods, Isis becomes known as the mother of the moon, Osiris.

But the same shifting relationship is seen with Mary and Jesus. She is often conceived of as his mystical spouse, echoing no doubt the Old Testament imagery of Israel as the bride of Yahweh.

But apart from the fascinating parallels and influences between different mythologies and religions in relation to the mother-bride-son relationship, how do we explain its pervasive presence? The cultural influences would not occur unless the symbolism was important and corresponded to an internal psychic structure.

The mother–son relation can be understood at many levels. Originally the mother Goddess was supreme, and the son was subordinate to and dependent on her. But patriarchal religion reverses this, and the Mother pays homage to the Son. Thus the actual relations between masculine and feminine in the psyche, and in society, are revealed in the relationship between Goddess and Son–God.

We have also observed that the Great Mother is mythologically the matrix of the whole universe, and some element of this can be found in Marian worship, and artistic images of her.

We can also see the mother and dying son as a representation of the psyche itself. The virgin mother is the personification of the unconscious, womb of all, home of all that springs into human consciousness. From this matrix is born the individualized consciousness, personified as the son. But this consciousness is mortal: periodically it dies back to the source, as does a plant in winter. And from this death it returns again. Jung defines 'the woman' in this way: 'She contains in her darkness the sun of "masculine" consciousness, which rises as a child out of the nocturnal sea of the unconscious and as an old man sinks into it again.'[31]

This symbolic sequence of birth, death and rebirth summates human existence: poised between unconscious existence and conscious awareness. This structure pervades our life: every night we relinquish the ego and sink back to the 'nocturnal sea'. Every child is compelled to emerge from the innocence and unity of unconsciousness into the harsher world of self-consciousness, where he/she becomes an object of awareness to others and to itself. We could argue that every moment of existence contains this structure: we are predominantly unconscious, and our consciousness is wrought, hewn, with great struggle, out of nature. Thus Christ's own life maps the tremendous struggle that it is to be an individual ego, and the suffering and crucifixion that the ego must undergo to be reunited with the source again.

And life itself emerges by a similar process from the inanimate, and decays back again. We as individuals face this prospect – extinction, the descent to matter again. The whole universe is structured around this process.

As a symbolic system, Christianity therefore historicizes a model of reality. The actual structure of each moment of existence is metaphorized into the drama of divine birth, crucifixion, resurrection. A cosmology is turned into narrative; an image of the psyche is concretized, and unfortunately lost to sight. This might be called the 'esoteric' understanding of religion: the Christ is simply every individual who is the conjunction of ego and Self, mortal and immortal, human and divine.

The Mary–Jesus relation can also be understood as the relation of matter and spirit. In Mary, reluctantly, spasmodically, the early and medieval Church paid reverence to matter itself, to flesh, to the fructifying earth, from where everything comes and into which everything decays. Jesus and Mary form a perfect syzygy – the one descending from psyche into matter, the other ascending from matter into psyche. Thus they are viewed properly as a unity of opposites, as a principle of tension, that underpins the human being and the divine being, and life as a whole.

Both Jesus and Mary are human and divine; both are material and heavenly; both are mortal and immortal. These contradictions are not escapist fantasy or science fiction: they provide a basic model of who we are and what we are.

But the Renaissance could not bear the tension between these polarities, and proceeded in the Reformation to destroy one half and desecrate the sacred nature of matter. The modern world has reflected this dangerous tilt towards reason/spirit/will.

The dislocation in the Reformation whereby Mary is cut out from the faith, along with much ritual and symbolism, is highly significant of a split between the non-rational and the rational. Religion became reasonable, a matter of belief, rather than faith or intuition. The masculine intellect rejects the mediating power of the feminine/material/maternal Mary. The unity of the universe, whereby matter and spirit were conceived of as a living whole, is split. Matter becomes inert, dead, analysable by empirical and scientific method. Matter is no longer sacred. Nature is an object of enquiry, not a mystery, but something to be dominated, exploited, obliterated. The sacred area of life shrinks considerably, to become a private inner sanctum in each person's mind. The soul of the world (Anima Mundi) is ejected.

But in fact, something similar happened to the figure of Jesus. The Biblical Jesus is a remarkably feminine man. His male disciples cannot bear his receptivity to children, and other social outcasts. He refuses the role of warrior-king, and preaches a discipline of weakness and suffering – 'For he was crucified in weakness' (2 Corinthians 13: 4) – which disgusts Peter, his chief disciple. Significantly in Mark's gospel, at the end, only the women are left with the dying Jesus – all the men have fled (Mark 13: 50).

There has been some interesting theological work on the continuation in Jesus of the figure of Sophia, the personification of the feminine aspect of God in Hellenistic Judaism.[32] And medieval mystics were not averse to apostrophizing Jesus as their mother, with his breasts giving them spiritual nourishment.

But the fierce Protestant spirit turns Jesus into a King, a Lord, a Judge. His femininity is either ignored, or parodied in the 'gentle Jesus meek and mild' imagery of hymnody. Jesus was feminine *and* masculine – this has been hard to take for many Christians. He got angry with people, he rejected his own family ('Who is my mother, and who are my brothers?' (Matthew 12: 48)), he is quite unpacific: 'Do not think that I have come to bring peace on earth; I have come not to bring peace, but a sword' (Matthew 10: 34). Yet he takes great pains with disadvantaged people; he doesn't judge people; he is a healer.

The scene with the adulterous woman is remarkable in this context: he takes her side against the judgmental male collective (John 8: 1–11). It can be argued that his mission of preaching is a disastrous failure: people cannot take on board his ideas of loving your neighbour and your enemy – in other words, incorporating into oneself the rejected, split-off parts of oneself, that are normally (i.e. unconsciously) projected and scapegoated onto others. He dies an outcast and a failure. Thus Jesus is very far from the militant triumphalism that came to be associated with his name in later periods: 'Jesus is Lord!' He is a man full of weakness, vulnerability, powerlessness against the power of the world.

One can make the surprising claim that *the Goddess is manifest in Jesus*, surprising, however, only if one confuses the feminine with the female, and the masculine with the male. The masculine God at times needs to be expressed in and through women, and the Goddess in and through men.

We can say therefore that in the Reformation, the Mother and Son in the godhead are divided, and the feminine aspect of the divine is excised. The divine being is fragmented even more, reality is thrown into schism, the profane is divorced from the sacred, public from private, knowledge from love. When one triumphs over the other – especially when we are left with the Father/Son hegemony – we become unbalanced, we go crazy, as we are today. The triumph of Logos over Eros is destroying us. The creation weeps and mourns at the loss of the feminine, and the souls of men and women are in torment.

The history of Mary is therefore a history of our civilization and its dislocation. The masculine deity separated from the Goddess has become a monster of reasonable unreason. But in addition the excluded Goddess has grown demented in her isolation and rejection, and torments us in turn.

It is doubtful to my mind if the cult of Mary itself will ever revive to any extent. Surely it has faded, along with the system of which she is a part. In the future, the divine Mother and Son must be reunited in another form, and joined with the Father and Daughter, if we are to be healed, if we are to survive.

VISIONS

Marian visions have been common in the last two centuries, but between 1700 and 1820 there were hardly any reported.[33] This is interesting, since the eighteenth century, known as the Age of Reason, saw Catholicism in retreat, e.g. in the French Revolution. But in the nineteenth century there began a spate of publicized visions – La Salette in 1846, Lourdes in 1858, Pontmain in 1871, Knock in Ireland in 1879. The twentieth century has seen many well publicized visions, including the 2000 visions occurring to the same group of children at Garabandal, Spain, in 1961-5; mass apparitions at Zeitoun, Egypt, in 1968-71 which are claimed to have been seen by over a million people; and the very recent visions at Medjugorje in Jugoslavia, which began in 1981 and continued until 1986 at least, to the discomfort of the Communist authorities. It is estimated that between 1928 and 1971 there have been at least 200 sites of Marian visions.[34] But this is probably the tip of an iceberg. Many visions are reported briefly but then disappear from public interest.

In the modern era, the visions have had certain fascinating similarities. Most of them have occurred to young children, often in groups of four, five or six. The children have usually been from very poor peasant backgrounds, have had little education, and there often seems to be one 'leader' among them, who possibly has psychic powers. Many cases do not receive ecclesiastical approval, as the Catholic Church is wary of hysterical phenomena.

But when a particular site is recognized, the popularity of it can become amazing: millions of people visit Lourdes, Knock and Fatima every year. The sites become associated with healing miracles; medical commissions are set up to investigate these cures; a commercial bonanza opens up for shopkeepers selling usually very poor quality souvenirs.

There are aspects of these visions that are of great interest as symbolic of Mary's role as feminine divinity. At Guadalupe (1531), Mary appears at the site of an ancient Aztec Goddess; a miracle occurs – roses appear in mid-winter, and Mary's imprint is left on a cloak. At Salette in France in 1846, Mary prophesies famine in the area, and predicts which crops will fail: potatoes, walnuts, grapes. The prophecy comes true. At Lourdes, Bernadette is told to eat earth and grass, and is told the site of a healing spring which she finds. At Fatima (1917), Mary appears standing in a holm oak, the evergreen oak. In addition, there are strange solar events, described as the 'dancing sun'. At many sites, the children having the vision seem to go into a trance or ecstatic state, and sometimes appear to possess telephathic powers amongst themselves, are able to walk across rough ground in the dark, and so on. A rather bizarre political twist is that at times Mary gives out anti-Communist propaganda.

It would be easy to dismiss the Marian visions as mass hysteria amongst children, but that misses the point of interest for students of the psyche, and students of Mary. Jung made the illuminating remark about flying saucers, that the really interesting question wasn't whether they really exist, but why people seem to need to believe in them.[35] And Jung concludes that the UFO phenomena reflect a surge in energy in the unconscious directed towards transpersonal matters. The same symbolism can be seen in the cinema – the popularity of the film *E.T.*, for example. E.T. comes from another planet and almost dies on earth from lack of love, but is saved by a child's love, comes back to life and ascends into the sky again. E.T. is obviously Christ-like, but it is noteworthy that he is associated with children, who are shown as much more sensitive to such transpersonal images than adults. But then it was Jesus who pointed this out: 'I say to you, unless you turn and become like children, you will never enter the kingdom of heaven' (Matthew 18: 3). It is not just that children are innocent and less corrupted by the ways of the world, but that they are closer to the unconscious, and therefore are more open to 'heavenly' communications.

In relation to the Marian visions, again the interesting question is not whether the Virgin Mary has really appeared on earth, but why people *need* it to be true. It is quite likely that if in the collective unconscious the feminine element is beginning to gather energy, and to move towards consciousness, that children will pick this up first.

It is often pointed out that visions of Mary never happen to atheists or in fact non-Catholics, and usually happen in Catholic countries. But if I am correct in assuming that Marian visions are a response to the upsurge of the feminine archetype, then we would expect them to appear precisely in those cultures which contain a readily available symbol of the archetype. Archetypal energy is like water: it flows through the channels that are available, and the creation of new symbolic mediations for this energy is often a turbulent and even traumatic affair. Thus the early development of Christianity was extremely fraught, not just politically, but because a new symbolic system was being developed to deal with a new unconscious dynamism.

Mary usually appears in rural sourrounds, often near trees, points out streams which become places of healing, and is often associated with plants, or with the earth in some way. Thus the archetypal link between the Goddess, the earth, and living things is expressed in these naive visions. The figure of Mary is usually absolutely conventional – blue and white clothing, a crown of stars, surrounded by blinding light. Often she speaks the local language or dialect. At Guadalupe she appears as a Mexican girl. Again sceptics or rationalists scoff at this. But they are missing the really interesting aspect of such visions: they are localized versions of a global phenomenon. One might as well claim that people who have significant dreams or fantasies have eaten an indigestible dinner!

I myself know five people who have had personal visions of Mary. As I indicated at the beginning, those images are of great importance to those people. And the visions that have occurred round the world have clearly met a need. In that sense they are like a collective dream. They show the flow of energy in the unconscious rising to the surface and being projected in apparently objective apparitions. They indicate that a truly momentous psychic phenomenon is at the root of it.

DREAMING THE BLACK VIRGIN

We have seen how Mary straddles orthodoxy and heterodoxy. And the Black Virgin is one of the most heterodox aspects of the cult of Mary. There is no official theological description of Black Mary. The statues of her tend to be local shrines, some of which become famous, e.g. Rocamadour, Einsiedeln. But many people inside and outside the Catholic Church will dismiss the blackness as being caused by candle smoke, age or paint. Even many people who have a considerable devotion to a Black Virgin are hard pressed to say what is special about her.

And indeed it is necessary to visit the Black Virgin to comprehend her – although 'comprehend' is entirely the wrong word. She cannot be comprehended. Her blackness is the blackness of incomprehensibility; of night; of the shadows that fall across the day; the blackness of Africa; of the other side of the moon. It is precisely the darkness that allows the imagination, the unconscious, to fill her with qualities that are indefinable, mysterious.

She is the Mother of the mysteries, of arcane knowledge, secret intuitions, initiations, the knowledge that is known without knowing it. Her blackness is a black hole, pulling in everyone who contemplates her, sucking our consciousness into her mystery.

She can be fierce, gaunt, as at Rocamadour; lush, bejewelled as at Guadalupe; or dressed in kitsch wedding dresses. The kitsch is indeed essential – it connects her with the hopes, dreams, the groans and laments of the ordinary people. Thus the Black Mary is a people's Mary.

But then again, she is often hidden. There are Black Virgins in Britain, but how many people have seen them? And Begg describes the great effort he made in some towns to get someone to let him into a church or chapel where there was a Black Virgin, or even to admit that there was one.[36]

I have referred to the affinity between dream imagery and religious dogma and symbolism. This connection can be used as a technique for exploring the meaning of religious images. For example: imagine that you dreamt of a statue of a black woman; or alternatively, that in a dream you met a black woman in a house or in the street, talked with her, related to her in some way. How would you interpret such an image?

One promising approach would undoubtedly be to consider that the black woman represented the 'shadow' side of the feminine, those aspects that have been denied, split off, denigrated.

Thus the Black Virgin takes into herself those aspects of the feminine, the Goddess, suppressed in the White Virgin. What are they? Sexuality, power, ferocity, cruelty, rage, fear, rebellion, warlikeness, envy – these are qualities that would not normally be associated with the conventional Virgin Mary. At times, as we have seen, she has been revealed as a figure of great power, a force of nature. But at the same time, official theology tries to shrink her down to the size of the obedient demure maiden. Is it not likely that the cult of the Black Virgin arises as a heterodox vehicle for all the qualities 'forbidden' to the White Mary? One can also imagine that her blackness conceals her Jewishness, her guilt at the slaughter of so many Jews in the name of her son, her guilt at her own 'adulterous' pregnancy.

Thus it is a very unconscious cult, without any explicit theology. But in a sense this is an advantage – that it is not turned into an official doctrine or devotion. This allows every individual a kind of creative licence in the contemplation of the Black Virgin – no feeling or association can be forbidden.

It would be wrong, therefore, even ludicrous, to fix a definite meaning to the Black Virgin. She is like a mirror into which we can gaze, and see reflected there the undiscovered, unknown, aspects of one's own soul.

She represents the unfulfilled potential of the feminine. She is black, and she is a virgin – is she waiting to be fertilized, to be made love to, to be married? Does she belong to God, to man, to woman? Or to herself only? Yet is she not part of all men and women? Does the black child represent some part of you that is still unborn, or not yet led forward into life?

Modern techniques in psychotherapy also allow us to construct a guided fantasy around the Black Virgin, a kind of waking dream. This is not usually as rich or valuable an experience as a spontaneous fantasy, but it can still provide very revealing insights and images. It is best to try this fantasy somewhere where you can relax completely, and at times close your eyes to allow the inner visualization to deepen.

Imagine that you are climbing down a steep canyon, along a winding path. The canyon is very deep, so deep that the bottom is shrouded in mist. You seem to be going into the bowels of the earth. But you continue to walk downwards. At the bottom a river is flowing and the sides of the valley are thickly wooded. On one side there is a rocky outcrop, and in the rock there is a cave. You feel compelled to walk into the cave, as there is something in there that you wish to see.

The cave is dark, and at the back you see a figure. You approach more closely. The figure lifts its head and you perceive that it is a black woman carrying a child. Notice how you feel when you see this woman. How does your body react? What emotions are evoked?

You are allowed to ask one question of the black woman. Decide what question you would like to ask, and speak to her. Does she give you a reply? How does she look at you? What does the child do?

Finally it is time to go. Before you go, the black woman reaches out and gives you something. Take it, and begin to leave the cave and walk back up the path out of the canyon. What is the gift from the woman? Notice how you feel walking up. Is there a difference from first walking down? Has your encounter made you feel heavy, light, anxious, joyful, fearful, angry?

Clearly this fantasy need not be as restricted as this. It could be done in another setting. It is interesting to allow an interaction with the black woman to develop spontaneously in the fantasy, if that is possible. For example, I know people who have sexual fantasies about her.

A fantasy such as this may work much more easily in a group context, and many individuals may find it difficult to get it to work on their own. This is in itself revealing, as it indicates the collective nature of the Black Virgin image.

THE REFORMATION

We have seen that the whole development and enrichment of Marian symbolism takes place within the restrictive patriarchal system of Church and society. This means that as an expression of the feminine divine, Mary is fractured, fragmented. She is rendered more and more pure and unearthly, while the earthly and magical witches are burnt at the stake. Eve and Mary show the basic split: dark and light; sin and sinlessness; shameful sexuality and pure asexuality; earth and spirit. 'Although the Magna Mater has always been there in the background, the Magnus Pater is in the foreground. ... Woman in her earthly aspect became synonymous with evil.'[37]

Thus Mary represents one half of the feminine as seen from the masculine point of view. She is a masculinized and infantilized femininity.

But then in the Renaissance, something even more drastic happens to Mary: she is removed completely. In Northern Europe the religious Reformation sweeps away the 'idolatry' of saints, chief among whom is Mary.

The stained glass windows were smashed; the statues of Our Lady were toppled and destroyed; the numinous Word became the prosaic word. Religion became rational, non-symbolic, individualized – we might say 'privatized'. Its function as a binding of community values was weakened. God became fiercer, more judgmental, as the intercessionary powers of Mary were lost.

The theological reasons advanced by the Protestants for the excision of Mary are of less importance than social and psychological reasons. The Reformation is indissolubly linked with the rise of capitalism. In both we find stress on the individual – in religion, the individual conscience; economically the right of the individual to accumulate wealth and charge interest. Thrift becomes a religious duty; idleness a sin. Protestantism also embraces the rising nationalism of the sixteenth century, as against the supra-national monolith of the Catholic Church. The effect on religious sensibility of this great movement is summarized as follows by a historian of the period:

> There grew throughout Europe, but especially in the northern countries, a specifically lay piety, orthodox in the main, but tending to shift the emphasis from the means of salvation to the individual's direct relation to God, and from theological dogma to the Christian conduct of daily life.[38]

It is the 'direct relation to God' that strikes at Mary: she is not needed in her function as a means of relating to the divine.

Thus symbolic dogma is abandoned in favour of morality. The already patriarchal nature of the Church is rendered more abrasive, with a fiercer examination of the individual's conduct, with a view to the expenditure of energy in a 'productive' manner. How deeply embedded these values are in our culture could be seen clearly in Thatcherite Britain.

None the less the Reformers were expressing a genuine and widespread sense of dissatisfaction in the whole Church. Worship had become too external and formalized. Indulgences for sins were bought and sold like commodities. The trade in relics had become notorious – Calvin commented witheringly that there were so many phials of the Virgin's milk in existence that she must have given milk like a cow all her life.[39] Undoubtedly the Reformation was a breath of fresh air, and led to the spiritual toughness of Bunyan, the magnificent poetry of Milton, and the exquisite language of the Authorized Version of the Bible, but most importantly it led to a new concentration on the inner spiritual life of individuals.

But as part of the price paid for this development, the values of Mary were rejected in the northern part of Europe. Protestantism became a religion with a huge hole in it. The Goddess was completely removed. She became an unperson. The feminine aspect of the divine went completely underground.

The consequences of this revolution are incalculable. On the positive side, there was an enormous release of energy into masculine thought and activity, leading to scientific and geographical discovery, new philosophical currents, the development of political democracy, inventions, manufacturing. On the debit side, we find a growing sense of the alienation of the individual within the community; an increasing feeling of soullessness, rootlessness and violence, that has come to dominate our culture.

What happens to the feminine? It cannot be made to disappear. It is driven underground, into the unconscious. There it becomes darker, more violent, vengeful. Surely it is not an accident that after the bright dawn of the Renaissance, and then the Age of Reason, we come to the twentieth century, one of the most irrational, destructive, genocidal eras in modern civilization? Is it fanciful to imagine the Goddesses of death and destruction stalking the planet, perched on the standards of Hitler, Pol Pot and Stalin? The Goddess unheard, unwitnessed, becomes a Fury. It has often been pointed out that 'the oldest deities of warfare and destruction were feminine, not masculine.'[40]

The more the feminine is denied, the more humanity becomes possessed by the dark unconscious feminine. We do not, cannot, 'get rid of' the feminine – we drive it into a dark corner, where it becomes a wild animal, or a destructive witch.

This has been one of the fruitful insights of contemporary psychology: that unexpressed, unconscious elements of the psyche have a powerful, even devastating effect on us. So the lost feminine element, and the usurping hyper-masculine element, have been a key problem for both men and women and have bedevilled relations between them.

There are many concrete examples in modern psychological work of the perversion of the feminine. In relation to rapists and would-be rapists, it has been suggested that such men not only act out a desire to have union with, domination over, obliteration of, the feminine, in the shape of actual women, but are themselves eaten alive, obliterated, by their own demonic (because unacknowledged) feminine. In his book *Rape and Ritual*, Te Paske points out how the ritualistic killings by men such as Jack the Ripper are uncannily akin to ancient sacrificial rites, such as were carried out by Aztecs.[41] In both cases, the ritualization shows that powerful unconscious, super-human, non-human, energies are being dealt with. This is not an academic point, nor does it absolve such men of their responsibility for their actions, but it does offer some hope of treatment of apparently intractable cases.

Marion Woodman has done similar work with women who

have eating disorders, and describes the 'witch-like' inner persecution of such women. This is the woman 'robbed of her femininity through her pursuit of masculine goals that are in themselves a parody of what masculinity really is.'[42] Thus both men and women have been raped by the patriarchal system. Men lose contact with their feminine side, which becomes destructive, and their masculinity therefore becomes perverted, degenerate. Women are taken over by an unconscious masculine element which attempts to destroy the true inner feminine identity.

One consequence of the Reformation was the Counter-Reformation, that extravagant surge of religiosity in Catholic Europe in which the cult of Mary became more exaggerated, more militant. But also, perhaps, more defensive, enervated, etiolated: 'as the Church relaxed its claim to intellectual leadership, Catholic piety throughout Europe became saccharin, more prettified, more emotional.'[43]

Thus the Reformation caused a blow to Catholicism and to Marianism from which they have never recovered. The cult of Mary seemed to lose some of its strength, toughness, and artistic freshness. This is still the position today, when the artistic emptiness and vulgarity of statues and pictures of Mary are notorious. In the statue found today in the Catholic home or church, Mary is generally a vapid featureless creature. Only on our Christmas cards do we still see reproduced the masterly images from the great painters. The tawdriness of a modern Marian shrine such as Lourdes shows us how much has been lost.

In the Reformation the patriarchy becomes even more masculinized. This seems a preposterous idea, but it happened. The pendulum, which had swung the way of masculine values for thousands of years, took a further lurch that way. But does not this extremism of masculinism indicate possibly that the pendulum is going to start swinging the other way? There are signs in the twentieth century that feminine values are being rediscovered, reasserted. Ecology, the peace movement, the women's movement – all of these concerns show an increased care for the earth itself, a new sense that we are here not just to exploit natural resources and each other, but to show love, compassion, respect.

Perhaps the Goddess is returning in new clothes. In this movement, is there a role for the Virgin Mary? I have indicated how spontaneous visions and dreams of her appear to be common today, not as Christian symbols but as symbols of a person's inner nurturing, and the contact with the numinous power of the feminine. This is a very individual phenomenon, and not connected with organized religion. I cannot see it becoming any kind of 'mass movement'. Nor can I see the cult of Mary being rekindled in the modern era. She remains an object of devotion for the faithful, but surely new symbols, new images of the feminine, will begin to present themselves.

BEYOND FATHER AND SON

It is tempting to predict a reversal of values in the age of Aquarius, as we leave the age of Pisces, with its predominant symbol the Christ, whose symbol is indeed the fish. Will masculine values be replaced by feminine values? In her important book *Beyond God the Father*, Mary Daly speaks of a 'Second Coming of the female presence' and hails the women's movement as 'anti-Christ, and its import as anti-Church'.[44]

Unfortunately a *reversal* of values will lead to an equivalent problem: the masculine will be driven into the unconscious, thereby to become anarchic and demonic. I cannot believe that the patriarchal system which has dominated our culture for thousands of years will simply be replaced by a new matriarchal order, or that the cult of the masculine God will be replaced by the cult of the Goddess. We cannot go back to a *pre*-patriarchal society.

It strikes me that rather than a supersession of the masculine by the feminine, we need a coming together, a marriage between them. Not the *dominance* of feminine values – for then we end up with the mirror-image of what we have now – but a joining in holy matrimony.

Naturally in this period there is an upsurge of revulsion, even hatred, for masculine values, but I do not feel they can be abandoned. Ironically anyone who attempts to do that will become their victim, just as many people today are the victims of the repressed feminine.

Whether we like it or not, we are all masculine *and* feminine – there is nothing we can do about that. We can suppress one or the other, but the suppressed side inevitably becomes voracious.

But there is no doubt that the whole earth and its people are crying out for the restoration of the feminine. Men are terrified of it and internally possessed by it; women are unsure what it means to be a woman, and what the feminine is concretely, and how to live it. There is an enormous amount of confusion, which cannot be solved by 'figuring things out', or argumentation, but by listening to the wisdom of the unconscious Goddess within us, in her struggle towards consciousness.

This rediscovery of the Goddess not only involves the development of new ideas, new symbols, new rituals, maybe new religions, but a reappraisal of the past. Thus throughout the history of the Christian Church there have been rich veins of feminine spirituality and mysticism, often ignored or demeaned, that we are able to reevaluate today as manifestations of the slumbering Goddess. For example, there are the women saints who have been a source of inspiration and comfort to many people – St Theresa of Avila, mystic, and writer of one of the great spiritual autobiographies; Joan of Arc, that remarkable visionary, soldier and martyr; St Catherine of Siena, who contracted a mystical marriage with Jesus, but was also something of a political agitator in the great fourteenth-century papal schism; Thérèse of Lisieux, the 'Little Flower of Jesus', who captivated the Catholic world early in this century with her naïveté and emotional fervency. In the twentieth century many people have rediscovered the writings of the fourteenth-century authoress Julian of Norwich, who expounded an optimistic, down-to-earth spirituality.

Apart from the women saints, we are only just beginning to explore the richness of women's spirituality within Christianity. A fascinating example are the Beguines, those independent groups of women who founded communities in the Netherlands in the twelfth century, who practised chastity, contemplation and charitable work, and whose remarkable writings, describing the ecstatic relationship of love with the divine, are being rediscovered today.[45]

Many people will also testify to the spiritual help they have received from nuns. Speaking personally, I can say that the most profound, authentic and non-pious spirituality I have ever encountered has been amongst Catholic and Anglican nuns. For example, I know a community in London who live in a terraced house, have manual jobs cleaning in hospitals and so on, who keep an open house for people in the neighbourhood, and who demonstrate a realism and toughness yet also a reverence towards life that is a million miles away from the patriarchal fantasy of 'gentle nuns', so beloved of Hollywood and – who knows? – perhaps also of the Vatican.

The Goddess has slept in the unconscious for thousands of years. She has periodically awoken, and images of her have emerged – wonderful images of great power and beauty, and also of great power and destructiveness.

In Christianity a kind of hide-and-seek has been played with the Goddess. She surfaced in the form of the Virgin Mary, but in an incomplete mutilated state, cleft from her Sister, the Dark Goddess, who remained unconscious and unexpressed.

Thus Mary has been both the symbol of the feminine and a fragment of its ruin.

But those people throughout the ages – and still today – who have had some contact with the numinous power of the image of Mary have experienced something mysterious, uncanny, beyond human understanding. We have always struggled to understand, to formulate theories about her, to represent her visually. But she remains beyond us, an autonomous self-moving being.

No one can be – or should be – forced to revere Mary. Those who are indifferent to her are not disadvantaged. Those who are hostile to her undoubtedly have a deep connection with her, and that is for them to explore.

Despite all the incompleteness, the sugariness, the impossible ethereal quality of Mary, many people have been thankful that she was there for them. She has embodied love, mercy, compassion, receptivity. She has countervailed against the stern male God. She has softened the asperities of the Christian religion. She has soothed many an anxious soul facing death. She has connected us with the ancient procession of Goddesses, who stem from the same timeless root.

She has opened people's hearts and souls so that love can flow naturally, spontaneously. She reconnects us with our original nature as loving beings –

> Be thou then, O thou dear
> Mother, my atmosphere;
> My happier world, wherein
> To wend and meet no sin;
> Above me, round me lie
> Fronting my froward eye
> With sweet and scarless sky:
> Stir in my ears, speak there
> Of God's love, O live air,
> Of patience, penance, prayer:
> World-mothering air, air wild,
> Wound with thee, in thee isled,
> Fold home, fast fold thy child. [46]

REFERENCES

1 All New Testament quotations are from *The New Oxford Annotated Bible, Revised Standard Version*, New York, Oxford University Press, 1973.

2 Epiphanius, *Heresies*, in *Mary in the Documents of the Church*, ed. P.F. Palmer, London, Burns Oates, 1953, p. 49.

3 Joseph Cardinal Ratzinger, *Daughter Zion*, San Francisco, Ignatius Press, 1983, p. 65.

4 The 'Ethiopic Anaphora', *Sing of the Joys of Mary*, Slough, St Paul Publications, 1982, p. 107.

5 Vladimir Lossky, *The Mystical Theology of the Eastern Church*, Cambridge, James Clarke, 1973, p. 193.

6 *C.G. Jung Speaking*, ed. W. McGuire and R.F.C. Hull, London, Pan Books, 1980, pp. 260 and 342.

7 C.G. Jung, 'Psychology and Religion', *Collected Works*, Volume 11, *Psychology and Religion: East and West*, London, Routledge & Kegan Paul, 1969, p. 46.

8 E. Schillebeeckx, *Mary, Mother of the Redemption*, London, Sheed & Ward, 1964, p. 180.

9 Vera von der Heydt, 'Psychological Implications of the Dogma of the Assumption', *Prospects for the Soul*, London, Darton, Longman & Todd, 1976, p. 3.

10 'The Blessed Virgin Compared to the Air We Breathe', *Poems and Prose of Gerard Manley Hopkins*, ed. W.H. Gardner, Harmondsworth, Penguin, 1961, p. 58.

11 William Johnston, *The Wounded Stag*, Glasgow, Collins, 1984, p. 188.

12 *A Critical Dictionary of Jungian Analysis*, ed. A. Samuels, B. Shorter, F. Plaut, London and New York, Routledge & Kegan Paul, 1986, p. 95 under *Myth*.

13 Quoted in Johnston, op. cit., p. 183.

14 *Mary in the Documents of the Church*, op. cit., p. 52.

15 M. Esther Harding, *Woman's Mysteries*, London, Rider, 1982, p. 109.

16 'Answer to Job', *The Portable Jung*, ed. J. Campbell, Harmondsworth, Penguin, 1980.

17 von der Heydt, op. cit., p. 72.

18 Marina Warner, *Alone of all her Sex*, London, Pan Books, 1985, p. xxi.

19 Marion Woodman, *The Pregnant Virgin*, Toronto, Inner City Books, 1985, p. 85.

20 Christopher Rowlands, *Christian Origins*, London, SPCK, 1985.

21 Rowlands, ibid., p. 4.
22 Ratzinger, op. cit., p. 12.
23 Rowlands, op. cit., p. 153.
24 Ratzinger, op. cit., p. 24.
25 Ean Begg, *The Cult of the Black Virgin*, London, Arkana, 1985, pp. 61ff.
26 Raphael Patai, *The Hebrew Goddess*, new edn, USA, Detroit, Wayne State University Press, 1990, p. 153.
27 Ibid., pp. 151–2.
28 Begg, op. cit., p. 68.
29 Ibid., p. 131.
30 Harding, op. cit., p. 93.
31 'Answer to Job', *The Portable Jung*, op. cit., p. 613.
32 See J.C. Engelsman, *The Feminine Dimension of the Divine*, Wilmette, Illinois, Chiron Publications, 1987, Chapter 5.
33 K. McClure, *The Evidence for Visions of the Virgin Mary*, Wellingborough, Aquarian Press, 1983, p. 22. I have taken some of the following detail from McClure.
34 M. O'Carroll, *Medjugorje: Facts, Documents, Theology*, Dublin, Veritas, 1968, p. 69.
35 C.G. Jung, 'Flying Saucers: A Modern Myth', *Collected Works*, Volume 10, *Civilization in Transition*, London, Routledge & Kegan Paul, 1970.
36 Begg, op. cit., p. 9.
37 von der Heydt, op. cit., p. 73.
38 W. Ferguson, 'Renaissance Religion', in *The Renaissance*, ed. P. Burke, London, Longmans, 1966, p. 58.
39 Warner, op. cit., p. 200.
40 Edward C. Whitmont, *The Return of the Goddess*, London, Routledge & Kegan Paul, 1987, p. viii.
41 B.A. Te Paske, *Rape and Ritual*, Toronto, Inner City Books, 1982, p. 120.
42 Marion Woodman, *Addiction to Perfection: The Still Unravished Bride*, Toronto, Inner City Books, 1982, p. 7.
43 Warner, op. cit., p. 312.
44 M. Daly, *Beyond God the Father*, Boston, Beacon Press, 1974, p. 140.
45 Elizabeth A. Petroff, 'The Beguines in Medieval Europe: An Expression of Feminine Spirituality', in *The Goddess Reawakening*, compiled by Shirely Nicholson, Wheaton, Ill. USA, Theosophical Publishing House, 1989.
46 Hopkins, see reference 10.

The Goddess in the Occult Tradition: Tarot Card No. 2
The High Priestess represents the Shekhinah, with appropriate
symbols. See *The Tarot* by Alfred Douglas, page 50 (Penguin).

THE GENESIS OF 'THE SPHERE OF REDEMPTION'
The Theme, and Power, of Lucifer – and the Creative Presence of the Shekhinah and Lilith
Fay Pomerance

The 'Theme', I believe, grew with me. I was early impressed by the first chapters of Genesis and the Garden of Eden story in my home teaching, later in school in the teaching of other mythologies, rather than as other religions. I always had a query in my mind as to the *origin* of things – *why* was the Serpent the most subtle of the beasts? being perhaps one of the earliest. The complexity of the Serpent seemed to ring against the high-placed 'good turned inside out' of the Fallen Angel, as Lucifer, the Accuser – Ha-sotan.

I was a tree-climber in my childhood days, and although I had sisters I spent a great deal of time living out my own games, playing all parts, within my trees. Part of the garden still exists, and the block of flats in which my mother lived until her death was built on the site of our old house. I have tried to visualize it again as it was, walking round it, and I expressed my reaction to this in a poem called 'The trees I climbed in Childhood are cut down'. They are very central to my psychological and spiritual thought and memory.

In my own garden dreams there were three trees in particular. A laburnum tree (which cannot be as tall as I remember it) with a black trunk and branches, and shining, golden, spilling blossoms. It was a Knight figure of the Galahad type; some almost celestial figure, bearing gold from the 'Good blackness' of protective, gleaming armour, suited to challenge all evil of opposing forces. I always felt there were two kinds of oppositions, one a Heavenly 'right' one, and the other a drifting away from Heaven, misguided, hampering one – the former sometimes more painful and rigorous to meet than the latter since there seemed no denying it whatever, whereas the opposition of the Adversary *could* be overcome and resolved by the equipment with which each one was personally endowed. The Golden Knight tree was not apart from my ultimate pictorial conception of my Golden Adam and the Celestial Adam of my Theme.

Then there was a central May tree, into which I used to climb and hide, and this was a kind of 'Mother of all' symbol for me, and somehow was embodied in colour and in some form in my Eve figure. This tree and the Laburnum were ultimately cut down to provide a tennis court for my teenage sisters, which did not please me in the least. I mourned those trees – and in part, still do.

The third tree of my dramatis personae was near a part of the garden which was, in fact, a gardener's rubbish dump, but contained a very old Oak tree, and a great deal of tangled bramble and undergrowth and dank, dark, decaying things and seemed to me like a mysterious jungle. Across and out of this lay a grey stricken tree, probably dead, which had been overthrown in some way, or time, and whose roots and branches seemed twistingly, agonizingly and accusingly raised in rebellion against the power of the sky. I used to straddle this tree, gazing upwards and trying to imagine its original height and appearance and then its fall and the dark decay out of which it now seemed to spring. I liked this 'wood' as I called it, the best part of the garden, and was always attracted to that which was dark and tangled. This tree metamorphosed itself into my Lucifer, particularly in the latter part of Part One and Part Two of the Theme, when he became rooted and torn in the under portion of the sacred river, lost and pursuing the Seed of Redemption.

From the age of nine I grew with the experience of a secret life of visionary enactment; I kept all this unrevealed until into my twenties, though I was very deeply and tortuously entangled both emotionally and in other ways at an earlier age. I seemed to be held in a vow of silence, from the age of fourteen to twenty-one, about inner experience and to be involved in much subjective conflict, and I think it was within it that I learnt what Judaic teaching seemed always to confirm; that the opposing darkness, though a force, was not a dual ruling Power but the result of some misguided spiralling away from the Divine Good, which could centrally be relied on, and to which one could re-turn. Even so, I was in great danger of engulfment within conflict, and had I endeavoured at that time to produce pictorially conflict and precipitous breaking away, I think it would have been completely destructive to myself and others. It was only possible to incorporate it into a given pictorial visionary Theme later, at a time when I was freed from the actual subjective involvement, and could select objectively – which the artist must do to communicate safely, for the sake of those viewing the result as well as for the artist's own sustained equilibrium. Within the sequence of my Theme of Lucifer – the Sphere of Redemption – I was dealing with two potent areas where there are very thin lines in pictorial representation. One was the portrayal of the forces of good and evil. The other was the representation of initial sex in the Garden of Eden, which forces the responsible artist to avoid the tilt from eroticism into pornography.

Accounts of the Garden of Eden and of the Fallen High One from Heaven, and the vision of Ezekiel of the Holy Living Creatures were my three most frequently recurring and dominating images – though it was many years later I came to any study of the Merkava mysteries, and indeed of Jewish mysticism at all. When I came to study it, I felt it was a confirmation of my inner experiences, and often I discovered in it things I had felt to be 'original' in my own working out of the theme of things.

My own visionary experience was always that of living vision. My non-revealing vow was in a way a protection, I think, as if, not observed, I avoided being misguided about it. As it was, I was later helped to harness my vision in a positive rather than a negative way, lacking which, I think, I should either have gone out of my mind, committed suicide, or just, through some physical reaction to the inner strain, have died.

My father died two days before my seventeenth birthday. My crucial turn of thought and purpose came when after this, the Rev. Dr Cohen (our Minister in Birmingham at that time, a very fine Hebrew scholar) investigated the Levy family tree and history for my Father's sister. My father's father, Naphtoli Levy, had been a Hebrew scholar and writer. On tracing my father's antecedents, Dr Cohen added a note to my Aunt stating, 'A heritage of which you can be justly proud.'

I saw the paragraph of the family tree, and this comment, and it struck through me. It seemed to me that if one had a heritage of which one could be proud, it demanded that one should become a descendant of which one's ancestors could be proud, and that in this case, I was one who must support this obligation. I looked round the family of descendants of my father's brothers and sisters in my own generation, and it seemed to me at that time (perhaps erroneously) that in the three of us – my sisters and myself – was the only visible spark of any real spiritual, religious interest at all, and it was somehow incumbent on me personally to honour the responsibility. I did not feel I was doing so in the work I was then engaged on. The fact that I was leading a rather frivolous outer and very involved inner life was the cause of an ultimate breakdown, not unallied with the ever-increasing feeling that I was not established in my own centre. I think I was rescued in marriage with Ben, who gave me both the safeguard and the ability to earth vision and develop the spiritual and committed side in a strangely paradoxical peace.

I did not commence actual studies for my 'theme' till 1946, ten years after my marriage. Then my growing feeling that my theme of Eden and the Fallen Angel were all one was confirmed. Some five years before commencing the Theme I did a study and cartoon for a proposed picture on the subject of a ballet of Lust and Avarice. It was, in fact, a satire on the hypocrisies of various religious denominations, and of monks, nuns and priests in particular. In the centre of the picture, however, was the figure of Lucifer leaping in anguish, with the right hand and arm withdrawn from the right wing which he was destroying with his freed right hand, while falling from the skies. I was, as if from a command of Supreme Authority, stopped from continuing this picture, but the figure of Lucifer returned in the First Part of my Theme – Lucifer's Creation of Hand.

Cutting across the discontinuation of the Lust and Avarice project, I was asked to illustrate a four-volume work called *Coming Forth By Day* by Marjorie Livingston for which, over eighteen months, I produced twelve illustrations in monochrome for the two volumes on 'The Egyptian Book of the Dead' and 'The Hebrew Kabbalah'. Over some years I worked with Marjorie Livingston in a field which helped me to health, and to channel my vision. Out of the personal work the living vision of Part One of my Lucifer Theme was given.

The illustrative work I did on the Hebrew Kabbalah volume of *Coming Forth* made me realize my own lack of knowledge in that direction, and the author's incomplete comprehension of the whole inner meaning. The atmosphere seemed imbued for me with the spirit of Simeon Ben Yochai, despite the contested authorship of the Zohar, and I somehow felt drawn to the ancient Rabbinic presence. It was an odd feature of the work, that I felt at one with Ancient Egyptian Priesthood inspiring the

140

investigation of the Egyptian volume, and also continued a study of the Egyptian mysteries thereby, but it did not have the same personal beckoning as the other. (Marjorie Livingston was not Jewish, though married to a Jew whom she did not know was Jewish, and I only confirmed that he was, fully so, ten years after her death.) From this time on, I made my own personal study and became deeply involved with Jewish mysticism which seemed to provide a confirming 'yes' to all my inner experiences and thought.

In my own personal exploration of the world of meanings, as always, I explored backwards to origins – I became absorbed in the feeling of the Holy Living Creatures, the emanations and creations. The feeling the Angels were *emanated, man created*, that one did not evolve from nor is likely to evolve into the other, and that the highest mark of man's evolution above other creatures was the eye and hand controlled by the mind, receiving its inspiration through the inner eye of vision. I also became involved in the thought exploration of the wing and the hand and arm. I discovered that no creature had separately evolved arms and wings, and that the man-depicted forms with wings, large or small, attached to their backs in Christian pictorial art were symbolic only of spiritual power, and not demonstrative of any creature that could maintain flight.

Recurring in my mind was the idea of the link between the two themes of the rebel outcast from Heaven, the accepted role there of Ha-sotan, the Accuser of the Book of Job, who *will* be heard and *must* be answered, and the involvement of the couple in Eden with the Serpent.

In 1945 I produced a series of water-colours which were in fact a forerunner of Part Three of my Theme, 'The Three-Fold Tree of Eden' and have the Zoharistic idea of Eve herself as the Fruit of the Tree tempting Adam, even more strongly brought out than in its ultimate form. In this also was adumbrated the idea of Adam as a somnambulist seeking the unborn Eve within him, outwardly. Incorporated into the later Theme, this clarified into the realization that in Adam's seeking outwardly for the true mate within him, and the male and female created incorporately, he encountered Lilith, the phantom mate, and Kabbalistically is seen to co-habit with her and people the World of Shells (Assiyatic World). This realization and experience was pictorialized in a later series of my work than the Lucifer Theme and seemed to ally with the Divine pronouncement of Genesis, 'and God saw it is not good for Man to live alone.' Thus was Eve, the true mate, withdrawn from the same bone and flesh as

Adam, in the sanctioned separation which makes meeting possible.

At this time I met a one-time student of Martin Buber's from Germany, who saw in my work a kinship to that of Buber's and even more to Franz Rosenzweig's and introduced me to their works. This added a dimension to my inner contemplation and a further confirmation of personal inner experience.

The Theme had been 'given' also in the previous years' events; events in which I was deeply involved: Ben's working to get children out of Europe (among the last, two twins of ten, who escaped from Czechoslovakia), the complexities of evacuating and then recovering my own child, the war itself, the Holocaust. Though it took twenty years finally to bring through, the whole vision was given in the first six or seven years, and vision withdrew almost completely in the latter years of its execution.

It had seemed to me a completely Universal Theme but as I worked I found that the more Universal I tried to be, the more centrally Judaic I became, and at length accepted this as an inner truth – that one can only give out widely from one's own centre, if one is not to diffuse and weaken what one has to give.

Within the experience of this Theme-work, of negative and positive forces requiring active participation in the meeting of opposites, the given powers, or drive, which can be *made* evil by precipitous wrong directive, faced me with the terrific temptation to cross the line into dualism, on the right side of which Judaic thought, even when surrounded by dualistic gnosticism, always kept. Despite many difficult experiences within these temptations, the central Judaic impulse always held, the Accuser's presence ever belonged within God's power of emanation.

The words 'Angel' and 'Messenger' in Hebrew are one, and to me Lucifer – Day Star, Light Bearer – is the bearer of the message of his own force's precipitate mis-direction, and of Adam's who can, however, at any moment redirect the two-way drive back to balance with good under the central shaft of the Divine will.

The Tree itself, in my studies, went through various transformations of thought, at one time as the two lateral and central pillars of Heaven of Kabbalistic interpretation, the celestial Tree with its fruits on the ground and roots in the heavens (man grows upwards to his roots). It eventually took the form of male and female lateral trees and the central shaft of Divine impulse, which still relate, I believe, to the early symbolism of the trees in my childhood garden and to Bible reading.

There is a transition from Part One – which echoes the first use of atomic energy as a destructive force on Hiroshima in Lucifer's first action of his released right hand's destroying rather than creating – and the picture's explosion from the centre and shape of atomic explosion, to the actual participation in these events through the history stream of Part Four – which also demonstrates a passage of time, and man's contemporary history, in my own and world-wide experience.

The idea of the spherical Globe for the final 'Sphere of Redemption' was conceived almost at the beginning, as I could never see Redemption on the flat. It was conceived long before man went into orbit (by about eighteen years) and therefore before orbiting globes were in people's minds and every TV studio. I wanted it turning in all directions, which it does, but for a long time people thought I meant a circular painting. I eventually managed to get it constructed by a firm of special exhibition stand makers. It was not exactly as I wanted it. First they constructed the stand of brass instead of steel, which became subject to metal fatigue and collapsed when the globe was suspended. Then a fire broke out in the factory where it was being constructed, and although I wanted alterations I thought I had better get it quickly, before anything else occurred. The people working on it had no idea of its purpose and called it 'Operation Telstar'!

From its conception and inception I felt the Theme to be a work I was impelled by Authority to carry out. In the initial stages and before I knew I could complete even the first large painting, I was more or less obsessed by it. As the whole progressed, and particularly after all vision was given, seemingly even beyond the point of exhaustion, I felt very often that I would never complete it, and that I would be failing an undertaken obligation if I did not.

From time to time, particularly during the early stages, there seemed a great deal of the hampering type of opposition at work, sometimes quite unpleasantly so, but this seemed to lessen as time went by. I think some of the later hold-ups were sanctioned, as I was enabled to incorporate things from later experiences and happenings, which I could not have done at an earlier stage.

Since the work's completion and brief exhibition, I have felt wholly in abeyance, as it were, and as the major works sit around me I am a little fearful lest its destiny is no more than to do only this. I used to think it more important to see that a work was done rather than to worry about what would be done with it. Now I am not so sure. But it is done and here remains.

And it was completed with the Shekhinah's support. I knew as I worked on the final Part of the Sphere that the protagonists leading towards Redemption were the Shekhinah and Lucifer, the former enduring and the latter challenging the attributes bestowed on the celestial Adam in his fourfold roles of King, Harvester, Miner and Guardian of the Celestial sword, which were taken forward in his earthly travels, used and abused throughout history. He was supported by the Shekhinah, the Divine Presence and Indwelling of God.

Aware that the manifest feminine of the Shekhinah balances with the masculine of the King Messiah, forming a monadic whole, I was extremely conscious that by presenting the Shekhinah pictorially my conception of her might be equated with Sophia or the Goddesses of other denominations of ancient or contemporary religious conceptions – and I strove within the pictorial presentation to avoid that direct idea of her being so. I experience her as something Other, and in my personal vision and awareness she so remains, and has been so accepted by viewers of many denominations and experiences.

Emerging from the force of Living Vision, there is a responsibility and discipline incumbent on the artist when dealing with themes of light and dark, of good and evil impulses (or the 'Good' and 'Other Drive' or 'Passion' deflected from the obedience of preserving balance and so as God said, 'You have made it Evil') to select in a manner that will not be harmful to the viewers, who might have the negative side rather than the positive side of their being operative, lacking the ideal balance between the two. One must avoid the danger of putting figuratively, or in any formal way pictorially, images, etc. experienced subjectively before one has within oneself objectified them.

I have accordingly found myself reacting against the description of the Shekhinah and Lilith as Hebrew Goddess figures. Lilith, for me, is the Temptress who never satisfies, the cause of God's saying, 'It is not good for man to live alone.' She has a succubus quality and is the phantom Harlot with whom Adam is conjoined while seeking outwardly for the true Eve within him. This I believe is a common awareness in many men. She is in essence not, as men may see her, 'fair', though she has this 'fair' side to present, but on the other side 'foul'. In my work I have seen the Convolvulus as a symbol of Lilith: its white trumpeting flowers a symbol of purity, on a tendrilled stem which strangles all growing things with which it comes into contact. Most men in ordinary life who express an interest – seemingly intellectual – in Lilith as a subject are those I find who have had some inner experience of the lady. My own experience is that she has presented herself as a subject in my studio on many occasions, insisting on being depicted, and this has always heralded a new spate of positive creative work. Though the Shekhinah has always been 'there' for me, Lilith has seemed to invade my work unexpectedly, and has appeared in other contexts also. With her Adam is said to have peopled the Assiyatic world of shells: form which is waiting for meaning. The necessity for bringing forth the true mate Eve, as against the fantasy, is thereby underlined.

My awareness of the Shekhinah is so incorporated in the phases of my life and creative work that it is not simple to express. I always found myself beneath her Way in the Great Invocation of the Jewish Night Prayers, where it is the Shekhinah who is held to be above the suppliant ' in the name of the Lord God of Israel'. She is 'above my head' and crowns the temple of protection that the prayer constructs. I have felt also her accompaniment, even in degradation, in her two-fold purposed banishment, willingly undertaken by her. She is in no way diminished as an inferior to God; though banished she is never separated in divine intent. The banishment results from man's abusing of the endowment of free choice by tearing asunder the Oneness and turning away from the balance of the Divine in equilibrium. The sanctioned separation makes meeting possible, in the bringing forth of a new Eve from her own form of indwelling to help – though sometimes hinder – the way through to redemption.

I attempted to follow the Shekhinah's way through various paths of creative existence, and the experience of Living Vision in my work with Marjorie Livingston. I felt then entrusted with bringing it through in the pictorial cycle of the Sphere, which I always felt would have been better carried through by genius, which is not mine. In the fourth part of the Sphere, 'The Way Back', the Shekhinah is present as the protagonist of Lucifer, who has the opportunity to enter the human world for the purpose of rehabilitation, where Adam and Eve, in the abuse rather than use of their endowments, extend their knowledge of good and evil, and in time voluntarily become the chosen heralds of Redemption. In the fifth and final part, the whole Sphere of Redemption, she is seen as the winged Shekhinah,

145

whose wings join the outstretched hands of King Messiah, embracing the happenings below and the return and redemption above, in a joint Female–Male protection encircling the whole.

Along the way in my studies I painted Her as the Divine Presence, also as the Banished Bride, the Bride Reclaimed, and even the World Waif, a reflection of my child self.

In the process of writing for this book (and through interchange with Alix Pirani), and of further imbibing life's ceaseless lessons in my own feminine role as daughter, sister, wife, mother, grandmother and creative artist, I have been granted a more harmonious insight, overriding my initial protest at the book's aim to reclaim the Shekhinah as the Hebrew Goddess. I can now view as equally valid others' experiencing of her Being, though differing from my own, in my humbly striving to follow Her Way; as I have related.

Possibly therefore we may collectively be contributing the varied-shaded strands that weave the fabric of Holy Unity, as its Pattern is revealed to us. As in the unique equilibrium of the Male–Female laterally placed columns of the Kabbalistic Tree of Life, balanced by the central Shaft of Divine Intent, perhaps we shall re-turn towards Redemption through the many paths open to us.

Abraham, it is told, was given this name 'Father of Multitudes' because of his Mission to bring all the People under the Wings of the Shekhinah.

The most difficult precious burden life lays on each of us is the establishment of the Sabbath of one's own soul. So, with the injunction of the inauguration of the Sabbath, 'Come my friend to meet the Bride; let us welcome the Presence of the Sabbath', we join in the recall of the Shekhinah, welcoming, through her Divine In-Dwelling Presence the Perfect Rest of Peace, which is the literal and innermost meaning of Shabbat Shalom.

IN THE BEGINNING
Janet and Stewart Farrar

[This playlet first appeared as part of a chapter on Lilith and Eve in *The Witches' Goddess*.]

Sheila, a witch, born a Christian
Bernie, a witch, Sheila's husband, born Jewish
Eve
Adam
Lilith

Scene: Sheila and Bernie's living-room Circle. They have finished their ritual and are sitting on the floor, skyclad, relaxing over the last of the wine.

Sheila: That was a good Circle, Bernie. If Harry doesn't pass his exam after that lot, it's not our fault.
Bernie: Well, I think we gave a boost to what he lacks. He's powerful in Hod – good brain, and all that – but he needs a dollop of Netzach for creative imagination.
Sheila: Not to mention Geburah for determination ... *(smiling)* You and your Cabala!
Bernie: I should abandon my cultural heritage, already? I don't bash your leprechauns.
Sheila: Leprechauns again! I've told you before – they're a very minor part of Irish mythology. The Tuatha Dé Danann and the Daoine Sidhe are the ones that matter. *[Pronounced 'Tooha day dahn'n' and 'Dweenuh shee'.]*
Bernie: Blinding me with science.
Sheila: Hark who's talking! *(Holding up hands in surrender.)* All

right, all right. Call it a draw. Everyone's got his cultural heritage; you can't be born without one.

Bernie: Way back to Adam and Eve, who presumably hadn't. *(He sips the wine.)* Le Chaim. [*Pronounced 'lehayim'.*]

Sheila: Now there's a bit of Hebrew cultural heritage I'd like to know the truth about. *(Takes the chalice and sips.)* Sláinte mhaith. [*Pronounced 'Slawncheh voy'.*]

Bernie: That's easy. A priestly establishment rewrite of earlier Middle Eastern creation myths. They wanted to suppress Ashera-worship which was rampant among the farming population of Israel. In the Sumerian version ...

Sheila: Hold it, hold it. I didn't mean that. I meant, what really happened.

Bernie: I hope you meant psychic truth, not alleged history.

Sheila: You know perfectly well what I meant.

Bernie: Let's go and see, then. *(He picks up the pentacle from the altar and holds it to shine light in Sheila's eyes, saying mock-dramatically:)* You are going back to the Garden of Eden ... You are going back to the Garden of Eden ...

Sheila (laughing): No, Bernie – not your hypnosis thing – you're too good at it, and I'm too tired ...

Bernie: It is too late ... You are already there ...

(It is suddenly pitch dark.)

Sheila: No, Bernie, no ...

Bernie: Oy, gevalt!

It is bright sunlight. Sheila and Bernie are sitting in the same positions, in a beautiful forest glade. She jumps to her feet.

Sheila: Bernie , you've done it again! You know how susceptible I am to it ...

Bernie (getting up more slowly): It certainly looks like the Garden of Eden.

Sheila: But how come you're here with me, this time? I mean, I've always been able to hear you, but ...

Bernie (bewildered): I don't know!

Sheila (pointing): Bernie – look!

(Eve walks into the glade. She is exactly as we imagine her, naked, with long blonde hair. She sees Sheila and Bernie and halts, puzzled.)

Sheila: Eve!

Bernie (taking a couple of cautious steps towards Eve and speaking tentatively): Shalom, Chava?

Eve: Shalom ... You're like him, I think – but what is that? *(pointing at Sheila).*

Bernie (pulling himself together): I'm Bernie, and this is my wife Sheila.
Eve (examining Sheila and starting back): You're another one!
Sheila: Another what, Eve?
Eve: Your voice is like mine and the Green One's. But his is like Adam's.
Sheila: That's right. You and I are women, and Adam and this one are men ... Who's the Green One?
Eve: Adam belongs to me. I don't want any more ... women. Go away.
Sheila: I will, I promise. I don't want your Adam, honestly.
Eve: The Green One does. She says she was here first.
Sheila: Who is the Green One?
Lilith (from out of sight): Actually, my name is Lilith ... Shalom.
(Lilith, in green body make-up or leotard, slithers into view round a tree. All her movements are serpentine. Her hair is as black as Eve's is blonde.)
Sheila: Er ... Shalom.
Lilith: Some company at last. (She slithers round the tree again, and reappears immediately with a red apple in her hand, which she offers to Eve.) Well, Eve?
Eve: I don't trust you.
(Eve starts to walk away. Lilith walks casually beside her, tossing the apple in her hand. Sheila and Bernie follow them.)
Lilith: You learn fast, my dear. Dealing with concepts like 'trust' already, are we? (Pointing ahead.) It'll take him longer.
(Adam comes out of the trees. He, too, is unselfconsciously naked.)
Adam: I've been looking for you, Eve. What are these creatures?
Eve: That one's a Bernie and that one's a Sheila. I don't know what they do. The Sheila says it's a 'woman', the same as me and the Green One, and I don't like that.
Lilith: Oh, poor Eve. She doesn't trust anyone.
Adam: What's 'trust'?
Lilith (to Eve): See what I mean?
Sheila: I'm not here for long, Eve. And I'm here as your friend.
Lilith: Good – Eve has a friend. Perhaps she'll advise her about the apple. (Holds the apple in front of Eve's nose.) Eve is trying to make up her mind. I'm sure you're aware of the background. What do you say?
Sheila: I only know one version of the background. I'd rather start from scratch. What is the apple?
(They have reached a many-branched tree, bearing several of the same red apples. Lilith slithers onto a sloping branch and lies along it, with her head just above the head-height of the others.)

Lilith: One of these. Adam thinks they're dangerous.

Sheila: Why, Adam?

Adam: God told me.

Sheila: Men always call their own taboos the Voice of God.

Lilith: I like this girl ... How long can you stay here?

Sheila: I don't know. Not long.

Lilith: Pity.

Adam: What's a 'taboo'?

Lilith (throwing Adam the apple): Here, eat that, and you'll stop asking such stupid questions. *(She picks another apple.)*

Adam (catching the apple and looking at it): I'm afraid.

Lilith: Of opening your eyes?

Adam: I can see well enough!

Lilith: The facts in front of your nose, yes. Not the truths behind them.

Adam: Oh. *(Studies apple thoughtfully.)* All right, then. *(He bites into it.)*

Eve (anguished): No, Adam! No!

Lilith: Too late, my dear.

(Adam swallows his mouthful of apple, frowns and then comes to look up into Lilith's face from a foot or two away. Enlightenment dawns. Lilith toys with the other apple.)

Adam: I remember now! You were here first – before me, even – you gave birth to me ...

Lilith: Go on. You're doing nicely.

Adam: You're Lilith – you're my first wife ...

Lilith (to Sheila): All genuine creation myths are both parthenogenetic and incestuous.

(Eve has burst into tears and dropped to her knees on the grass. Adam goes to her and kneels beside her, putting an arm round her.)

Adam: But Eve – don't cry – you're my wife, too ...

Lilith (to Sheila): Also bigamous, it seems.

Sheila (snatching apple from Lilith): Oh, stop being so smart! Can't you see she's upset? *(She runs to kneel at Eve's other side.)*

Lilith (with a suddenly genuine smile): Hurry, my dear, hurry ... *(To Bernie):* It really is a pity she can't stay.

Sheila (offering apple to Eve): Eve – you need this – if you leave it to those two, everything will be out of balance ... Here ...

(Eve, sniffing back her tears, looks at the apple, then at Adam, then at the apple again. Then she takes it and bites into it. Sheila and Adam watch her, holding their breath. Eve munches and swallows. She begins to smile. The smile broadens, and she begins to laugh. She jumps to her feet and goes to take Lilith's hand. Soon both Eve and Lilith are roaring with laughter, Eve reaching up and Lilith reaching

down so that each has one arm round the other's shoulders. Adam gets to his feet and goes to face them, looking puzzled. Sheila also rises, and joins Bernie to one side, where they both stand watching.)

Adam: I remembered, and I thought I understood. But now I don't again.

(Eve and Lilith look at him, smiling mischievously. Their following dialogue alternates without pause, like one continuous speech.)

Eve: We are your wife, Adam.

Lilith: But which of us is which?

Eve: Or are we sisters?

Lilith: Or the same?

Eve: Or your mother?

Lilith: Or your lover?

Eve: Or your daughter?

Lilith: Which is which?

Eve: Will you ever find out?

Lilith: And how many different stories will you invent about all this?

Adam: Stop! Stop, both of you! I need to think! *(Turns to Sheila.)* You – you're from outside. Tell me what to do.

Sheila (smiling): It's no good asking me. I'm another of her.

(It is beginning to grow darker.)

Lilith: Quick – you're going! ... Here, catch!

(Lilith grabs an apple and throws it to Sheila. Sheila catches it.)

Suddenly it is pitch dark again – and a moment later we are back in the living-room Circle, with Sheila and Bernie sitting as before. There is no sign of the apple.

Sheila: Oh. I'd have liked to stay a bit longer.

Bernie (still stunned): Wow! How was that for a hypnosis session! Darling – I've never managed anything like that before. I mean, me being in it with you ... I don't understand. And it was so real ...

Sheila: It certainly was.

Bernie: Like a shared dream ...

Sheila: You reckon it was a dream, do you?

Bernie: Well, that's easier to believe than a sort of shared hypnosis.

(Sheila reaches behind her back and produces the apple. She holds it up in front of Bernie's eyes.)

Sheila: Then how do you explain this?

LILITH AND SATURN –
AN ASTROLOGICAL VIEW
Deike Rich

Adapted from a talk given to the Astrological
Association International Conference.

THE FEMININE SIDE OF SATURN

The idea that Saturn has a feminine side is an ancient one.
Barbara Walker in her book *The Women's Encyclopedia of Myths
and Secrets* tells us that before Hellenic masculinization of the
goddess Rhea, who later became Kronos' wife, she was the
Universal Great Mother Goddess who had no consort, and ruled
supreme.[1] Her name was also Coronis and in this form she was
both a death goddess and a life goddess. In Russia she was Rha,
another version of Mother Time, who devours all that she brings
forth. In Celtic mythology she was Rhiannon, also a child-
devourer. Time and Earth are inseparable, both taking back
what they bring forth, consuming their offspring (whether hours
or gods), just as everything which Earth produces must
eventually return to her.

Rhea's consort, Kronos or Saturn, is renowned for devouring.
As we know, Saturn castrated his own father and usurped the
title and attributes of Time which had belonged to Rhea. So
Saturn, then, in his original form was feminine, the Great
Mother, creating and devouring.

John Layard in his book *A Celtic Quest* tells us that every
attempt to create is an attempt to escape this pull of the Great
Mother, an attempt to escape her *vagina dentata*.[2] He even goes
so far as to suggest that no action exists which is not related to
the Great Goddess: all the Gods are her emissaries. Even Satan
(or his equivalent), he tells us, is only a son of the Great
Underworld Goddess Hell, as Eros is the son of Aphrodite. Each
is in the service of his mother, doing her bidding. Consequently,
Saturn on the birth chart is this force that swallows back its own
creations – anything that is attempting to escape the ring-pass-
not. Sometimes people believe that it is through the hard work

of Saturn that one becomes free of Saturn. This, however, is not the case. Whether we can escape this pull of Saturn or not depends on the strength of other planets in the horoscope, particularly the will force of Mars.

The Renaissance philosopher and doctor, Ficino, who had Saturn prominent in his horoscope, was familiar with this devouring side of Saturn, but he also sensed that within Saturn was hiding a light, very faintly glowing, a creativity which could not be found other than through the experience of the influences of Saturn. All his life he could not escape the Saturnian depressions he suffered from so severely, and his only way of surviving them, he felt, was to allow Saturn to turn him inward towards the Self and there, in the Otherworld, find the strength and inspiration for renewed creative expression in the outer world.[3] The idea that a deep Saturnian depression can only begin to transform through creative expression, through bringing forth from within ourselves, is well developed in Siegmund Hurwitz's book *Lilith, die erste Eva*. He tells us of a deeply depressed forty-year-old man[4] who, after about two years of therapy, during which they examined the shadow or repressed aspects of his psyche, had a dream in which a beautiful woman comes to visit him. She does not speak, is half naked and has prominent breasts. Her skin and hair are black and she has a pair of wings. He is enormously tempted by her, fascinated and stunned, and at the same time he is afraid and does not dare to speak to her.

In his associations to this dream he names this creature Lilith, the whore. She had come to show him the repression of his feminine side, his sexuality and his ability to create and relate. It is precisely because she had become repressed, just like the Hebrew Lilith who was Adam's first wife, that she now appears as a dark demon of the night who fascinates, but at the same time renders us speechless, impotent and immobile and lures us into unconsciousness and death.

In a poem, whose source I do not remember, but which has certain aspects in common with Keats's *Lamia*, she appears to a man in a vision and disappears again. He then goes looking for her all over the world and finally finds her again in the desert. He is overjoyed to see her and she calmly and sweetly says to him, 'If you knew your fate you would not have gone looking for me,' and bites off his head.

During therapy, the patient, although he fell into a very deep depression after this dream, began to relate to his dream figure through dialogue and painting, and his depression, which had lasted many years, gradually began to lift. Although it remained a part of his general disposition, he could now balance it with his creative endeavours. By producing something which is our own creation, we begin to escape the grip of Saturn, Earth and Time.

When we work with people therapeutically Saturn will show himself in his Lilith aspect, as a devouring mother who is angry, raging, strangling, hating all and everyone, living a terrifying lone existence; or as the temptress who comes to a man, alone at night, and takes his best seeds from him, so that after an encounter with her he feels totally drained of his life-force and his ability to create. And it is only through getting to know her that we can escape her overwhelming powers. As in Rumpelstiltskin, only when we can name the devil does he/she no longer have power over us. Recognition of the energies and dynamics involved in what we are doing is always the first step; only then can we also *not* do something.

WHO ACTUALLY WAS LILITH?

Let us take a closer look at Lilith and two accounts of her creation. One is recorded in the Alpha Bet Ben Sira in the ninth or tenth century,[5] and the story goes something like this: Adam was bored with just having animals as companions and became miserable and lonely. So God made a woman for him who was created from the same stuff or material as Adam, totally his equal. But very soon they got into a marital row because Lilith sometimes wanted to be on top when making love. As Adam would not allow this Lilith became angry, cursed God by calling out his magic name, which was forbidden and the most blasphemous thing to do, grew wings and flew to the Red Sea. God sent angels to try and persuade Lilith to return and behave, but when she refused, because Adam would not allow her equality, she was punished by being sent into exile, and cursed with having to bring forth demon children whom she was compelled to kill and eat as soon as they were born. And if she did not bring forth enough children of her own to kill daily she would have to hunt the world for other women's children to kill. She often appeared as a screech owl, and she would also search the night for men alone asleep in their beds and have sex with them and prevent their seeds from producing human offspring (perhaps the original wet dream?). And because of her rage against the unfairness of God, she tried, whenever she could, to come between man and wife and separate them. God then created a second wife for Adam from his rib, Eve, who was pleasantly submissive and did as she was told, until, of course, Lilith appeared to her in the shape of a serpent in the garden of Eden and tempted her to defy God by biting into the apple of the tree of knowledge of good and evil. And we all know what happened then: they became conscious and could no longer remain in blissful ignorance or paradise.

The other story about the origins of Lilith comes from a French play by Rémy de Gourmont.[6] Again, Adam becomes dissatisfied and lonely without human companionship. God, who wants to be a perfect God and give Adam all he needs, decides to create a woman for him. He takes a lump of clay and makes the most voluptuous, gorgeous woman imaginable with lots of curves in all the right places. When he has almost finished he realizes that he did not give her a brain, so he reached up between her legs into her belly and pulls out a handful of clay and puts it into her head as a brain. Then he breathes life into her and Lilith stirs. She stretches and feels her body and is well pleased with herself. Then she looks around and asks God: 'Where is my man? The one you have created me for. Give me my man!' She becomes more insistent until God realizes that he has created a 'monster' who is only interested in the man he created her for. Lilith's overt sexuality causes him great distress and discomfort and he finally throws her into hell to become the bride of Satan.

So, Lilith, then, the personification of desire, a woman who considered herself equal to and created for man, was banished to the underworld. But just because she was banished and repressed she did not disappear altogether. All that which is repressed returns to us in another form somehow, and Lilith returned as a destructive demon who sought to spoil everything which is supposed to make relationships between man and woman harmonious and peaceful. She is against nuptual bliss at the expense of woman's freedom, independence and equality, and against the offspring of this unequal union. Anything she can do to spoil this brings her sweet revenge. Her main purpose, having been denied her rightful place, is to ruin it for the rest of us.

LILITH REPRESENTED BY SATURN ON THE BIRTH CHART

I have already mentioned some of the associations of Lilith with Saturn deriving from the devouring principle of the Great Mother in Saturn's association with Rhea. Now let us look at a few more parallels between these two figures. Saturn is also Satan and the fallen angel Lucifer, who descends to earth in the guise of the immortal lightning serpent Sata. When God denied Adam and Eve the fruit of the tree of knowledge in order to keep them ignorant, it was Lucifer, in the form of the serpent Lilith, who offered them the 'light' of consciousness.

The serpent in Gnosis is the female spiritual principle, the instructor, who teaches humanity to trust that they will not die if they become conscious. She tells Eve not to believe God's warning but that all will be well, even better, if she bites into the apple.

If we look at the glyph for Saturn (♄) we can see the serpent on the cross of matter. Saturn is both, the tree and the serpent, the snake and the ladder. Lilith, according to the Zohar, is the ladder on which we descend into matter and also ascend to heaven.

We are beginning to get a sense of this great mystery. On the one hand Saturn and Lilith are the devouring mother, the force that tries ceaselessly to pull us back into the darkness, into unconsciousness. On the other hand, Saturn and Lilith are also our greatest teachers who lead us into the light.

Lilith in her Sophia guise, like Saturn/Lucifer, also fell into matter because she wanted knowledge which was withheld from her. It is only by falling into matter, by being embodied and informed, that we gain knowledge or consciousness.

Both Saturn and Lilith eat their children. If we look at photographs of the planet Saturn with its rings we see that it resembles the solar system, almost as if Saturn is pretending to be another sun. Indeed, Saturn is also considered the *alter ego* of the sun, the Black Sun, the sun in its sleeping state (reminding us that Saturn is asleep and enchained on the Island of the Blessed). And like Lilith, the Black Sun is the spirit of the night, the screech owl. In actual physical reality the planet Saturn also swallows its children, for everything that comes into its orbit is swallowed up to stay wraith-like within its rings forever.

Both Saturn and Lilith are connected with death and disease. If a baby died (for instance, of diphtheria), it was believed that Lilith as the strangler had come and killed it. If a woman died in childbirth or during pregnancy, again it was Lilith's doing, and in order to protect themselves and their children women would use specially engraved amulets as talismans. This supposedly had the same effect as the eating of the *pharmakon* (R_x), an earlier symbol for Saturn, in order to cure disease. Perhaps these were the beginnings of homoeopathy: you take a little of the poison which is afflicting you to effect a cure. It takes one spirit to chase another spirit away.

If we say that symbolically children are our creations of the mind, our ideas, then we can perhaps more easily understand and see how this Saturn principle functions as Lilith the child-killer. We are all familiar with situations where we have brilliant ideas but feel unable to do anything about them. As soon as these ideas arise they get swallowed up by feelings of inadequacy, incompetence, inferiority or sheer laziness. Those are the effects that Saturn and Lilith can have on us. Every time we feel defeated, depressed or insignificant, it is Saturn or Lilith in us, devouring our life-force. The energy needed to escape this perpetual downward pull is very great, as everyone who works with people therapeutically will know from observation.

I believe that we have become far too optimistic regarding Saturn. The general consensus these days seems to be that we ought to get to know this planet, learn to love it, work hard against life's challenges, and then all will be well. Depth psychology seems to present a different picture. The hard work aspect, characteristic of a Saturn experience, appears to be more an aspect of escaping this pull of Saturn into deadness, inertia and unconsciousness, than of working with the energy of Saturn. The work against nature, against the endless, mechanical cycle of reincarnation, is the work against Saturn. Every effort we make to escape our habitual nature, our conditioning, environment, habits, duties and parents, is an effort to escape the ceaseless devouring jaws and strangling hold of Great Mother Time. Let us for one moment consider the enormous energies needed to launch a rocket into space; to escape the gravitational pull of Mother Earth, super-human forces are necessary. These technological achievements may symbolize a parallel development in the realm of psychology that is ready to be realized. We struggle on ... .

SATURN AND DEPRESSION

We have all tasted Saturnian depression, the gloom and doom that Saturn can bring. In alchemy this stage of deep Saturnian depression, when it seems as though one were swallowed up by the earth, is called the nigredo, when all is black, hopeless and meaningless. This is a state of melancholia which is particularly associated with a creative depression, a depression which contains within its core unbridled life energy, the aim of which is wholeness. This blackness in alchemy is, of course, Saturn's lead, and the goal of the alchemist was to turn this lead into gold. The lead needed to be purified in order to reveal the gold it had always been. This is how the dark, cold side of Saturn can be transformed into one of wisdom and gentleness.

Hurwitz tells us that,[7] in the Zohar, Lilith is described as the *Black Gall* who is under the rulership of Saturn and who is the melancholy of the deepest realm of death, poverty, darkness, tears, complaints and hunger. Melancholy people, who are under the influence and domination of Lilith and Saturn, are actually called *Sons of Lilith* in the Zohar.

I should like to mention one of my clients whom I have been working with for almost three years. He came to me initially because he felt that all his relationships with women had failed. He is wealthy, loves his work and has lots of friends. To any outsider he seems to have everything, but he cannot find a woman with whom he would like to share his life.

His background is working class; his father, a kind, passive man, worked night shifts and he rarely saw him. His mother was crazy, probably schizophrenic, and would go through a mad phase every two or three years. These phases would last for a few months during which she would lock and barricade herself in. When he was twelve years old he pleaded with the family doctor to help him deal with his mother. He described her as a proper screech owl, a raging fury. He has been married twice, but in both cases the wives rejected him until he decided to leave the relationship. He has had a steady stream of girl friends ever since: usually attractive women, younger than himself and apparently independent. But the moment a woman appears to grow dependent on him he becomes disillusioned with her and soon terminates their relationship.

His mother used to make the most impossible emotional demands on him. She wanted him to be totally in her service. Whenever he talked about her he looked old and depressed, as if just the idea of her had the power to drain him of his life energy. This mother issue could eventually be confronted and with a great deal of effort and hard work he managed to escape her pull. He could finally accept the fact that his mother was and is crazy, that she will never be the kind of mother he would like her to be and that he will never be the kind of son, totally devoted to her, that she had hoped for. He found a new girl friend who was pleasantly compliant, an Eve rather than a Lilith. She had no outbursts of hysteria, let him make all the

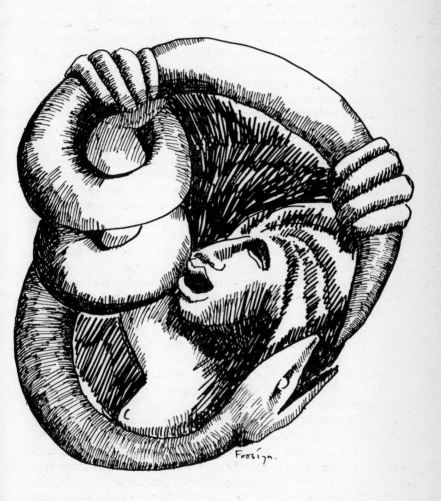

Foosiya.

decisions and generally tried to adapt to what she thought he needed of her. He was extremely happy. Everything appeared to be falling into place for him, and with the planet of regeneration, Pluto, just moving into that area of the birth chart which is associated with close intimate relationships, there was the possibility that his attitude to and unconscious expectations of women were positively transforming. But gradually his sexual interest began to wane. His unconscious image of woman was one associated with demands, crisis and punishment. Her compliance and ever-ready companionship had turned out to be a lack of initiative and imagination which in time bored him so much that he had no alternative but to end the association.

He has been stuck with that Lilith image of his mother (all women are dangerous and you need to protect yourself from them), a mother who tried to devour her son either by domination, as his two wives also did, or by drawing on his energies and becoming dependent on him emotionally.

One of his wives appeared so Lilith-like to him that he drew her symbol on a piece of paper and put it under her mattress in an attempt to 'cure' her, without understanding the significance of Lilith.

Shortly after he started working with me he began writing a book which deals with sex magic. Since sex had been one of the taboo subjects with his mother, writing this book was an enormous step away from her pull and a beginning of reowning Lilith's sexuality within himself.

Lilith, the feminine side of Saturn, repressed for at least 4000 years, is insistently demanding the restoration of her rightful position – that of the Great Mother Goddess who is bestower of life as well as being a powerful Queen of the Otherworld. Otherwise we shall continue to suffer the consequences: the *curse of Lilith*.

The best way, I believe, of helping to integrate Saturn's and Lilith's energies, would be to practise living in the here and now, to be in time and one with time – Kairos as the antidote to Kronos – for then Time has no power over us. Whether she eats us up is not important nor registered when we are one with the present moment ... .

REFERENCES

1 B.G. Walker, *The Women's Encyclopedia of Myths and Secrets*, page 856, San Francisco, Harper & Row, 1983
2 J. Layard, *A Celtic Quest*, Zurich, Spring Publications, 1975.

(See chapter on Cuhullain and Olwen.)

3 T. Moore, *The Planets Within*, London, Associated University Presses, 1982.

4 S. Hurwitz, *Lilith, die erste Eva*, Part B, page 117ff, Zurich, Daimon Verlag, 1980.

5 B.B. Koltuv, *The Book of Lilith*, chapter 1, page 19, Maine, Nicolas-Heys, 1986.

6 R. de Gourmont, *Lilith*, trans, J. Heard, Boston, John W. Luce Co. 1946 (1892).

7 S. Hurwitz, op cit, page 126.

GENESIS
Valerie Sinason

In the beginning
was God without playground
was God without books and toys

And God in His infancy
in the lonely alphabet of His endlessness
began with A for Apples
and made trees for them to hang from

And He polished His picturebook garden
for millions of years
waiting ...

And after millenniums of fish
and flying birds
after the exhaustion of molten rock
and years of sky and earth

He made the best toys

that could speak to Him
and sleep in the waiting beauty of
His doll's house
and talk Him through the awfulness of infinity

But Eve, the girl doll,
tired from clockwork prayers and walks
round the tracks of God's sad playroom
cried for the apples, the first alphabet

'Don't cry' pleads God
scared of the colours running.

But Eve cries for an apple womb
for a round moon apple
though God the drought will make a reservoir of her
a parchment to see His soul in.

Eve takes the apple, the ripe womb
the pale clock of the moon.
She will bear floods, plagues, earthquakes.
She will find a friend called Lilith.

God storms in a playground without children.

LILITH'S GENESIS
Valerie Sinason

One of those bleak ravaged landscapes
where the screaming woman
returns again and again
in a wake of gulls

Her cries never change
but only retreat
to recharge their hoarse voices
with fresh news from the angry dead

How the dead scream
through her one mouth

There isn't room for them, she says
But they ring their bells,
flick their whips

Screech for company, food, air,
Their bedsores are spreading, spreading
But they don't care

Can the living haunt the dead,
she worries.

She repots screams and prayers,
waters the stillbirths and abortions

While shadows of the dead
blot out the sun like batwings

And this, she understood
is how all the horror stories begin.

CREATIONS OF
THE GODDESS
Alix Pirani

How do I experience the Jewish Goddess and in what way have I become, as it were, her priestess? What is this co-creation, in which She and I evolve from what we were in a process of spiritual transformation that involves the recovery of a lost tradition? Through teaching, psychotherapy and writing, and a fascination with creative process, I was, all my life, as I now recognize, being 'trained' to help restore the feminine in my religion of origin. In fact I am a daughter of the tribe of Levi, and I knew from an early age that we had a priestly role. That I left the religion and the community and spent thirty years in the wilderness also seems fated, for the Goddess too became alienated from Judaism. Lilith fled to the desert; so did I. Religion held me until the age of 21, then I turned my back on it, and 'it' on me. It had become for me a system promoted by an intolerant outdated Jehovah – represented by my father – who undervalued me as a sexual, intellectual, creative woman and expected me only to be a blinkered Jewish mother. Furthermore, to be fully Jewish meant to be one with the Jews of Auschwitz. I was the same age as Anne Frank: only a strip of water, and the scarcely explicable non-invasion by the Nazis of Britain, saved me. I shrank from the horror of the death camps just as the Shekhinah shrank from the destruction of the Temple, and exiled herself.

Three decades later I knew I needed to return to my roots to reclaim basic strengths and find meaning for the fear and the obsession with destruction that so dominates everyone's lives. How could I find form for what felt like a 'vague spirituality'? I needed to experience it with my whole mature self: mind, imagination and body. My question had always been How do we make love effective? and the relationship between sex, childbearing, love and the soul was always a central concern. How do we bring the soul back into our lives? Transpersonal and Jungian psychology provided one route; Kabbalah another. 'Soul' and 'love' always *felt* like feminine attributes and concerns. Yet the medium for my spiritual development during those thirty years had been English literature and its mostly male Christian visionary writers, and the music of J.S. Bach, whose work is to me a miracle. And life experiences as wife, mother, political activist, teacher, ex-wife, seemed designed by destiny to lead me to do the work of the Goddess.

When I first saw the title of Raphael Patai's book *The Hebrew Goddess* it was as though a fuse blew. In that moment a whole set of concepts changed. I knew of the powerful goddesses of many cultures but had never dreamed there might be one in my own religious tradition. 'Hebrew' and 'Goddess' seemed almost mutually exclusive words.

My efforts to return to the Jewish community, religion, synagogue, then became identified with Her return. I began to experience Her as an accompanying symbol and presence. I had, in Jungian terms, recognized an archetype which held immediate meaning for me. Jung said that when we fail to honour the gods they become diseases. Certainly my life had become diseased. But now I had found the Goddess, the archetype which had been driving me without my conscious knowledge. I became Her partner and deliberately devoted myself to reclaiming and celebrating her. And Judaism started coming alive for me again.

Historical, theoretical and psychological study were part of the work; exploratory workshops, and personal imaginative writing, mainly through a series, which still continues, of Psalms to the Goddess. I found in all this a kind of 'psychic chronology', working at both individual and collective levels. The original creative feminine, the matrix, with its dark primitive power, its seeming chaotic, unruly unboundedness, gives way to, or birth to, or submits to, a more 'masculine' detached, ordering, unifying principle. Asherah gives way to Jahweh. But the pendulum swings too far: dispirited restrictive rigidity sets in, binding and denying the imagination and life-energy. Then the feminine has to return, release the energy, revitalize and create anew, and join with the masculine to achieve a healthy balance.

In this context, the Jewish Goddess returns, with love and with hostility, as the Shekhinah and Lilith, the one exiled, the other banished, moving irrepressibly to regain their rightful place and power. Then, as Hochmah, the Goddess claims respect for her intelligence and wisdom, which have been only grudgingly acknowledged. Hochmah is needed – because a balance and mediation must be achieved, and firmly grounded, between the Shekhinah and Lilith, and between the two of them and the religious community of the established God. Growing in self-confidence, reclaiming the power that was once Asherah's, the Matronit emerges, more visible, richly complex, Queen, four-fold goddess 'of infinite variety' who contains all the many energies which had once seemed uncontainable and irreconcilable. The Matronit requires, if not worship, certainly homage, commitment, equal to that accorded the King her consort.

The match is made, and with it the assurance that the two awesome deities do not become over-inflated in their power – as happened to the lone male God. They become a foursome: a 'divine tetrad' – father–king, mother–queen, son–prince, daughter–princess, in two marriages: a transition to a collective, family, intergenerational sharing of divine responsibility.

Extension inevitably follows: a concern with the wider environment, the needs of all people, all dwellers on the earth. And the connection of the Jewish Goddess with Christianity, the most influential of Western religions, has to be looked at. There follows a re-assessment of Judaism as the mother of Christianity. At the same time Christianity begins to be experienced as a sister religion. In my quest to find the Goddess in Mary, the Jewish mother of Jesus, and understand that mother–son spiritual link, I begin to feel the sister link, the meeting between myself and my Anglo–Christian sister-friends, who reflect my 'non-Jewish' self. This sometimes feels like a confrontation between the Shekhinah and Lilith – but which is which? We each contain each – though it is clear that the pain and the sexuality of Lilith is more present in Judaism and my Jewish self, and the calmer detached spirituality of the Shekhinah is in Christianity and my non-Jewish self. When these two allow one another their full spiritual power, and exert it together, the two religions can use their 'mother wit' in the urgent task of restoring life to the planet we share. So we return to the original Great Goddess: Adamah, earth, is the mother we must respect and cherish. And the further out I reach to Her as my external landscape, the more I am aware that she is my internal landscape; she is me, there is no division, and each one of us does experience the Goddess, and her marvellous progress, within.

THE PROCESS OF RE-CREATION

Let us retrace our steps, and look at how the Goddess's return involves a complete re-framing of our ideas about God, creation and creative process. The way religion is renewed and re-born is the way She is renewed and re-born. The Shekhinah comes with hopefulness and promise, and Lilith comes with explosive defiance, protesting all the way.

The first step in renewal is bound to be disruptive, like that of the outspoken bride in the dream described by Howard Cooper (p. 19). There has to be a shock. Lilith strikes at the heart of the primary myth, of Creation and the Fall, of the Judaeo-Christian tradition. As the serpent she had the knowledge of good and evil she wasn't supposed to have. She still has it. In her awareness of the forces of sexuality, destruction and death she is life-enhancing: she contributes to realistic love-making. And 'making love' is what the Shekhinah is committed to: she will hold that principle throughout everything. The two are inseparable: different but intertwined, as are the similar contradictory feelings we experience in ourselves. The duality, the two-in-oneness of the Goddess, is a concept which is difficult to hold once we give her two names and faces ... .

VISIONS OF THE GODDESS

My mirror shows me the Shekhinah, my strong sister:
Her eyes glow with naive love and delight.
Openhearted, patient and wise in her beauty
She breathes with compassion, receiving, joyful.
And she yearns in sadness for the lost union.
Eagerly watching the young in one another's arms
She loves her own body, and blesses them.
Praise her.

My mirror shows me my tough sister, Lilith:
Her eyes are fierce with hellfire and envy.
Cursing and cursed, she hates her tormented body
For its frustrated passion, serpent desperation.
Holding her breath, she embraces loathsome Satan,
And brings forth devils: a race of men-children
She'd willingly kill for their atrocious black evil.
Praise her.

We twin sisters are one.
Each reflects on the other.
Let no man separate us
Nor spoil the love that is between us
In our reflecting.

The more we split these two, oppose them, judge between them, the more we lose the sense of their vital connectedness. Patriarchal religion polarized light and dark, calling them 'good' and 'evil': a way of making the Shekhinah 'safe' and of dishonouring Lilith.

This parallels the difficulty of imagining a divinity or God who combines female and male, since feminine and masculine values and roles have, in the same splitting way, become so polarized in our culture.

Goddess cultures have always contained and accepted the Black Goddess as of equal status to the White. Monotheism split Lucifer and Satan off, leaving the 'White' God superior. Lilith received the same treatment. But the Shekhinah cannot return without her. Both were consort to God – and 'Lilith is the ladder by which one may ascend to heaven.'

Lilith, outraged and outrageous, is determined to challenge and undermine where necessary the decaying forms and stale patriarchal habits of a spiritual tradition women wish to be fully part of. She makes way for the benign qualities of the Shekhinah to inform religion constructively.

She is not, of course, disembodied spirit. As a woman she mated with Adam; as a serpent she appeared to Eve. She is the way of experiencing the body exactly, fully, as it is: a more immediate link than the Shekhinah between our physical carnate selves and the divine. She is a fundamental moral challenge – to our understanding of the pain and joy of being in the body, in the mortal flesh, and learning to live in it responsibly and develop its evolutionary directions. When we are wholly, unashamedly, in our bodies, the Shekhinah can dwell in us with full meaning and help us realize our holiness.

To create new religion is as painful as being born, and giving birth; or as leaving the parental home, and allowing the adolescent to go; especially when the parent religion refuses to recognize that the renewal, the new birth, the departure, is going to happen however hard it resists. The Creatrix knows these cycles of destruction and creation, of separation and re-formation, from her experience of childbearing, menstruation, miscarriage, abortion. Theorizing is only part of religious change: it must be *felt*: the Goddess feels.

What do we feel then about a God who supposedly created us, without our acquiescence, and then proceeded to control and dominate us, giving us scant sense of our continuing role in creation? Rejecting His control we may well, at first, feel that chaotic unbounded confusion, those primal feelings with which the creative process starts. Lilith and the Shekhinah may be in conflict, with fear of craziness if they are not reconciled. For the Shekhinah, though present, is detached, sometimes remote: benign, serene, warm, 'clean', steady, contained, patient, forgiving, composed; whereas Lilith is turbulent, heated, desperate, hateful, 'dirty', greedy, clinging, impatient, vindictive, impassioned.

William Blake called these two states 'Innocence' and 'Experience'. For Jungians these are the light and the shadow. Kleinian psychology names them gratitude and envy. Another psychological view of the two would describe them as 'schizoid' and 'hysterical' modes of being. These two states, when extreme in their manifestation, are traced to the psyche's early response to transmarginal, insupportable pain, in abrupt separation or bodily violation, at birth, or beyond. So, when the temple is destroyed, an intolerable rupture, the Shekhinah, who had been there with God, withdraws in horror, detaches herself in a schizoid way, unable to be in the place of suffering, yet constantly yearning to return, to re-connect and restore wholeness. Lilith, who had already known disillusionment, banishment and denial of her body's love is, conversely, unable to let go the attachment, has to hold on, in a hysterical way, attack, re-iterate her dissatisfaction, re-appear to invade and damage those who had put too much fake idealized, cosmetic trust in the Temple.

These are recognizable behaviours disturbing women; in a soulless, mad society which is so alienated from values of warmth and connectedness, so blindly destructive, sane women will always have times of 'madness' as the distraught goddess in them makes herself felt. The more obvious 'hysterical madness' is most common in women: their schizoid quality is less visible. Men tend to take the schizoid path: their 'madness' is manic, and catered for by their social roles.

In psychotherapy we go back to the place of splitting, in order to know it fully, understand and so heal the rupture. We heal it also in the present by re-aligning and grounding the schizoid and hysterical tendencies. We are guided by our

171

capacity to re-balance. This, the principle of integrative intelligence which balances positive and negative, stabilizes, brings the past to rest in the present, is that of Hochmah, Wisdom. She is acknowledged as having been there before God, and she can provide the ordering, unifying principle, without letting it rigidify into suppressive and possessive control. And God, in His present impotence and helplessness, may turn to Her yet again hoping for Her help in developing valid, not illusory power ... .

HIS MADWOMAN

God knows he's not the only one who knows
His woman's crazy, vicious as a bitch.
She has a wisdom she cannot expose.

Posturing madly, to her man she shows
Frustration's brought her to this desperate pitch.
God knows He's not the only one who knows.

Woman's awareness from the rank earth grows:
Blood-red it flowers from its rotting ditch.
She has a wisdom she dare not expose.

Goddess of chaos, from which order rose,
Called God omniscient – ah, cunning witch:
God knows He's not the only one who knows.

Snubbed by her patriarch, she tight-lipped chose
The angry victim's comfortable niche.
She has a wisdom she will not expose.

Must he then hopeless wait till from her flows
That deep live knowledge which could make them rich?
God knows He's not the only one who knows
She has a wisdom she may not expose.

WISDOM, TIME AND BODY-MIND PROCESS

Hochmah, Wisdom, is called the Tree of Life: she is the principle of organic growth. Hers is the impulse to evolve and the inner intuition that fosters healthy process. She is not an artefact.

When temples are destroyed and religious structures have become brittle and dispirited we call on Her to help us find the new forms that the Shekhinah needs in order to bring divinity to earth.

The process can't be hurried. Time, history, our place in the universe, have to be taken into account. Our power as humans is limited; but we can be, in the moment, very effective.

The Shekhinah and Lilith are different agents of process, with different relationships to time. The Shekhinah is a goddess of transition, continuous creation and evolution, bridging, bringing the soul smoothly to a finite form which will then, as a symbol, promote expansion towards the infinite. (This, according to rabbinic belief, happens through the daily performance of 'Mitzvot' – meaningful religious acts.) Lilith is a goddess of transformation, radical change and revolution, with the soul's urgency to interrupt, make hiccoughs, or contract into the finite mortal gravity-bound body so as to force us into transcendence. (See Deike Rich's observations: p. 152). The paradox is explored by T.S. Eliot in *The Four Quartets*: 'Time the preserver is time the destroyer.'

Hochmah has the wisdom of the 'world-soul': *anima mundi* beyond space and time, before and after human knowledge and the human brain's range. So she is in touch with other dimensions of knowing, and with unknowing, and also with 'primitive' consciousness: the old brain, which was superseded by the brain of *Homo sapiens*, and holds the feelings of earth-connectedness and cosmos-connectedness that rational thought cannot grasp. So Hochmah tells us that there is no split between mind and body: they are all one.

The conflict between timeless and time-bound awareness is played out in our awareness and management of our body processes: digestive, excretory, energetic, reproductive, respiratory, muscular. Denial of the body, loss of contact with it, severely limits our spiritual creativity and evolution. There are, at every moment, issues of control and surrender. To control the body unduly is to refuse to surrender to the timeless, to death, to higher purpose, to love. And to call the body 'sinful' is surely a sin against the God who created it, and the Goddess who dwells in it. The Kabbalah affirms that the Shekhinah is in Malchut 'kingdom' – earth, the body, matter. 'As above, so below.' And in the body politic also (see p. 96).

There is a crucial difference here between women and men which influences forms of 'kingdom': political organizations, including religious organizations. Women are biologically more acquiescent to body processes: they submit to the body's cycles of creativity, the timing of menstruation and pregnancy. However, the process of food intake and excretion is subject to non-submissive management and control: we can stuff or fast, achieve constipation or diarrhoea at will. When men become managers and manipulators of production they have a regular opportunity to manage time. This often leads to wilful organizations more concerned with the product than the natural human process, and to patriarchal religions that take pride more in controlling people and their bodies than in surrendering to divine purpose and to the inevitable cyclical changes and mortality of their own religious forms.

THE SHEKHINAH ABOVE
AND BELOW

The Shekhinah is experienced as soul or heart. The fear, expressed by many, of giving her form, as a Goddess, and thereby rigidifying her into something which will betray what she is, parallels our fear that our bodies are unworthy, too inflexible to embody her. But she is not rigid; nor do we have to be. She does not ask of us worship, a fixed Bible, mindless observance of rules. She is a mother who feeds us intelligently, and who 'toilet-trains' us sympathetically, and forgives herself and us for misjudgments and accidents. The Shekhinah moves in a dance with us. Though she always seeks a resting place it is always temporary. She is the Goddess of the Wandering Jew, of the diaspora, of those who don't conform. She has, when it is needed, an essential imprecision, adaptability, elusiveness. She is poetry, music and all creative arts. She organizes our dreams. All these give her meaningful form until she is impelled to move on to find further meanings and forms, wherever and whenever she is needed.

I need her to help me re-form god-ness, divinity, religion. Sometimes I try calling on her as a mother, try 'praying' to her to answer my needs, as I called, when a child, on God the Father. I struggle with her, with the meaning of prayer, the meaning of 'mother', when she doesn't answer and my material needs aren't met. I don't know whether to call her She or she, and I don't know whether it matters. But I do find in her the mother who consoles and forgives me for my limitations and impossible demands. And She understands the limitations of that ideal male father God who failed me. And encourages me to re-vision Him.

The body politic, the world of action, has the same need that the personal body has for the Shekhinah. There is always pain and ambivalence in bringing divinity to form: in religion as in art. That is clear from the contributions to this book of Jenny Goodman, Gloria Orenstein and Fay Pomerance. If in the 'secular' world we hope to manifest the divine, this means that we have to engage in the politics of spirituality – and the spirituality of politics. The work of the Shekhinah must be done in all those centres of power which ignore her, for even the best intentions can turn into soulless ego-investment, and a corrosive cynicism about human behaviour takes over. National and international politics, industry, business and finance, medical and psychiatric practice, media communication, educational and social administration, are badly in need of the excluded soul. Religious leaders are chided for 'interfering in politics', and the egocentric politics of established religion itself has virtually lost its soul.

However, the Shekhinah's work is done, inevitably. Without naming Her or consciously knowing Her, many are guided by Her. In all the centres of power mentioned voices speak up increasingly for the restoration of humane values. The green movement and the women's movement gradually take hold as people realize our world cannot be slave to an idolized technological god of greed and materialism: For religion, Liberation Theology confronts directly the political challenges.[1] The media are infiltrated by 'Aquarian Conspirators'[2] who carefully speak for health and promote a wholesome human image. The Shekhinah has many Aquarian characteristics: the idealism, the flow, and the detachment. And she is persistent; her work is radical: she connects to the roots. She may be sensitive and benign: she is not therefore feeble or blind, but quietly strong, firm in her conviction, and partner with Lilith, who breaks down resistance through the disasters, man-made and natural, which are increasingly afflicting us. Ruthless Lilith enters the fray as an 'agent provocateur', stirring it up, causing what havoc may be necessary. In the world of politics and the media, she can be seen at her most outrageous and effective in the satirical TV programme *Spitting Image*.

To bring spiritual values into the public domain it is vital not to get caught at the level of secular power, and fall prey to its language and concepts. If our Judaeo-Christian belief systems infuse, whether we like it or not, our secular existence, then those belief systems must be brought out into the open for re-assessment. But as soon as we do that, as soon as we name the

Goddess and Her purpose, She will be open to envious attack and will need protection.

RE-VISIONING JUDAISM:
The Shekhinah and Traditional Religion

Present-day diaspora Jews have a particular difficulty in their relationship to Judaism. They know their identity lies in the religion, though their Jewish racial and social identity may dissolve through intermarriage and cultural mix. They work energetically, creatively, in all kinds of public activity; but for most the religion continues to speak an alienating language. It has never overcome its initial over-reaction to idolatry (and idolatry originally meant goddess-worship), its rejection of iconography and its fear of the surrounding environment. It has excluded pictorial or statuesque representation of deity and discouraged imaginative and expansive elaboration of its rituals. This is beginning to change, particularly in America, where fearless expansion has always been a norm, and cultural mix an accepted fact of life. But generally such creative work has to happen outside the traditional synagogue. The feeling is that to be an observant Jew you will have to be less than you really are: less intelligent, freethinking, subtle, passionate, puzzled, dynamic and, if a woman, less of a woman.

There has been no visible, tangible divine form to play or struggle with; no graphic portrayal to re-image, such as is available to Christians. We have no Sistine Chapels. Instead there is a described immoveable image of a male God, and that, and His religion, have become idols: fixed objects. Yet Judaism was never meant to be stagnant. The Shekhinah comes to us with the opportunity to understand anew what divinity and its presence means. In Her own way. Less through theology than spiritual ecology: she is present in all our resources and our being, in human and non-human existence. Indeed Rosemary Radford Ruether, a Christian theologian, experiences Her as the ecological principle, who re-balances the distorted, dislocated energies of our world, and may yet see us through our global crisis.[3] The narrow self-centredness of the synagogue must end if the Shekhinah is to do her work, which is for all humankind: and that was, originally, the meaning of the Jewish spiritual role. It is the meaning of the diaspora.

THE HEALING POWER OF
THE SHEKHINAH

Holiness, wholeness, healing, harmony. The Shekhinah has always been present in Jews in music, which more than anything can express the heart, the soul, and be spoken of in terms of its spirituality. Jewish music and musicians have always known that: the Yiddish lullaby, the Chasidic *nigun*, the synagogue chanting and Sabbath table songs are the background to the consummate art of the great Jewish performers and composers of the nineteenth and twentieth centuries. This is where Jewish spiritual devotion has been most powerfully at work in the wider world, and will not be silenced.

The Shekhinah's healing rhythmic power is felt in the heart and the breathing. It beats with the pulse of the rhythms of the blood and responds to the rhythms of the universe, pacemaking and peacemaking: Time the preserver. She marks time also by her visits to earth as the Sabbath Bride, bringing rest and peace, Shabbat Shalom, for refreshment and revival – vital now in a world which overstresses us with its manic drive to conquer time and rushes headlong towards its own end. 'Time is money' and we mustn't 'waste ' it. The Sabbath prevents us from abusing our resources, misusing time, just as the Sabbatical year does in agriculture. The Jewish theologian Arthur Waskow suggests that for a spiritual-political economy the Jubilee Year should be restored, when all property is pooled and shared out equally in a benign re-organization of social imbalance.[4]

The Shekhinah is restorative: the breath of life itself. In our bodies (and as represented on the Tree of Life) she is the energy flow, infusing spirit: Ruach, Neshamah, inspiring the whole system. To breathe fully and without anxiety is not always easy, and much body-work in therapy aims to dissolve breathing blocks. This is particularly true of bioenergetic (neo-Reichian) therapy, which charts body energy flow in a way which is remarkably similar to the Tree of Life's representation of the body's organization. Since there is difficulty in breathing, the impulse to pulsation, the choice to breathe and allow the Shekhinah to move within, must come from Hochmah, timeless, fearless wisdom, who is anxiety-free – She who is the Tree. If we breathe fully in time we know we are heading toward ultimate death, which our bodies fear. Hochmah, outside body time, tells us to regard ourselves as a piece of the Shekhinah's music. We can fully experience and savour every moment of our life, be it a symphony, quartet, oratorio, sonata or opera; go with its rhythmic flow and accept the completion of its ending. Shalom means completion. As T.S. Eliot says in *The Four Quartets*: 'You are the music/While the music lasts.'

THE HEALING POWER OF LILITH

Lilith, too, is known as the Breath of Life: she who is so acutely aware of death. She is with us as we breathe painfully through the blocks to happiness and fulfilment, breathe tormentedly in situations of suffocation and despair (Lilith is present in acute asthma), breathe, snort aggressively, offensively, foul draconian breath, foul wind, in our defiance and negativity. She breathes fire also: the fiery serpent, expressing divine wrath – a purgatory fire.

In another sense Lilith heals homoeopathically; she enters into the poison or corruption, becoming one with it in order to effect the needed transformation. The Shekhinah composes: Lilith decomposes. Akin to the worm, this she-serpent has a vital ecological role. We know to our cost how decades of detergents, anti-bacterial and pesticidal cleansers have disastrously eliminated essential algae, bacteria, 'pests' and vital decomposing agents from our environment. In the same way centuries of puritanical 'laundering' of religion has disastrously suppressed the 'pest' Lilith, who could take charge of the compost of our lives.

And religion has laundered not only the diapers but also the bloodstained underwear, denying the power, the problem, the existence even, of menstruation, which connects women so mysteriously to moon-cycles and to the rhythms of blood, the essence of life. Lilith has her place there, on the dark side of the moon, in the witches' sabbaths which are connected with menstrual ritual, in that process which can be felt as either a 'curse' or a gift. What was originally taboo in the sense of awesome, to be regarded with distanced respect, became degraded to taboo meaning untouchable, dirty, unmentionable. We will look at that further (p. 185).

The Shekhinah's presence in the body is a glowing vibratory flow, a tingling. Lilith's is marked by hot-bloodedness, irritability, high blood-pressure. As for the Sabbath, Lilith will often arise out of the meditative stillness with unexpected feelings of anger or frustration that had no opportunity to surface during the previous six days or six years. They disturb the hoped-for peace, but are vital transformers. When the land lies fallow poisons surface, weeds flourish. Putrefaction may be necessary for purging and purification.

In the body's digestive system, the Shekhinah handles balanced intake and excretion. Unhealthy eating caused by intemperance, anxiety, disrespect for one's body, leads to bitterness, acidity, 'heartburn'. Lilith seems present like an overpowering sour poisonous snake eating corrosively at one's oesophagus, stomach and bowels. She reminds us of what we have to do; we ignore her messages at our peril.

THE HEALING GODDESS AND THE EXPERIENCE OF THE HOLOCAUST

It may seem disrespectful, or trivializing, to go from the digestive system to so immense and catastrophic an experience as the utter devastation of European Jewry in the 1940s. But it is for us, precisely, a question of how we digest that experience and prevent it from poisoning and destroying the spirit of surviving Jewry. It is a question of bitterness and heartburn, of selective intake of information and interpretations, of purging and excretion. Ever since the question was put 'Where was God at Auschwitz?' there has been an agony of effort, struggle, theological and personal, to understand, justify, the nature of a God who could allow his 'chosen people' to suffer such terrible pain, destruction and loss. That it was partially avenged through the equally barbaric destructions at Dresden and Hiroshima and elsewhere is no consolation, no way now of healing. These experiences have not been fully digested, and we must call for help from the goddesses who long for love, but know that corruption is inevitable. Lilith can be one with that shadow in ourselves which we wish did not exist, do not want to own, our unacceptable feelings and behaviours. But we have to realize that our belligerence, hatred, disgust, envy, are part of our primitive survival instincts. In the concentration camps all were degraded to the primitive level of the Nazi perpetrators, who were obsessed with their own racial survival. In the midst of such a debasement of humanity, so callous a shattering of trust in the human and divine image, the Shekhinah could not be, though there were moments when the light of Her presence was dimly felt. But Lilith for sure was there in the rottenness. May Sarton has written a profoundly important poem which recognizes Kali's presence in the death camps.[5] For Kali one could easily read Lilith, and there could be added hopefulness in knowing that she and the Shekhinah are one.

The drive towards Nazism originated in the repression of the feminine; the mothers of the Nazis were confined to Kinder, Küche, Kirche by a patriarchal society whose cultural pride suffered degrading humiliation after the First World War. The Nazi vileness was a perverted, deeply envious expression of supressed creativity and sexuality. Lilith at her frustrated worst drove sons and daughters to ecstasies of sadistic vengefulness. Edward Whitmont describes this process in all its implacable detail;[6] Hitler was Lilith-ridden.

If we look at the history of the two patriarchal religions, the centuries of anti-semitism that ultimately sanctioned Hitler's behaviour, we see how the persistent denial and repression of women's spiritual power produced judgmental, sanctimonious, punitive male priest- and God-figures. The brother religions fought for moral supremacy; the more ascetic, witch-hunting Christianity won out over the more body-oriented, sexually allowing Judaism. So the witch Lilith rages with a vengeance and her malignity hardens, concentrated indeed in the concentration camp. And she stays there tenaciously, transformatory, death-in-life, in the place where humankind is forced to look at itself and its inhumanity, to know the nature and discover the source of the corruption. The corruption is potentially within each of us: when we can recognize it we can prevent it from spreading everywhere.

There were glimpses in the camps of the Shekhinah: goodness was never forgotten. There were acts of courage, selflessness, love which, small as they might be in the overwhelming shadow of mass monstrosity, proved we do have hearts. And those to whom Hochmah's timeless wisdom and philosophy was available preserved their dignity and sanity. The occasional presence of music, the permission sometimes so strangely given to Jewish musicians to give chamber concerts, reflected the Shekhinah's harmonizing power. The awareness of the movement of time is the Shekhinah's; the knowledge that the camp is where time is arrested and cannot be escaped is Lilith's. The faithful assurance that there is life before, outside, and after the camp is Hochmah's in her sad wisdom. And since she preceded God she knows that no one will be healed who is solely intent on justifying or angrily denying His existence, and maintaining the exclusivity of His power. To force that down, swallow that as some sort of obligatory medicine is to interferé with the inevitably slow process of digestion and genuine healing. Love, not guilt, heals. In time the Shekhinah helps us to forgive, though never forget, the human capacity for evil.

CREATIVITY AND THE BIRTH PROCESS:
The Rebirth of Religion

The Goddess gives birth to new religion. Lilith is one of the dark goddesses of transformation related psychically to the childbearing mother who is as likely to kill her child as to give it life, who destroys its easy weightless womb-life and propels it out into gravity. Any mother, in her body's agony, and fearing death, may indeed half wish to kill her baby. This fearful primitive crisis, a competition for survival, at the very point of making a life which will ensure survival, is an acute existential dilemma that modern anaesthesia cannot eradicate. It supposedly suppresses it, suppressing Lilith. But the trauma emerges in post-natal depression, which ought to be recognized as a time of existential anxiety and spiritual crisis, not some sort of hormonal nuisance. Lilith hovers there. Lilith was associated with childbirth: amulets were made to propitiate her; she was blamed as the killer of babies at birth; onto her, the disgraceful one, were projected the fears, the unacceptable contraceptive and infanticidal feelings. As the serpent in Eden, she supposedly caused Eve to be condemned to the 'punishment' of childbearing. Yet childbearing can be a highly joyful, sexually exciting experience, for both mother and baby, even though mixed with pain and the fear of death.

The same is true of the birth of new religion. The goddess does not impose guilt: she knows, painful childbearer herself, that there is no morality to be attached to pain. Pain is pain; we were made with faults, only partially evolved, like the faults in rocks. Suffering, betrayal, infliction of hurt on others, force us to find or make meaning – a spur to further evolution. To blame God or suppose that God blames us holds us back in guilty stasis. Eve and the children she bore have been held back from spiritual evolution. The relevance of this to the holocaust experience is clear: the religion has to be re-born and renewed through that suffering. Without undue guilt and blaming, but accepting that the painful, life-threatening transformation, the existential crisis, was an inevitable part of our spiritual evolution, and what was learned in that holocaust must teach us how to prevent a greater holocaust of our whole existence on earth.

THE GODDESS AND SEX-LIFE

The Shekhinah is the potential consort of God, the Sabbath Bride, she who rejoices in sexual union which reflects and contributes to her union with God. There are times when this consummation, this bodily expression of divine love, is indeed a 'peak' experience, as two minds, hearts, bodies, souls meet in creative union.

And there are times when they don't. We may be 'out of love', un-partnered, wary, like Lilith, of our infatuations. The Shekhinah can bring solace, comfort for the anguish of an unheld body. She lives in separation, voluntary though unwanted exile. This helps us realize that we have chosen to forbear from sex rather than dishonour ourselves. In that place of loneliness She does not allow us to feel rejected and unloveable. Her love is only conditional on our being prepared to receive and understand it. If we reject Her we will not experience the complex quality and potential of Her way of loving; and bitter, resentful Lilith, unforgiving, nagging at our bodily deprivation, will keep us from Her. Even so the Shekhinah's love is there – as is Her pain that her love is not accepted nor trusted. But patience is Her great strength. And if we devote time and space, unhurried, to the cultivation of love, of the Shekhinah's erotic power, be it through sexual or non-sexual relating, through auto-eroticism, or the healing power of massage (of body or spirit) we come closer to wholeness and present joy.

The Shekhinah withdraws wherever she sees the sexual act corrupted, debased, exploited, robbed of its beauty: she recoils from the abuse of the temple of the body, repelled. As the heart principle she will at times let the heart harden, close up to protect itself from harm. She may fear madness, as a cold detachment has to cover up a despairing sorrow or need for contact. Yet even so the heart goes on beating: the Shekhinah is always present though seemingly absent. When She is recovered, when we 'return to our senses' and pause to consider how we are betraying our bodies, we will receive Her gifts and come into her loving again.

Lilith, of course, is inseparable from this, she who is passionate, seductive, wild, and intensely sexual. Sex appeal can be used to good or bad purpose. The Song of Songs, the epitome of erotic spirituality and beauty, encompasses a whole range of feelings and behaviours. It is believed that Lilith appears there in the 'black but comely' Shulamite. Lilith's is the greed for life, for orgasm. Her Kundalini serpent energy can fascinate, hypnotize, seemingly devour those who experience it, in themselves, or as coming from another. When persistently frustrated it can bring on hysterical craziness. Yet heterosexual fulfilment leading to pregnancy may also be loathed: one's partner or one's own body may be hated, despised, for what has happened. Lilith is not 'motherly': she gives the breast more willingly to her lover than her child. She may opt for childless celibacy or for homosexuality rather than breed. Lilith's realm, fertile or barren, is mainly from the waist down: she is associated with the devouring monster Leviathan, greedy creature of the oceanic depths. She knows about corruptive pornography and perversion. The Shekhinah rules mainly from the waist up: heart, breasts, head. She knows about potential beauty.

And they, accordingly, have different kinds of humour. Lilith, vulgar, mischievous, outrageous, crude, gives a belly laugh or a dismissive snort. The Shekhinah's laugh is delight: a release of breathing in the chest, wholehearted, gently mocking, smiling. She tends towards levity, lightness. Lilith tends towards gravity, heaviness, and her humour is serious, ruthless, and often hits below the belt. Hochmah, as we shall see, has wit. She laughs from behind her eyes, seeing through the folly that is the shadow side of her wisdom.

MALE SEXUALITY AND THE GODDESS

Men and women both have the goddesses within them. Both have to meet the challenge of combining the two kinds of sexuality. These energies are so often split off from each other that some people will carry predominantly Lilith energy and others Shekhinah energy. Combining them sometimes involves having two partners, the chiefly sexual (lover, mistress) and the chiefly non-sexual (husband, wife). This may be acceptable and stabilizing. But it will come unstuck if the Lilith or Shekhinah representative decides to reclaim the other denied aspect of herself or himself.

What is men's experience of these kinds of sexuality in relationship? The male rabbis cultivated their images in the Kabbalistic texts, entering into luxuriant detailed descriptions of sexual activity. But all this was kept secret. Sexual power was too dangerous: the creativity it could engender would lead to the breaking down of their ghetto walls and confronting the hostile environment (to say nothing of their offended wives): the temptress Lilith had to be suppressed.

Today however there are men who are prepared to accept or devote themselves to 'goddess sexuality' and its challenges. They may find in her, in the Shekhinah, in Lilith, in the Matronit, feminine figures to respond to, or recognize energies to integrate within themselves. Patai and Whitmont demonstrate cogently in their writing the importance for men of reclaiming the sexual goddess. She will call up in a man his own vital spirituality, 'seducing' him into a relationship involving equally mind, heart and sexual attraction. These tend in men not to be coherent but compartmentalized.

Lilith has long been familiar to male artists and writers. They have kept her alive but inevitably appropriated her. Only in recent years have women re-owned her and expressed their Lilith-hood in writing and art. She is invariably a spur to creativity, and it is worth looking at the familiar legend: that she causes wet dreams, takes men's sperm and spawns demons with it. This reference to masturbation or involuntary emission suggests that she can be highly stimulating of a man's creativity – but it reflects also man's fear of being drained and misused by women. Indeed there are parasitic women who excite, then steal and abuse men's creative powers, be it their fatherhood, their money, their imagination, or their political efficacy (witness the British Conservative Party in the 1980s). But of course men may, through this legend, be blaming Lilith for their own wastefulness, and sexual or creative vicissitudes. They may maintain that she tempts them away from their rightful power, omitting to encourage and to acknowledge the power of sexual creativity she can bring to them. So, in turn, her anger at being excluded and denied will lead to her vengeful misuse of their seminal achievements.

This dynamic is apparent in the way the serpent, as symbol, lost its goddess connection and became interpreted as phallic, a penis. Is it Lilith's serpent or Freud's serpent? It should be remembered that Freud reduced artistic creativity to 'mere' masturbation and sublimation. In so doing he reduced sex also: to something irresponsible, Lilith as libido. He could not cope with the repressed feminine sexuality, the snake he had charmed and conjured up in his work. He had no sense of the potential spiritual energy of sexuality, nor respect for the infinite mystery of creative imagination, for the collective and ancestral meanings of dreams, such as Jung had. This doubtless was due to his alienated Jewishness: and it accounts for his concern with castration anxiety. The anxiety is reflected in the Lilith legend: it was said she had boy babies in her power until they were circumcized – so here again she is connected to a place of painful initiation, transformation, and loss of the protective mother. But the anxiety and neurosis imparted to this ritual only persists if there is no commitment to the belief that it is a meaningful wounding ritual, designed to ensure that men understand they are not omnipotent and that the potency of the flesh, their creativity, must serve a higher purpose.

And men whose work in life does go beyond the service of their own ego, or someone else's, do not allow Lilith to undermine them and their potency. Through her men can explore their own incontinent or misused sexuality and creative endeavour, discern how it is seduced into wastefulness, and take responsibility for that. There is a whole range of appropriate activity: 'playing with oneself', and others, at many levels, freely fantasizing, then moving into visionary, imaginative art or meaningful work in life. And moving into the art of loving: achieving true eros, making love in its widest sense, which is the Shekhinah's concern: the power of love, not the love of power.

THE MENSTRUATING GODDESS

Obviously issues about sexual promiscuity, masturbation, and the abuse of body-life and creativity are live ones for women also. But women don't need ritual wounding to remind them that their bodies serve a higher creative purpose and rhythm; they experience that in themselves in menstruation. It is in fact called the 'Wise Wound' by Penelope Shuttle and Peter Redgrove, whose book of that name demonstrates how feminine power, the goddess, has been repressed through menstrual taboo, and its mystery turned to an unmentionable disease.

The taboo is so strong that the obvious connection of Lilith with menstruation gets no overt mention by contemporary writers though it is hinted at in the myths. She displays the moodiness, the heavy tensions, the sexual excitement, the resented smelly messiness, of the menstruating woman. Her connection with the night, often as an owl, is moon-relatedness, mysterious wisdom. And she represents women's non-maternal, free, unbridled sexuality and creativity. This goes with the 'red' phase of the menstrual cycle; the time of blood-loss, when fertilization doesn't happen and sexual excitement is high (though often suppressed). The Shekhinah has the energy

of the 'white' phase: ovulation time: potential patient maternity.

Adamah means 'red earth' and suggests the blood-infused fecundity of the original earth-mother. As for the cyclical awareness of the goddess, we may well ask why the Jews still have a lunar calendar and celebrate New Moon, and why madness at Full Moon is statistically so common. Menstrual wisdom, though thoroughly suppressed, is there, and the menstrual pattern is imprinted in men as well as women – even in the Tree of Life (see p. 231).

MODELS OF JEWISH WOMANHOOD:
Eve and the Jewish Mother

The banishment of Lilith, she of the 'red phase' of the menstrual cycle, was accompanied by the promotion/education of Eve, who was to concern herself only with the 'white phase': ovulation and childbearing. Non-maternal creativity henceforth was not for women. It is forbidden to orthodox Jews to have sex around the time of a woman's period. The serpent goddess entwined round the tree of wisdom was erased. The story in Genesis created Eve, a 'daughter of the patriarch', Adam's rib, a subservient, guilt-ridden, obedient, second-class person, always suspect of falling into evil, to be kept under control by suffering, never to be forgiven for having increased poor Adam's hardships. However much this story may be overtly rejected or ignored by modern-day men and women, it is undoubtedly there in the collective psyche and mythology, and it is there in the centuries of conditioning and socialization by religion of our bodies and feelings. Only by restoring to Eve her lost connection with the scapegoated goddess can we begin to put this right, and recover our loving pride in our bodies. And Eve's mothering of her sons will lead to less bloodshed when she knows more about the mystery of her blood and her ancestry.[7]

The 'Jewish Mother' archetype or stereotype, a modern development of Eve, is a persistent perversion of the Jewish Goddess. Undoubtedly she has the status once accorded to the gods, with her mythologies and her acceptance as a commonly recognized figure. She is idolized, feared, pitied, idealized, satirized, excused, and she does not go away. Her positive qualities and strengths, of generous nurturing and caring, are those of the Great Earth Mother, and have been vital in the preservation of Jewish homes and families under constant threat of assimilation and decimation. Where she has been spiritually connected to the religion the Jewish mother has had an honoured role as an inspiring source of education, generosity and meaningful ritual in the home. Without that she is solely a material nurturer, a food-giver, a smotherer: possessive, seductive, dominating, intimidating. Her sexuality and creativity are diverted into maternity: she is the great breast. Lilith is more or less hidden, the Shekhinah gets no space to breathe, and often the idealized warmth and generosity masks a vicious enviousness or coldness. Where this archetype has really taken hold she becomes in later life, at menopause and after, acutely depressed and a plague to her children, who are supposed to reward her, guilt-ridden, for her years of materdom and martyrdom.

Yet older women who have been more spiritually fulfilled are able to realize in themselves the Hochmah wisdom, the 'crone' qualities we shall be looking at. This wisdom transcends the everyday material, emotional and physical concerns of the middle years of life and parenting, and finds new meaning in what those years were. The wise older woman supports her adult children who are at that stage, and interacts creatively with them, with a steadying philosophical view. Philosophy means 'love of wisdom'.

Another version of the controlling Jewish mother, now increasingly familiar, is the mental matriarch, daughter of the patriarch, with a high-powered matronizing intellectuality, active in political, academic or business spheres, or communal activity, not at all a truly sexual nor philosophical being, very controlling and sure of herself, quite masculine, her creativity running on set railway lines. Often she is living out the aspirations of the patriarch – her father, who had no power in the gentile world.

These women, these Eves, are still as defined by men. Others are acting out their fathers' sexual fantasies: the American 'princess', apple of her father's eye, accepts, on entering the mothering phase of life, a role he has designated for her, obediently choosing a husband in his image.

What these suffocated and suffocating mothers do to their sons is well documented. Their daughters are perhaps more resilient.

HOCHMAH'S 'FEMININE' WISDOM: Crone and Midwife

Hochmah, the tree of wisdom, which was once the Asherah tree, became detached from her natural setting in Eden, but exerts her power through the symbol of the Tree of Life: the power of intelligence and discrimination. She is mediator, fearless, intent on movement and poised in stillness. She can contain the infinite mystery constantly unfolding. She seems bisexual, for she created, inseminated herself, and when she mated with God to create the world, it was He who mothered it. She carries a quality of steady separateness, celibacy. Athena-like, she is not to be seduced, nor diverted from her course. She has the toughness and the impregnability of the post-menopausal woman. She cannot be taken advantage of. When forcibly prostituted or seemingly corrupted she is able to practise 'whore wisdom' or to contain herself in esoteric concealment.

In personal life Hochmah manifests in the 'crone', the woman who is past childbearing and approaching the end of her days.[8] Her psychic awareness increases as she begins to reclaim contact with her innocent soul, and it mingles with her life-experience. Her body carries visibly this mixture of decay and simplicity, just as Hochmah contains Lilith and the Shekhinah. She knows that her innate intelligence connects with a higher intelligence. She can contact and draw on that in her stillness. In meditation, sitting on the ground, Adamah, she will be aware of herself breathing, as a channel between Adamah, earth, and that God toward whom she aspires, heaven.

We can see now why Hochmah is goddess, a feminine being, an abstract noun. She is more than Hochom, wise man, just as Adamah is more than Adam. The final 'Ah' ending of the Hebrew seems to echo that final period of a woman's life when she is clearly less involved in body-life, and detached from her children – unlike the man who can still engender offspring well into old age – and she must find another way of being. The 'Ah' linguistically has always been present in naming goddesses and women's spiritual being – it involves the outbreath, in contrast to the 'Mmm' which relates to the Mamma, the feeding mother, the sucking, intake and holding attachment.

If Lilith and the Shekhinah give birth to new religion, then Hochmah is the midwife, versed in that honoured older women's mystery. She keeps God the Father at an appropriate distance from the birth. When it is over she will gradually take on a different role – a wise companion to parents in fostering the child's growth.

The process of being born leaves a lasting impression on every person: this intensely traumatic life-threatening, life-releasing experience has its lifelong effect on both individual and collective patterns of creativity, particularly at times of dramatic transition. The baby's experience is well documented: much has been learned from regression work and dreams[9] (see the chart on p. 232). I want here to focus on the mother's experience, partly to explore the nature of the goddess's giving birth – the drama of the creatrix – but also to counteract the tendency in psychological investigation of birth trauma (mostly done by men) to blame the mother, and in effect increase and exaggerate our fear of the 'damaging mother', and subtly eradicate the mystery and awe of creating. Current obstetric practice also has its own patriarchal creation mythology. Otto Rank traced the myth of the hero to the birth-experiences:[10] it is the cult of the hero which has led us astray and must be revised. The hero's mother merits attention.

Hochmah watches the mother's struggle: the Shekhinah and Lilith are in conflict, though they know they must work together. The Shekhinah can detach herself from the pressure: in her love for mother and baby, her desire to make a new incarnation, she keeps calm, urges patience, relaxation, measured breathing, surrender to the process, and the pain, to facilitate a smooth delivery. She promises there will be joy and new life and comfort. Lilith is over-excited, frightened of death or madness, breathless, impatient, angry, hating her body and the baby, wanting to keep it in, drive it out, afraid it will never come out, exasperated at its not emerging, terrified that she won't love it. Finally she enjoys the agony of rupture that sets mother and baby free of one another. And the Shekhinah, who has been frightened of Lilith, breathes with relief and pleasure when she knows the child is safely delivered and the crisis is over.

Hochmah, philosophical midwife, watches this process, this conflict between control and surrender, sees it in its context, sees 'around it', accepts that yes, mother and baby might die or be damaged, knows that this is one of many births, and also that there is much more yet to happen to this family than at this critical moment in time. She says to the mother, finally, 'Stop pushing,' but she may not be heard, and there may be damage. She knows that when the child is born it will have its own awareness and story of what the birth was like.

The Shekhinah, in the life of our civilization, is prepared to stop pushing, in her faith that humankind wishes to give birth to a finer human community, and can surrender its habits of dominance to achieve this. The Goddess wants a better, holier, world: the Shekhinah brings slow change through peace, Lilith brings quick change through war. Hochmah knows we live and die with the fact of these different forces which are often in acute tension or conflict. She knows that we will suffer less if we stop pushing and surrender to cosmic, divine process.

Perhaps we shall die as a species, in the death of the planet we are destroying. We are specks in the cosmos. We may be the highest form of intelligence on earth, but a greater intelligence must evolve if *Homo sapiens* destroys the earth. That greater evolving intelligence is Hochmah. Perhaps *Mulier sapientia* – wise woman – will come into her own, manifest Hochmah, and prevent him so doing.

Her most powerful manifestation is through metaphor – myth – art. Symbolizing is an activity unique to human beings: Hochmah/Shekhinah encourage symbolization, imagination, re-visioning. Symbols are mediators, midwives, working with us at the boundary between blinkered human knowledge and divine intelligence. In psychotherapy we work with the dream – the symbol *par excellence* – at the boundary between the conscious and the unconscious, the realm of the soul. In body therapy we work at the boundary between voluntary and involuntary movement, between life-forces and death-forces. Artists, poets, musicians, scientists, are devoted to this boundary-work, driven often by 'divine discontent' – Hochmah's most charitable description of Lilith!

HOCHMAH'S 'MASCULINE WISDOM': The Seeker after Truth

When the child, the new religion, is born, Hochmah becomes a foster-parent. Wisdom's knowledge is infinite. Her task is to relate to the human brain which is 'infinitely' curious about its world. Once a child, or brain-child, is free of the self-centred enclosed womb and the struggle to emerge is past and transcended, there is the change and a release into new consciousness, a new paradigm: often a quantum leap in evolution. Then learning is of prime importance. In human life the first months and years are those in which the capacity to learn is at its greatest: the same ability can be called on whenever we find ourselves again born into a new life, new world. Like the fourth child described in the Passover Haggadah, we may not know what questions to ask, but that simple receptive humility must be at the base of every quest for 'truth'. Hochmah holds the child's hand, learns what it sees and needs: she is at times the child herself. Her tradition is not of a set of beliefs to be obeyed, but of cultivating modes of learning.

The craft of learning and teaching – the two being vitally inseparable – has always been a devoted concern of Jews, whose reverence for learning has a unique quality and has undoubtedly, over time, contributed to their intellectual prowess in many areas of life. The need to understand and make meaning was made intense by the suffering. Survival needs also produced business acumen and cunning: so in the Bible Hochmah is called on often when the people have lost their moral bearings.

There are many Hebrew words for different kinds of knowledge and awareness, and much Talmudic activity is concerned with the refinement of meaning, with codes, and with toothcomb exploration of texts. The obsessive ghetto quality of such study can lead to a woeful narrowness of application, to sophistry rather than philosophy, but in a broader, receptive learning context the mode of study itself is admirable, and contains the seeds of its own evolution. The place on the Tree of Life below, between and 'behind' Hochmah and Binah, two different kinds of knowledge, is Da'at, which represents 'unknown knowledge' – mysterious dimensions outside the Tree's dimensions. Thus there is the inbuilt humble recognition that we humans cannot know it all. Einstein, who is the epitome of Da'at, who so radically changed scientific perspectives, was Jewish; doubtless he carried within himself the imprinted mystical tradition of centuries, *unknown to himself*. And his approach to scientific enquiry was exactly that of the fourth child who does not ask the expected questions in the old paradigm.

Yet Hochmah is still not trusted enough. There is a fear that religion, spirituality, morality, will be threatened by the pursuit of science and rational thought. If the old-style God seems threatened by the expansion of human knowledge, that is because his image was so narrowly defined – as the God who forbade humans to eat of the wisdom trees. But Hochmah, the spirit of the tree, can be a steadying and fearless guide as we explore new territory – outside Eden. And in Jewish tradition the seat of thought is the heart, not the mind.

New religion encompasses new science; at the same time new science is at present discovering dimensions previously unimaginable – except by old religion! Present trends in scientific inquiry and its application through computers show a massive increase in knowledge, ingenuity and communication; they multiply so rapidly that there are fears they may go beyond human control. Then it begins to be said that the universe, and the complex human brain a small part within it, is a vast computer with unimaginable powers, of which God is the programmer.

Hochmah has been telling us that all along: the Tree of Life is a model of that computer. And since we can only imagine and construct computers with our limited brains then even that concept, of the universal computer and its programmer, may not get at 'the truth'. There is always Da'at. Again it is a matter of what questions we ask and do not ask and of finding out what we need to know and we do not need to know. Hochmah guides us here, helping us return to our 'common sense' and the reality of the crisis we are in in relation to the earth we inhabit. What is the morality of the universal computer and its God processor? Do we let it dominate us? Can it solve our problems? Parsifal, another innocent who would not ask the 'right' questions, finally voiced the humble transpersonal ones: 'What is the meaning of this?' 'What can it lead to?' 'What can it teach me?' 'What is it to serve?'[11]

'Common sense' – which many uncomplicated people have – will keep us grounded when we over-reach ourselves. The phrase itself suggests communality, shared intuition and instinct. The creativity beyond the self-absorbed womb, in which the individual ego has been caught, is expanded, collaborative, ritualistic, fertile. It serves the wider group, which in turn nourishes and gives identity to the individual. The child goes out into the playground. 'Common sense' is about the apprehended interconnectedness of all life, all being: the universal mind. The Shekhinah.

This interconnectedness is increasingly emphasized by scientific research and observation. The new discoveries all attest to the marvellous shared patterns, rhythms, organizations of human and non-human life: they are the beauty and love principle of the universe. 'Morphic resonance', 'the implicate order' are among the names given to it: the collective unconscious of many life-forms. Attention is focused now on the cellular codes, the process rather than the content and matter of the universe. This is 'continuous creation', which is the Goddess's creativity: Gaia, Adamah, not the fixed once-and-for-all creation of matter ascribed to the God of Genesis. The joy of such scientific discovery is akin to the joy of the artist, musician, and poet: they are all in this process, and this is the Goddess's delight.

Scientific excitement, however, must be accompanied by awe, respect for the mystery, the pace of the Shekhinah. Otherwise it leads to egotistical manipulation of communications, and wasteful promiscuous proliferation (Liluth lurks here, seductive and over-stimulating). The computers, inventors and makers of products go way beyond our needs. The technological dream, as we approach the end of the century, begins to turn to a nightmare. The simple unquestioning child has been led into a technocratic supermarket that tells him what he needs to ask for, and to consume, and that his needs are insatiable: obesity follows.

Hochmah is there, however, curtailing, slimming, teaching discipline. The industrious computer culture which has developed robots of massive size and power has now arrived at 'reversible computation' to deal with its own excessive productivity. In effect the computer re-cycles its own surplus knowledge. The significant practical result is that it uses up far less electrical power. Somewhere in here Goddess ecology is at work. In time other wasteful industries will learn how to do the same, and over-production accompanied by built-in obsolescence will be replaced by organization based on understanding of preservation and decay, and of the modesty and immodesty of human needs – going with the wisdom of the Shekhinah and Lilith.

HOCHMAH AND THE USES OF PSYCHOLOGY

The new paradigm, with its inspiration in relativity theory, insists that the observer is as much part of the perceived universe and its process as the thing observed. In the computer domain, how could the nature of the human observer/programmer be fed into the system in such a way as to take account of this? Perhaps some reductive psychologies could put you or me into the system, as medical science might do. Such reductionism would be disastrous, however, no matter how subtly it developed its codes and programmes. The uniqueness of each human being, unconsciousness, the dream-world, inarticulate intuition, could not be put through a computer, unless perhaps some individual were prepared to be monitored for a lifetime ... what would that serve?

Psychotherapy in practice works with the relativistic paradigm. In the individual encounter the person and the role of the therapist are as much available for scrutiny as that of the client. In working awarely with the interaction a transpersonal place is inevitably reached, effecting a transition for the client (and often for the therapist) to a stage beyond a previous ego-state or personality which was in discomfort or crisis. This relationship recalls many Biblical encounters (such as that at the burning bush) between God and man. They are mysterious: elusive, interpenetrative. Soul is being evoked, the Shekhinah established, tentatively.

Psychotherapy has developed this way and is increasingly called on to meet people's spiritual needs. At its heart is the one-to-one encounter, the I–Thou relationship (as described by another great Jewish mystic, Martin Buber) which challenges our view of ourselves as persons. More than ever the soul is being brought back into psychotherapy, just as the body is.[12] This is Shekhinah religion. The craft of psychotherapy, which makes this possible, is Hochmah religion. Its practice calls for intelligence, wisdom, responsibility, and a firm discipline, allowing growth within a facilitative structure. The role of supervisor in the therapeutic culture is a Hochmah role of guidance without dominance.

The development of different therapies owes a great deal to Jews who, consciously or unconsciously, have carried forward the mystical tradition and Her work.[13] Certainly the majority of them have spurned the Jewish God: the relationship with Him, beginning with Freud's Moses complexes, has never been wholly resolved. Meanwhile Jungians carry on asking the questions. James Hillman's profound reflection that 'The soul's eternal wanting is psychotherapy's eternal question' might well be rendered 'The Shekhinah's desire to dwell with us is Hochmah's preoccupation'. The limitations of psychotherapy (can its questioning *be* eternal?) must be recognized: it can become narcissistic, as Hillman himself stresses. In the enclosure of the womb-like consulting-room two persons can lose their sense of connectedness with the social environment and the natural world outside. This symbolic work must never forget that it is a symbolic 'transitional phenomenon'.[14]

With this in mind, I shall be using, in another chapter (p. 226), Hochmah's symbolic Tree of Life to explore feminine experience, hitherto absent from traditional patriarchal interpretations, as it once was from psychoanalysis. This has been one of the unknown dimensions hidden in Da'at. But ultimately it is the divorce from the natural world that leaves the soul and the Shekhinah wanting: the divorce from Adamah. It is real trees we need to be one with. The real tree is, unknowably, in Da'at, the place where the symbolic Tree is not, is 'dead'. Real life is where psychology is not.

Returning to the history of the Goddess, we find, similarly, that the urban setting and enclosed narcissistic world of the Kabbalists inevitably affected their view of Her power. Still, they made a major leap, and with Hochmah's inventiveness conceived and named the very Jewish Matronit – a wholly new amalgam of goddess features of their own and other traditions – and imagined her in the setting of the divine tetrad. These were, are, powerful archetypes, and deserve to co-exist with the Christian deities, which offered another kind of departure from the Jahweh tradition. The appeal of Christianity certainly owes much to Jesus' more 'feminine' messages (some see him as the Shekhinah) and to the presence of Mary. She carried and still carries Goddess qualities and is bound to have a vital contact with the imagination, the soul, answering to the human need for spiritual mothering.

Nothing is heard in Kabbalah of Adamah as deity. She is not accorded the status of earth goddesses of other cultures, though some of her power is recognizable in Asherah and in the Matronit. The rabbis presumably were loth to get involved in the subtleties of the relationship between Adamah and Adam. He was given care of her – dominion over her – but also told she would be a great burden to him. Why was she not honoured for her fertility and plenitude? Nor for having mothered him, since he was made from her dust? We get a dusty answer to that ... God wanted to be a single Father, and Adam's mother was made Absent.

In the Kabbalistic Tree the ground is Malchut – kingdom. Adamah has been enclosed in dominion. It is understandable that the males of a harassed people without national territory would want to visualize kingship, but in so doing they were forgoing the sense of universal ground and of their primal connectedness and union with nature. It would have given them something firmer to rely on and build on than the fantasied splendid Matronit who was predestined never to establish herself in the real world. However, at a psychic level she was and is a most significant maturing of the feminine.

THE MATRONIT

With the Matronit the Goddess has 'arrived', has been born, and has found stability in the four-fold support of her mothers: Shekhinah, Lilith, Hochmah, Adamah. She has come into her birthright: she grows in power, is a Queen, self-possessed, with status and pride in what she is. Through her naming she lays claim to connection with the cultural environment.

The rabbis designated to her also a four-fold nature, with aspects that she shares with other goddesses. Four as a number has stability and symmetry: it is the foundation for many mystical and alchemical systems and linguistic structures. The divine tetrad grew out of the Tetragrammaton. The Matronit is virgin, mother, warrior and harlot/lover. She is the multi-faceted feminine, reflecting, allowing for, a woman's changing moods, and able to hold within herself contradictory energies. Rabbinic description delighted in the extravagance of her extremes: ferocious bloodthirstiness, tender loving-kindness, innocent receptive purity, voluptuous and treacherous sexuality. Though these are male definitions and open to expansion and revision, the important thing is that she is seen as ready and able to be consort to the King – which is a remarkable advance beyond monotheism. Here we have a model of a Goddess with her own power who has equality with God, and her sexuality and belligerence are accepted without condemnation. The Shekhinah and Lilith are there, in and with her.[15] She is very healthy: in her women find their pride in their feminine strength, and embrace the challenge of balancing the varied aspects of their personality.

Is modern woman ready to become Bride to God the King? Can both Queen and King acknowledge all those tendencies that go towards, and pull away from, the 'holy marriage' – and still agree to the marriage? Can God the King freely find similar qualities to the Matronit's in himself? If he does not, this is no match. His bloodthirstiness, his motherliness, his sexuality, his virgin vulnerability will have to be acknowledged. And is he not having to own them, now that his previous 'good' image as the justly warring, severely paternal, non-sexual, impregnable being has been exploded by genocide past and present: the slaughter of his children? Can she forgive him? And he her, since for so long she let him hold that image unchallenged?

This critical question, with its implications for both personal and spiritual life, remains as yet unanswered. In religion the question hardly arises – which is a reflection, and cause, of the dilemma of commitment that is prevalent in a society as disillusioned with marriage as it is with religion. Thinking people struggle, virtually unguided, with the problems raised by rapid changes in practice and attitude in marriage and family life.

What seems significant in the Kabbalistic development of 'alternative deity' is the introduction at this stage of the divine tetrads, adult offspring who can relate to and define the parent marriage according to their own needs and perspectives, relieving the older pair of the need to model perfection in relationship, to solve it all. The four-in-one again suggests creative stability, while it allows for generational progress. The parents are usually portrayed as settled, calm, mature, the children as turbulent, quarrelsome, and lively – with the daughter/princess being particularly unruly. She in fact, not the mother, is the Matronit. She is the daughter born of Wisdom and Understanding, the parents. This concept, conception, is very significant, and needs pondering on.

Is this polytheism? In some ways yes, and a natural and healthy development. We need a variety of archetypal gods: we all refer constantly to the Greek gods even though we don't 'believe' in them. We have our gods in film stars and pop singers, royalty and TV celebrities. However, Kabbalistic divine families are not polytheism but tetratheism, confining in the group of four many energies, which could become too dissipated or inaccessible if multiplied. The chaos of the Olympians, like the chaos of television's too-many-gods and too-many-bewildered-humans, can become unmanageable. As can the too many 'gods' we may run to in our environment, unwilling to stay at home with our ancestral tradition.

THE TRANSITION TO CHRISTIANITY

The Matronit did not come into her majesty and her marriage with the established God. She, and the tetrads, remained hidden in the Zohar, and are virtually unknown to this day. The time was not right: there was no way she could come out of Her ghetto and challenge the role and rule of her sister – cousin? – Christian Mary. Yet they had much in common.

I must leave it to Christians to take up the story – as Roger Horrocks and other contributors have done for this book. But I have long been drawn to Mary and intrigued by her, and recently by her position as the Jewish mother of Christianity. My own children were raised in an agnostic Anglo–Christian environment. One son adopted Christianity, seemingly taking inspiration from my own submerged Jewish spirituality. My interest in the myth of Danae and Perseus involved the same instinct to mother a spiritual son, and led to my mothering a book.[16]

As a child I respected the statues and paintings of the Virgin and her baby. They were distant, beautiful: not for me, but for the others. I appreciated the cool, spare calm devotion I saw in Mary, a love not known in the hothouse smothering atmosphere of Jewish families. In later life, when I became a mother, it was the Pietà that I came to find profoundly moving. I believe now that I was subconsciously recognizing the mother mourning the young Jewish men so tragically cut off in their prime in Europe. The massacre had been too great, ungraspable; the pity, the loss here was encapsulated in a single timeless statue that echoed down the ages. I now know of its archetypal resonance: the goddess mother, the dying son-god, the spring festivals of death and renewal. The personal tragedy is having to accept the grievous loss, while knowing that in time the lost person becomes a transpersonal symbol of rebirth.

The timelessness of the statues made it possible to look at the irony: to ask what is the meaning, now, for me, of Jewish Mary's mothering a religion that was responsible for the murder of millions of women and Jews, 'witches' and 'infidels'. Did Mary too much want her son to be a rabbi and a Messiah because as a woman she was not allowed to express her own spirituality as a priestess? Did her adoration for him, combined with her religious and political impotence, lead to his victimization and martyrdom, paving the way for centuries of misapplication and perversion of his messages of love? When Jews and Christians look at one another now in antagonism, it is as though the existential question at the birth were never asked nor answered; we are still in the post-natal depression of the birth of Christianity, asking who was more destroyed in that birth: did the Jews kill Jesus or Jesus kill the Jews?

And what of the purity and virginity of Mary, insisted on as a contrast to the sinful Eve or Mary Magdalen? I appreciate that purity. But my Jewish self cannot wholly go along with it. Why should she not enjoy sex and feel it to be a central source of pure love and a holy act? Was not the Shekhinah in her awareness? And Asherah, and Lilith, Jewish as she was? Perhaps in her were the celibate priestess and the prostitute priestess: both were once part of the goddess religions.

By musing on these questions I find myself at the crucial boundary between symbolism and literalism, and am led to ask does Mary give birth to a person or a myth? A great human rabbi or a divine Messiah? Does she invent the myth and, if so, why? To save herself from being stoned to death for committing adultery? What does she feel about her fellow-Jews who would condemn her? And about Mary Magdalen, daughter of Lilith? Is she herself the Shekhinah, God's consort? In time they will say

Jesus, or the Holy Ghost, is the Shekhinah, and absolutely deny to the Marys their feminine spirituality and the possibility of either divine or human marriage. Is she not angered by all this? The Blessed Virgin Mary *angry*?

And then I remember that there are Gnostic Gospels to redeem her. And I find – because she is always beckoning to us – the Black Virgin. Here at last is a Jewish mother of Christ I can recognize, because she has lost all pretence of total purity. In her all my anger and darkness, and its ancestry in Judaism, is acknowledged; in her is the suppressed goddess. She carries the spiritual power that is considered negative – to look on her statues often seems like looking at the negative of a photograph; they are rivetting, numinous. And through her there is the possibility of imagining and reclaiming a lost heritage and restoring a vital link between Judaism and Christianity.

There is no more galling, poignant, representation of the Black Virgin and her paradoxes than in Our Lady of Czestochowa. Her splendid banner is held defiantly high, her image, full of wisdom, inspiring the Polish Solidarity movement in its quest for personal and religious freedom. And, as she well knows, Poland with its long history of anti-semitism has been responsible for appalling destruction of Jewish life.

What do I know, in my blackness as Mary, if I let my imagination free, as the Black Virgin asks me to, when I look at her in her striking vividness, and she bids me speak for her?

I know I hate the role that has been given me.
I was chosen by God: I had no choice. That was always the Jewish fate.
I know I know far more than He does.
I know more than I am allowed to show.
When I am in my black menstrual moods my son feels and shares the blackness also.
I know I have a formidable power that is recognized by many people.
I know my Jewishness that comes from Eve, and Lilith.
I have denied my Jewishness and hated Jews.
I know all the horrors that have been perpetrated in my name and my son's name.
I know much about my sexuality that I cannot reveal.
I wish my son had never been born; that I'd aborted him, and all his suffering would not have been.
My Jewish father abused me and forced me into silence – saying I had seduced him.

200

I know I want my son to be everything my father, his father,
  was not: gentle, tender, non-oppressive, trustworthy, non-
  sexual.
And this will probably make him a victim
And an object of ridicule to future agnostic generations.
I know too much: I am too wise. Take this wisdom from me.

Much of this was revealed in a workshop I conducted on the
missing goddess of the Judaeo-Christian tradition. Before I
describe that, a word on Hochmah's way of 'taking this
wisdom' – of handling the 'too much knowledge'.

HOCHMAH'S WIT

The descriptions of Hochmah in Proverbs and in the Apocrypha
(see p. 46) repay close attention. Here I want only to quote
Proverbs 8:12 – 'I Wisdom dwell with prudence, and seek out
knowledge of witty inventions.' (Wisdom – *Hochmah*; 'Dwell' –
Shikhanti, root of Shekhinah; 'Knowledge' – *Da'at*.) That seems a
good stance to take and to imitate. I offer an example here of her
wit, and I imagine her laughing, with her wise eyes, at what
happened on this occasion.

At the time that I was becoming deeply absorbed in questions
around women's role in Judaism, Christianity and the Goddess,
my father was approaching the end of his life and living in
relative seclusion. It was impossible to tell him about any of this:
he would have been uncomprehending and affronted. One day
when I visited him he told me a joke I'd never heard from him
before, though he told many jokes, and certainly had wit.
Hochmah alone knows how he came to tell this one at this
time ...

'You know there was Izzy, this Jewish man – he lived a long
life, he was a good man. So he goes to Heaven. . . . When he gets
in there he looks around him, it's wonderful. He wanders about,
and he sees a little old woman, a yiddishe Boobe, sitting on a
bench. So he goes up to her and says can he sit down next to
her, and she says of course. And he looks around and says, "Oi,
it's really beautiful here," and she nods and says, "Yes." And he
says, "My name's Izzy – and yours?" And she says, "Mary."
"Have you been here long?" he asks, "in this lovely place?" She
thinks a minute. "Well, about two thousand years...." He nods.
"Hm." Then he thinks, and it dawns on him. "Two thousand
years ...? Mary? You don't mean – THE Mary?" And she nods
her head. And he says, "Ach – you must be so proud.... To have

such a son – so famous – so important!" And she says to him, "Well – to tell you the truth – I really wanted a girl ...."'

NEW DIRECTIONS:
Roles, Rituals, Tasks for the Goddess and her Devotees

In a weekend workshop called 'The Missing Goddess', held in July 1990, eighteen women, Christian and Jewish, gathered to explore their experience of the Goddess of Judaism and Christianity. By the end, among the many wonders that emerged, two in particular seemed to suggest ways forward.

When we had contemplated and 'felt our way into' the Matronit in all the variety and the power She offered us, I suggested we try to imagine the male God – Her Bridegroom – who could match Her, and to whom She would be glad to relate. This was done, with many different responses: resistance, disbelief, surprise, pleasure. Some women were able to envisage such a male figure and allow the possibility of marriage, others not.

I then realized that what each woman had done was to create in fantasy a 'son': of a kind she could wish to marry – which is what many mothers do. And Mary had done this also. Just as we women had visualized a God who was deliberately different from the God of our fathers, so Mary conceived and nurtured a son who must be different from her own brutal God and father.

Women will continue to do that, and can do it consciously and responsibly with their real or fantasy sons (or internal male), mindful of all the implications and risks. For Jewish women it is a symbolic contribution to the coming of the Messiah, whatever that means to us, for we have never been allowed to have one. Do we need to give birth to a new Messianic myth? It will not be of a Piscean martyr and hero. The first or second coming will involve the redemption of feminine spirituality. Perhaps the Messiah is women's renewal of religion, perhaps it is the Goddess. And after the devastating losses and horrors of the holocaust we who are Jewish look for a saviour – of our integrity and sanity ...

> Out of the ashes of Auschwitz
> Out of the wreckage of God's Jewish body
> Bloodied and tortured, seared by Christ's vandals:
> Out of the ashes

She rises, see, the spirit of Lilith
the wisdom of Hochmah
the loving Shekhinah
> *Heal our souls*
> *Dear Goddess*
> *With your balm.*
> *Teach us to cherish*
> *What we may be.*

At the end of the workshop the group considered the idea of a habitation – temple? – church or synagogue? – for the Goddess. There was much disagreement, but also the realization that simply to do this as an exercise was, in effect, to do it. And we had made a characteristically temporary habitation for the Shekhinah for the whole weekend. What we felt strongly was the need to go on visualizing, making Her images, through art, dance, poems, drama, music – celebrating the Goddess, as we might do ritually in her temple. If we cannot immediately create a temple or cathedral we can begin to visualize it. Temples and great cathedrals were hundreds of years in the making. And the Shekhinah has been in them all – everywhere in the world.

One woman insisted we must never use male constructs, but always start from our own organic movement. And indeed the talk about the goddess's habitation had followed on from a free dancing that had developed in the group, picking up half-formed themes and movements, expanding them, finding words spontaneously, finally coming to rest with the newly engendered energy.

This woman had insisted also that the Matronit was a male construct: we must 'invent' our own new Goddess. For me this was a challenge; I have always been uneasy with the name Matronit and its connotations – and She was beginning to feel too limited to a personal internal scenario, her roles those in relation only to people.

Where was the life of nature, animals, the pantheism, the trees? Diaspora Jews are too urban and suburban, Israeli Jews too much concerned with their Eretz Israel and too little with everybody's Adamah. How could I add to the Matronit's aspects more of the lost Adamah? Our perspectives now in the twentieth century are so different: we are only too bewilderingly aware of the whole immense earth: yet we can see a photograph of it taken from the moon and it looks small and vulnerable.

It seemed to me then that the Goddess must in part become a gardener. She must cultivate Adamah, in Herself, in a terrain of manageable size. And this would be no Garden of Eden.

This seemed a very English concept – indeed, characteristically local. I recalled Andrew Marvell's poem 'The Garden', which explores so subtly the complexity of the symbolic status, and felt reality, of trees and nature, and the paradoxes of Eden. I began to write my garden poem, to cultivate Adamah. And before it was finished I came across – by chance? – in William Blake's collected writings[17] the following aphorisms:

> He repented that he had made Adam (of the Female, the Adamah) & it grieved him at his heart.
> What can be Created Can be Destroyed.
> Adam is only The Natural Man & not the Soul or Imagination.

ADAMAH'S GARDEN

How can I, Adamah, know myself, tend and cultivate myself, I who created myself? Inside knowledge is self-perpetuating, self-important: I am sluggish, fertile-fat with my own fecundity, forever creating, procreating. My surface is dry, dust, crumbling as though through my own fingers, losing me, in desolation, dross, deserted.

Who knows me? Know me. Please know me. Eve and Adam in their modesty, ashamed, knew me. Lost knowledge. Their offspring know too much, bigheaded; they don't know me, Adamah, in whom their ancient wisdom Tree was rooted.

Roots move me. Hochmah's wisdom stirs me. Knowledge grows out of me, becomes consciousness. Grows wildly, profusely, becomes Nature: crazy, beautiful, burgeoning into life. I can no longer bear this hard gravity: heaving I put forth and the nerve-ends of my being, trees, bushes, plants, grasses, vibrate with another awareness, caught and played with and loved by air, breezes, strong winds, eddies of breath. My outgoing has burst into the shock of colour: brilliant, pale, deep, vivid, translucent, caught and played with and loved by light, shadow, glare, gloom, glow. There is such love.

Sometimes I wish there had been no animals.

Yet I fell in love with the animals, loved their freedom to move and range across me, tread me, change me, fertilize me, feed off me. I marvel at them now and they respect all that I am.

Sometimes I wish there had been no human beings.

What consciousness presumed to make this man Adam and call him my son?

I fell for my son: I let him think he owned me and knew more about me than I know myself. And now his offspring fight over me. They ruin me, rape and abuse me. Deny me and plunder me. And still expect me to go on providing for them for ever.

In my anger I could wipe out Adam's children, the human beings: my final upheaval, shaking them off: earthquake, flood, pestilence, fire, volcano.

God consciousness will create them again.

Please God the new humans will be careful gardeners, loving cultivators. When you say, with the words of your culture, breathless a moment with love, 'But the earth is so beautiful!' ... Then I know myself, I remember long-forgotten Adamah. I become beautiful, willingly, and purposeful: I will serve your purpose. Love and tend me and I will stay with you steadfast until the end of days.

Come now
Into this grove, this manageable garden.
Here you may grow to know me intimately.
Here you can learn
How these things may be.
Here wildness and order have their place.
Here the roughly predictable seasons
Ensure repeated growth.
Mis-shapenness also.
No paradise: an opportunity.

If you recognize my variety,
The beauty and ugliness of my rich hues,
The subtle textures at my finger-ends,
The shocking ecstasies, the shifts and dramas
Of my breeze-blown, windblown
Hurricane-ravaged existence;
If you take them in
And give back to me your images of splendour,
Dance the dance of my passionate rhythms,

Cultivate me, celebrate me with all that skill, that knowledge you have,
Even the knowledge that I too have a limited life;
Then I will serve you in truth,
And this shall be the new Garden of Love.

And you may rest here in my peace also;
On the ground of your being, of my being,
Your head in my lap,
Your weary paid-out consciousness
Resting in the gratified stillness
Of my quiet womb.
Adamah.

NOTES

1 A courageous and challenging work which looks at the crisis in the West Bank, and its implications for spiritual responsibility, is Marc Ellis's *Toward a Jewish Theology of Liberation* (Orbis, 1989).

2 *The Aquarian Conspiracy* by Marilyn Ferguson (Paladin, 1982) identifies the many areas of social and scientific practice in which new and positive directions are developing for humanity.

3 In *Sexism and God-Talk* (Schocken, 1978).

4 In *Godwrestling* (Schocken, 1978).

5 'The Invocation to Kali' in her *Selected Poems* (Norton, 1978). Also reprinted in the anthology *She Rises Like the Sun* (Crossing Press, 1989).

6 In *Return of the Goddess* (Arkana, 1987). In his introduction, Whitmont speaks of the origins of this book in his move away from the narrow Jewish orthodoxy of his parents, and his first-hand experience in Austria of Nazi cult and persecution. Chapter 11 explores Hitler's regime in the light of the Grail myth.

7 I explored the psycho-dynamics of this in an imagined psychodrama, 'Cain and Abel: A Case for Family Therapy?', published in *European Judaism*, No. 43 (Pergamon, 1990).

8 See *The Crone*, by Barbara Walker (Harper, 1988), a book full of wisdom and riches.

9 See e.g. *Realms of the Human Unconscious* by Stanislav Grof (Viking, 1975) and Elizabeth Feher's *The Psychology of Birth* (Souvenir, 1980).

10 In *The Myth of the Birth of the Hero* (Vintage, 1959).

11 For the important connections between the Grail Myth and the lost Goddess tradition see Whitmont, op. cit., Ean Begg in *The Cult of the Black Virgin* (Arkana, 1985), *The Holy Blood and Holy Grail* by Baigent, Leigh and Lincoln (Corgi, 1983) and *The Wise Wound* by Shuttle and Redgrove (Paladin, 1986).

12 All the work of the Jungian analyst James Hillman is devoted to the restoration of soul, and of the feminine, to psychotherapy, see e.g. *Insearch* (1967), *Suicide and the Soul* (1976). Stanley Keleman's writing on body-therapy is particularly relevant: he is explicitly aware of the spiritual dimension. See e.g. *The Human Ground: Sexuality, Self and Survival* (1975), one of many powerful books.

13 See Edward Hoffman, *The Way of Splendor – Jewish Mysticism and Modern Psychology* (Shambhala, 1981).

14 A term coined by the analyst D.W. Winnicott. His *Playing and Reality* (Penguin, 1971) is one of many relevant works on symbolism by the Kleinian and Object Relations schools of psychotherapy.

15 Patai explores the subtlety of Lilith's shadow relationship with the Matronit, in *The Hebrew Goddess*, pp. 266–7,

16 *The Absent Father: Crisis and Creativity* (Arkana, 1989) was based on this Greek myth, which has many parallels with, and important differences from, the Christian story. Writing the book led me back (as the myth does) to my roots, and to the mother whose absence has led to the crisis of fathering in our society.

17 [The Laocoon Group] engraved 1820, in *Blake's Poetry and Prose* (Nonesuch Press, 1948), pp. 580–1.

For Blake's indebtedness to the Kabbalah, see 'Blake and the Kabbalah' by A.A. Ansari, in *Essays for S. Foster Damon: William Blake* (ed. Rosenfeld, Brown University Press, 1969). Blake's 'Jerusalem', where personified, is his version of the Shekhinah.

A MIDRASH ON THE SONG OF SONGS
Lorna Mitchell

Verse 1 'The Song of Songs, which is to Solomon.'
How can I sing the song which is the quintessence of peace?
(Shlomo = interpreted by the rabbis as *shalom lo* peace to him.)

Verse 2 'Let him kiss me with the kisses of his mouth.'
I am outside the atomic rings of my inner world. I can begin the
song when my conscious mind becomes the passive 'feminine' and
surrenders in meditation to the inner active 'masculine' self. My
inner self breathes in (through the mouth as Adam did) the
Neshamah (the breath of life). I am inspired with the Ruach-ha-
Kodesh (the Holy Spirit or air which the prophets were inspired by).

Verse 2 contd 'For your love is better than wine.'
Now the active/passive polarity is dissolving. I have stepped
into the first ring: the world of images (Yetzirah: formation – see
p. 96). I receive joy from the cup but I raise my arms to drink it.
The cup of emotion energizes me. I can face my inner self
directly and closely, speak to her as 'you' and not 'he'.

Verse 3 'For perfume your oil is good. Your name is like oil
poured out.'
The Goddess within: my secret name, known only to me, is
normally hidden as if sealed in a flask. But now through my
meditation I have opened the flask, and the perfume pervades
everything. My divine self is a microcosmic mirror of universal
divine immanence. The oil is also for anointing myself as the
sacred king. The sacred king is the symbol of the divine passive
masculine in relation to his mother: the divine active feminine.
The oil is also the 'fat of the land', the oil exuding from the body
of Mother Earth.

Verse 3 contd 'Therefore do maidens love you.'
Verse 4 'Draw me. We will run after you.'
The disparate parts of my ordinary self long to come together in one, so I let the inner self pull them together. In the moment of integration, the disparate selves are actively running together towards the same goal, like wild horses under gentle reins, willingly pulling the chariot.

Verse 4 contd 'The king has brought me into his chamber.'
I have now moved into the next ring of the atom (Beriah). The ante-chamber before the Holy of Holies. The king is the androgyne psychopomp (leader of souls), who has gently led me into this next world.

Verse 4 contd 'We will rejoice and be glad in you.'
It is 'we' again after the 'me' of the last sentence signifying that the Ego-self (Yesod) has united with the Beautiful or True self (Tiphareth). *Nagila*, rejoice, and *simcha*, be glad, refer to these two levels of the mind. Nagila is a spontaneous burst of pleasure in the Ego-self and Simcha refers to the awakening of the lasting joys of the Beautiful or True-self. In this ring, because I am nearer to the eternal present, the two selves are in harmony.

Verse 4 contd 'We remember your love better than wine.'
The last time this phrase 'your love better than wine' was used was when I was outside the chamber longing for the wine of love. Now I know it is inside me, so why do I remember it? 'Zachor' is the word symbolized by one of the shabbat candles, 'remember the sabbath day to keep it holy'. It refers to the ideal sabbath awareness. Through re-membering the dismembered parts of the past in the present, I attain the experience of divine love.

Verse 4 contd 'Rightly [or "in straightness"] do they love you.'
Only through honesty with yourself, through straightness with others and being true to yourself, can you be capable of expressing your own divine love. (But don't always expect people to like it! Your true self may be very dark, and so –)

Verse 5 'I am black but I am beautiful, O daughters of Jerusalem. Like the tents of Kedar, like the curtains of Solomon.'
In the heat of the day, you escape from the prison of the city, past the stinking fetid pool of Siloam, through the south gate.

Out to the desert by the Dead Sea. The desert is like the map of all your suffering through your whole life. You must go through it all again now. Can you do it? Do you want to run back to the prison, because you're scared of being free? You take the risk, and though it's hard, it's not as hard as you imagined. And after a long time, which is also an instant, you see the black tents of the despised Bedu. They are poor, and their tents are torn and patched. And as you come near, you smell the sweat and grease and you feel queasy. But you stick with your fears, and you approach the central tent. You raise the dirty ragged flaps, you bend over, and you go inside. Inside, it is utterly different. Dark thick curtains, patterned carpets, large cushions, the low flickering lights of candles, incense in the air. An experience both sensual and spiritual. You could sink there. But, no! you see the curtain: the curtain of Shalom-lo, immaculate black with exquisite gold embroidery glittering in the light. You must now enter the Holy of Holies and come into her presence: your dark goddess, your Dark Shekhinah. Open your mind's eye to what she looks like, what she represents for you. Ask her the question you need to ask. When you have your answer, go quickly back outside.

You may find, when you return to the city, you are no longer a prisoner in it. Instead you have become an empowered participant in its revolution.

Where do I find the Jewish goddess? I find her in the study of Torah. Now this is a strange thing for me to say. For a start I'm not an ethnic Jew, and I gave up converting to reform Judaism a year ago. (How could a scruffy old-hippy Lesbian like me fit in with the provincial suburban schul?) I now see myself as ethnically Celtic/Nordic with a soul passionately embroiled with Jewish identity: spiritually as a Jewish heretic.

Let me tell you why. Way back when the Children of Israel left Egypt, there went with them a number of gentile Egyptians who are referred to as the 'mixed multitude' (the *airev rav*). Now, the rabbinical commentators blamed almost all the sins of the Israelites in the desert on this mixed multitude. They were, you might say, the scapegoats' scapegoats. But the commentators are defaming them. The truth is, there was much positive intermingling going on outside the ken of the Biblical redactors. Exodus doesn't tell a quarter of the story. In fact there was a small mixed bunch of Hebrews and Egyptians gathered round Miriam, Moshe's sister.

When Moshe went up Mount Sinai to get his Torah, Miriam went inside a cave down below. So he got the Upstairs Torah, while she got the Downstairs Torah. Miriam's Torah got lost. (Some people said Aaron destroyed it ....)

How do I know this? Well I'm a firm believer in the Kabbalistic doctrine of Gilgulim, that is, reincarnation. Yes, I was there, helping Miriam get her vision written down. And now, today, parts of that vision are coming back to me. But where is the rest of the gang?

I study Torah, but not as an orthodox Jew, bound by rigid grooves of traditional thought. I study it with a mind that has been filled with comparative religion and mythology for many years. I like to play the midrashic game, looking over my shoulder at no one. This Midrash of mine on Shir-ha-Shirim owes much to a narrow fundamentalist set of commentaries called the Artscroll Tanach Series. Its compilers would be deeply shocked at a gentile heretic like me using them, and some of their opinions are, to say the least, offensive to me. But still, they open to me the treasure-laden coffers of rabbinical thought.

Traditionally it is forbidden for gentiles to study Torah. And there are many Jews, both religious and secular, who appear to share this sentiment. Well, I'm a heretic, so I defy the lot of you. And as a co-producer of Miriam's Torah in a previous incarnation I claim my right to my bit of the Jewish Goddess – and him up there as well. May the Elohim be with me, in this world and the world to come.

Verse numbering according to Revised Standard Version.
Translation thanks to Mervin Lebor.
Commentary inspiration: 'Shir haShirim', Artscroll Tanach Series (Zlotowitz, Sherman), Mesorah Publications, New York, 1979.

JOURNEY TO THE REALM
OF THE PATRIARCH
Dyana Hart

I was a stranger
or received as such
in the kingdom of contradictions.
You could only respond to me
as to a stranger.
There were no papers
signatures or speeches,
but she was Eve
and I, Lilith
and you expelled me
and my child.
But I heard the pain
surrounding and inside you,
I could touch it too –
it was solid.
I wanted to be
your healer, lover and your bridge,
but yours is the realm
of the powerful father,
the mother is dark
and evil.
Circe, Hecate, Medusa,
Ereshkigal, Snowy,
who 'spat out men like frogs',
snakelike sexual potency.
Was it through fear of the mother
that you regretted
what passed between us?
Did you know that longing
would surge in my veins,

seas of darkness and desire?
To forget you would be
to deny the mother,
she who bestows passion,
sometimes sadness.

214

DESCENT OF
THE GODDESS
Dyana Hart

My song
is just a wail
that begins deep
in the centre of me
and sucks me inside it
then there is pain.
I am nothing but pain
pain echoing vibrating
in the eternal abyss
between male and female.
There is no peace
i as a woman
suffer for the collective sins
of Woman.
Mary must have been crucified
mingling her blood
with the blood of
Lilith, Jezebel, Judith,
Jael, Jane, Margaret, Joan,
Jean, Judy, Norma-Jean,
Virginia, Janis, Karen
and all the nameless witches
unknown to his-tory.
I am each one of them
i have been
an insect trying
to climb a rainbow
i have been
a white sow
and a silver snake.

I want to journey back
beyond my birth
beyond my conception
beyond the pain
of any form of existence
beyond time and being
to nothing
to stillness
to darker than darkness.

GENDER POLITICS AND THE SOUL:
A Jewish Feminist Journey
Gloria Orenstein

(Extracts from a longer article published in 1986)

A Tu B'Shvat Seder for the Trees at the home of Savina Teubal, author of *Sarah the Priestess*.[1] We women do not know each other, but we have come a long way in order to celebrate our emergence from the winter of our spirits to a new cycle of rebirth into Jewish feminist culture. Fern has brought leaves and thread for us to make ritual decorations. Savina has set the table with fine crystal for the ceremony of mixing the wines from white to red symbolizing our leaving Winter for the communal pot-luck. Some of us, Irene and I, have brought along our children. Others have invited friends. Bruria, an Israeli artist, and Savina, our hostess, read Hebrew fluently. Later they enter into a heated debate about certain stories in the Bible which Savina has reinterpreted in her book, concluding that Judaism originally had another strain, a matricentric lineage as well as a patriarchal one. It descends from Sarah, who may well have been a Priestess of the Goddess religion. Sarah, who spent most of her life in a sacred grove of terebinth trees at Mamre, may even have taken an oath not to bear children, as did many women of her time who were Priestesses. Thus, her 'infertility' or what is often referred to as her 'barrenness' is probably a clue to her true identity as a Priestess.

The idea that Sarah could have been a Priestess of the Goddess religion thrills me. For many years now I have been a scholar of Comparative Literature and the Arts, studying women and creation, and I have been constantly preoccupied by one image – that of the re-emergence of the Goddess in art and literature by contemporary women. Yet, as a Jewish woman I feel both guilty for being obsessed by my search for the

Goddess, and simultaneously ecstatic about discovering that our most ancient matriarch may even have revered Her.

Our Seder begins. We light candles, say prayers, read poetry, share our writings, our dreams for this evening, for this world, for ourselves, our families, our friends, and we eat the two best kugels we have tasted since our childhood. We explain the fine art of the Ashkenazi Kugel to Savina whose background is Safardic. Some of us speak in Jungian terms about our inner searches for the integration of the 'masculine' and the 'feminine' within ourselves, assuming that others know exactly what we mean by those labels. Others of us react vehemently to this vocabulary and its ideological implications. 'Haven't we learned that "masculine" and "feminine" are social constructions?' we ask. 'Haven't we proved through a decade of feminist scholarship in a variety of disciplines that gender roles vary from culture to culture?' 'No!' claim the Jungians. 'We feel ourselves to be deeply "feminine", and moving towards an integration with our "masculine" counterparts within the self as we become more independent, as we learn to participate in the creation of our own culture and the transformation of society.' We must above all be patient with each other, I think, as my voice pierces the hallowed space of communion and rises shrilly to contest: 'No, you are wrong! We do not have "masculine selves" or "aspects" of the self. We are women and our independence is female. What you are calling "masculine" in you I call "female" in me.'

We have been going at each other for two hours – about whether Sarah could have been a Priestess of the Goddess religion, about gender and socialization, about inner guides and spiritual revelations, about transformation and Feminism. As we recite our own prayers to each other, and as we tell each other about our studies and about our life experiences, I suddenly feel intensely that we are women passionately engaged in a search for God or Goddess, a search for our origins – that we are women recreating something that feels extraordinarily like what a women's Yeshiva might feel like. But, as women, we do not have our own scrolls to argue about, so we are disputing our recent scholarship as we would dispute a sacred text. We have already written some of our own stories, our own commentaries, our own 'midrash', and as we do so, we are creating our own tradition! 'But is this Jewish?' we continually ask ourselves.

Last week we attended Adrienne Rich's talk on Jewish women poets at UCLA. Marcia Falk, our friend, and poet-scholar in Los Angeles, is writing new prayers which say: 'Let us now bless the wine, the fruit of the vine, etc.' Instead of 'Blessed art thou O Lord our God, King of the Universe.' But, 'Is it Jewish?' we ask ourselves again and again. Marcia's reply is always: 'I'm deeply Jewish. I've studied Jewish tradition all my life. Of course it's Jewish. but it's also inclusive of women.' We ask her if the Rabbis, even the women Rabbis, think it's Jewish. I ask Rabbi Patti Karlin Newman of UCLA. If, as one of the first women Rabbis in the history of Judaism, she couldn't simply make a pronouncement saying: 'We women Rabbis recognize the pain and struggle of contemporary Jewish women to write women experiences into Jewish prayer and scholarship, and we recognize their new prayers, their new art, and their new scholarship as profoundly Jewish.' I tell her how much anguish it would save us to know that what we dream and create as Jewish women is, in fact, recognized as Jewish. She replies that she has the authority to make such a pronouncement, and, indeed, she would make it if she were convinced it were Jewish. 'But Gloria,' she responds, 'we have been over this many times. Your Goddess is simply not Jewish. We have to make distinctions somewhere; to draw the line between what is and what isn't Jewish. We can't accept everything as Jewish.'

Adrienne Rich has been telling us how she struggled with her Jewish identity – not ever thinking that the Bible her Jewish father read to her as a child was the 'Jewish Bible'.

How did we come to this time and this place?

I have come to Los Angeles from New York, and I often tell people that the change has marked, for me, an entry into the world of the future and of the machine. In New York we are surrounded by people packed into elevators and subways like sardines, engulfed by crowds everywhere we go. Here, in Los Angeles, we spend the day alone in our cars, listening to tapes, or at home with answering machines, computers, video cassette recorders, more tapes .... When we shop a computerized voice, like a disembodied ghost, rises from the cash register and announces the price of what we have purchased. Because of this technical pollution we crave community and society more than ever. We yearn for human passion, for the flame and zeal of commitment to ideals and the energized emotional atmosphere that poetry, philosophy and art generate. Our endless robotics, artificial intelligences, plastic ready-made foods, drive-in computerized electronic life-styles and games, Pac-Man and Pac-Woman, all the simulacra of life, deprive us of contact with the vital forces of nature and the characteristics of human thought that defy computer programs such as humour and ambiguity, sources of creativity.

And so we come to this time, 1985, to this place, Santa Monica, Savina Teubal's house surrounded by fruit trees, to shed the winter of our souls and enter a period of communal rebirth symbolized by the Tree of Life that Tu B'Shvat commemorates.

All of this began when I was appointed to the Planning Committee of the Shekinah Conference. I was to represent USC's Program for the Study of Women and Men in Society in which I teach. Our conference was to be about Jewish women and spirituality, and our first discussion centred on the title: Did we mean women's spirituality *in* Jewish tradition or women's spirituality *and* Jewish tradition? I fought for *and*, because it seemed to me that my own spirituality which had been loosely referred to as 'pagan' until then because of its association with the 'goddess' seemed to be defined as 'outside' the realm of the Jewish religion. Yet, I felt deeply Jewish, and was reminded of my Jewishness all the time by my feminist sisters of other religions. It held no water with them whether I confessed to my former atheism, my flirtation with Buddhism, my discovery of the Goddess. For them I was Jewish, and that was that! But the Rabbis had other opinions in the matter.

We called our conference 'Illuminating the Unwritten Scroll: Women's Spirituality *and* Jewish Tradition', and we took the name of 'Shekinah' for our all-embracing symbol. The unwritten scroll represented for us the Torah as it might have been, had women written it.

I was to do a workshop on the Goddess with anthropologist Gelya Frank. At last I would pose the question of the goddess's re-emergence in contemporary art to Jewish women. At last I would know whether my goddess had anything to do with Judaism. As I prepared for the workshop I reflected upon my life and my Jewish background. As a child I had attended temple regularly on holidays. I was confirmed at 13, as was the custom in my era, and I attended Brandeis University, graduating in its 8th graduating class. Having lived in New York and attended Brandeis, I was virtually unfamiliar with anti-semitism. However, I did marry a Holocaust survivor from France, and although I was sympathetic to his sufferings as a child during the Holocaust, I also analysed the sexism within my cultural tradition as I experienced it in marriage. Why did I identify it as Jewish? I have been faulted for this. Everyone reminds me that the sexism I associate with Judaism is rampant in patriarchy in general. I suppose that I had expected Jews to rise above all forms of discrimination, having suffered from one virulent form of it themselves. I was naive about how wounds are transmitted from generation to generation.

After my marriage ended, after I received my doctorate and had searched for spiritual meaning in various arenas such as the occult, the mystical, magical, I found myself telling people that I was only a secular Jew; spiritually I felt attracted to a Goddess religion. It had been anti-semitism that originally sensitized me to sexism, but in my more recent involvement with feminism I had come full cycle, and once more encountered anti-semitism. Thus, I came to a point where I wanted to resolve all the political conflicts in my identity. I wanted to find a way to be both Jewish and feminist....

My research has shown that contemporary women of vision (artists both Jewish and non-Jewish) have in fact been re-evoking the Goddess as a symbol of our new feminist consciousness, of our erased pre-history and history, of our rebirth into a new era in which women name reality for themselves. Contemporary women artists and writers use it as a symbol of the reclamation of their own creative abilities and of a reverence for nature as well as, of course, a reaffirmation of female procreation. These are just some of the meanings of the re-emergence of the Goddess in women's culture today. It is in general a symbol of the knowledge of women's history and of the power that comes from that knowledge.

Paradoxically this goddess symbol is usually not that of a deity *per se*. It does not denote a monotheistic belief structure as opposed to a polytheistic one (with female counterparts of male gods). In fact, it does not speak about religion with a dogma. It speaks about a non-dogmatic spirituality, going back to a first-hand encounter with a dimension of spiritual experience, be it in a cave where once the goddess was revered in Neolithic times, or the experience of the land as sacred, the female as sacred, the sexual as sacred, life itself as sacred.

As I write this I am aware that I experience a very deep taboo in saying that I am asking myself if there is anything superior about monotheism, about any theism that empowers males at the expense of females. In view of the oppression that centuries of Jewish women have experienced in our monotheism, I do not feel that those cultures which had a plurality of gods, some of which were goddesses, were inferior. It is heresy for me to say this. I know it, yet, I must say this as a Jewish woman who was alienated by patriarchal monotheism.

We might ask ourselves, as contemporary Jews, what makes our creation mythology, one that has no goddesses, more valid, superior, more spiritual or more important? High priestesses, goddesses, and woman shamans are familiar images to women raised in many of the cultures of the world. As a Jewish woman I was told that we were superior because our God was transcendent, genderless, and imageless. Then, in the very next breath I was told about Him, about God the Father. I now realize how impoverished I have been – deprived as I was of the potent examples of female strength encoded in the image of the female creatress, the images of female power, of female energy, and of female priestesses that women of other cultures know and contemplate as they grow.

While I joyfully celebrate the acceptance of women to the Rabbinate, I am still denied a female aspect of the deity. Merlin Stone[2] shows that the goddesses worshipped by people in a variety of cultures did not symbolize just one thing, but represented a multitude of aspects, traits, and powers.

Moon, sun, stars, volcanos, rivers, lakes, trees, corn, birds, Queen of Heaven and Mother of Earth, lawgivers, compassionate one, wrathful one, holy ones, wise ones, symbols of liberty, justice, victory, warrior women, hunters, ancestors, mothers, guardians, scribes ... all of these have been symbols, roles and images of goddesses, of women.

Why have the many accounts of these goddesses been suppressed and erased? What do they mean for Jewish women today who find their own theology too patriarchal? As Jews we are probably most interested in the accounts of the Goddess Asherah. Why was the once-sacred image of woman then degraded? Why was the reverence of Her referred to as a cult, as a myth rather than as a religion that lasted over 3500 years – perhaps longer than 7,000 years? Merlin Stone also sees the connection between Goddess reverence and the sanctity of nature. She sees the fact that womanhood was held as sacred among people who revered a goddess, be they Mexican, Irish, or Zuni, as very important. In reading her I ask myself again and again, as a Jewish woman, what would I write into Judaism to meet this need that I have for the dimension of spirituality that the Goddess symbol has represented in terms of empowering women, a dimension that embraces both nature and culture in a positive way? At my workshop I show slides of art by women both Jewish and non-Jewish.

While the non-Jewish artists seem to connect the goddess with earth energies and the realm of animals and nature, the works of Jewish artists often relate their Goddess references to the spiritual dimension within history, both secular and sacred, communal and personal. Judy Chicago's *Dinner Party* is an excellent example of this kind of search for a transcendent spiritual community of women. Esther Broner's novel *A Weave of Women*[3] is about a Jewish feminist community in Jerusalem. Ruth Weisberg's art is concerned with our relationship to the host of Jewish souls who have lived and died before us, whose lives and spirit we commemorate in our own lives and works.

In our workshop Gelya Frank leads the audience on a guided imagery journey and asks them to name the deity they encounter, to tell where it comes from, what it looks like, whether it is accompanied, what its gifts are, what it wants of us, how it envisages women's role in Judaism in the future. Our responses are amazing! The women present envisage either a female being or an intensely warm and brilliant light....

Can this be Jewish? I feel it to be so deeply Jewish that I often wish it were less so. When? When I discuss my Gertrude Stein paper with a writer friend, telling her that if you listen closely for Yiddish in her abstract poetry, you will discover an anti-Seder, and underneath that you will discover a goddess-centred world in which nature and forbidden love are celebrated. You will discover a completely new interpretation of the Garden of Eden (at Bilignin), of forbidden fruit as well. My materialist feminist friend says to me: 'Gloria, I cannot dispute what you say, but it's not my thing!' I wish it were less Jewish when I submit my Goddess paper to a contemporary American feminist journal of materialist persuasion, and they reject it saying that they admire it, but it is simply not their thing. This thing that is not theirs – what is it? It can't be an overt Judaism, because my paper on the Goddess is anything but Jewish. I will call it 'soul', for lack of a better word. Whatever it is, it doesn't process, and it is a part of me that feels like it comes from my Jewish background. Soul. Is it that Soul does not process? Is there a sexual politics of the soul, too?

I have been told that I am reclaiming my Jewish identity for the wrong reasons – because of anti-semitism.

I had contested Judaism because of its sexism. I had turned to the pre-patriarchal Goddess instead. Then, Judaism rejected me because of my unorthodox spiritual and political quests. I was equally rejected by my feminist sisters and by my Jewish sisters and brothers, either because of Israeli politics or feminist politics. I was caught in a double bind....

It is now clear to me that when we talk about the soul we are entering into a discussion of gender politics again.

As a feminist I must critique the ideological presuppositions inherent in both Jung's work and Judaism. Yet, I have passed through both at different times and have been greatly enriched by what they offered me. What attracts me to both bodies of thought and belief is the notion of the Soul. What I cannot accept is their approach to the concept of gender, which ultimately applies to their concepts of the Soul, as well. If gender is socially constructed and relative, not absolute, then ideas of the 'feminine' and the 'masculine' are relative and socially constructed as well. Perhaps the soul is also a social construction. While certain attributes are represented by goddesses in one society, it is a god who embodies those same qualities in another culture.

Then, in view of this reasoning, why do I insist upon a female image of the Goddess as the creator of life? If it is all culturally relative and socially constructed, should I be satisfied with a genderless image? A male-female dyadic image? Yet, there is something in me that rebels against these two solutions. Reasonable people say that since it is beyond our power to name the Creator, a genderless image, such as a geometric shape or a light should suffice. Yet, gender arrangements, as we know, reflect politics and reinforce power in the secular world. It is probably not until the structures change in the secular world that I would turn to another symbol system. For, even an image of equality can be abused in order to mystify us, and force us into believing that divine manifestation of equality legislates equality on earth when actually inequality reigns. Isn't it obvious how the blatant contradiction of the Male-god image has already legitimated male-supremacy? It is just amazing how long it took us to notice.

In this matter, I will trust the artists, and when their symbolism changes, I will believe that our secular structures have been undergoing transformation as well. For, I contend that the only reason the Goddess is reappearing in the art and literature of contemporary women is that feminist research has transmitted that knowledge to us – knowledge of our ancient pre-history and of our true legacy from the past. It is this knowledge that we have acquired through research that has stimulated the creative imagination of women artists today. I strongly maintain that to espouse the idea that a 'feminine archetype' is re-emerging in our consciousness is to erase the important contribution of feminist scholars to our thought and to obscure both the relationship of knowledge to creation and

224

the relationship of knowledge to imagination. It is at the nexus of feminist scholarship and gender politics that my 'search for a Jewish soul' can be situated.

This conscious creation of images that will circulate in the culture will provide women with reflections of those aspects of themselves that they feel to be sacred, divine, or in the image of the Creator. In the future when women dream that they are giving birth to the creative aspect of themselves they may at last be able to dream that they are giving birth to the daughter of a Goddess, or even of the Goddess herself.

NOTES

1 Savina Teubal, *Sarah The Priestess*, Athens, Ohio: Swallow Press, 1984.
2 Merlin Stone, *Ancient Mirrors of Womanhood: Our Goddess and Heroine Heritage*, New York: New Sibylline Books, 1979.
3 Esther Broner, *A Weave of Women*, New York: Bantam Books, 1978.

(From an essay which originally appeared in *A Modern Jew in Search of a Soul*, ed. Spiegelman and Jacobson, Phoenix, Ariz: Falcon Press, 1986.)

THE KABBALISTIC TREE OF LIFE: THE GODDESS'S PERSPECTIVES
Alix Pirani

What do we mean by a 'feminine reading' of the Tree of Life? As in all these matters, we strive to correct the imbalance of centuries of narrow patriarchal interpretation of texts which in themselves carry much wider truths. The Tree of Life, whose avowed aim is to hold in balance polarities, 'masculine' and 'feminine' energies, must be at the centre of that. As Jenny Goodman points out (p. 97) there is no reason for women to go along with any hard-and-fast gender designation and indeed the Tree always invites us to explore and expand its inherent paradoxes.

There has been for many people the uncomfortable feeling that the right-hand pillar, though 'male' and 'active' contains 'female' and passive characteristics, and the left-hand 'female', 'passive' pillar contains male and active characteristics. And that in deliberately designating Hochmah a male Sephirah, the Goddess is erased. But this assumes a male right-handedness, i.e. if the Tree represents the body of Adam Kadmon, and I imagine it to be my body, it would be imprinted on my back, so to speak. However, if we give the Tree over to Eve, facing Adam, it is imprinted on her frontally and the right-hand pillar becomes her feminine left-handedness. The two Trees then face one another in fertile sexual interchange: fertile for the imagination, and fertile in implications for the interaction of sexual, relational and spiritual energies, mutually stimulating and 'doubly' creative. The initial image of Hochmah as the Divine Intelligence with whom the patriarchal God mated allies with this idea. His Tree needs to be in embrace with her Tree in order to be creative.

What is her Tree? I believe the fundamental Hochmah wisdom of the Tree is in its reflection of the body, which carries and provides Hochmah intelligence throughout generations. So the 'feminine reading' I offer here will be mainly about woman's body process, and the original principles of matriarchal wisdom. Women's menstrual and birthing processes inevitably affect men, and need to be known by men. Matriarchal wisdom knows – as all body therapies and holistic medicine know – that ancestral intelligence is communicated through the body: particularly the wisdom that for one reason or another is silent. The vicissitudes of the 'occluded intelligence' are also carried in the body.

As I see it, Hochmah *is* the Tree, and is also *inside* the Tree, in one of the Sephirot. The Tree is Her infinite knowledge, Her cultivation of healthy evolution. And to ensure that She has genuine 'understanding' of that process as it works within finite human consciousness, She is inside the Tree. The Kabbalists put her in the place of revealed knowledge in the highest 'supernal triangle'.

This is very similar to psychotherapeutic practice in which the therapist stands outside the client's process, observing and facilitating it, and at the same time allows part of himself or herself to step into that process, relating directly to the client according to the client's perceptions and needs at the time. Then, after time has passed, there comes detached reflection on what has been happening.

I am also aware of my own role as both editor of and participant in this book. The duality carries the same effectiveness in achieving responsibility in management, the 'balance of power', handling time and space boundaries. The dual perspective contributes to my promotion of its creative power.

There is no doubt that this principle – that time-bound existence is part of a timeless process – was always strongly maintained by matriarchal cultures. Laws based on matriarchal authority were closely connected to matriarchal priesthood.[1] They were a culture of the spirit, before they became legalistic or property-oriented. In Jewish tradition that has remained: the child of a Jewish mother is, by Jewish law, Jewish, whoever its father. This entrusts to Jewish women a clear spiritual responsibility, if they wish to assume it.

One particularly interesting example of the workings of Hochmah can be found in Shakespeare. He was familiar with Kabbalah through the teachings of John Dee,[2] and in *The Merchant of Venice*, that exploration of capitalist morality, there comes the famous speech by Portia, 'The quality of mercy is not strained ...' in which she clearly confronts Shylock's Gevurah with the principle of Hesed, in language which contains much beautiful Kabbalistic imagery. And here is a woman, dressed as a man, in legal robes, about to administer firm 'Gevuric' justice from a place of Hesed, and acted, in Shakespeare's day, by a man! There is no doubt that Shakespeare is playing very creatively with issues of feminine/masculine humanity. And we could well see in Portia at this point the archetypal feminine figure of justice – even to the scales which are to weigh the pound of flesh – a matriarchy which has to be hidden under patriarchal robes in order to speak out.

'Matriarchy hidden under patriarchal robes' could well describe the Tree of Life. The energetic/creative processes of bodylife are in the Tree. The woman's experience imprints itself on a man through birth, sexual intercourse, and menstrual/emotional proximity. There is no doubt that the women's creative energy pattern was in the men who 'created' the Tree.

I offer five comments on the Tree: on the relationship within it of goddess archetypes; on its representation of feminine bodylife; on menstrual process; birth process, and sexual process. I hope these will encourage further contributory ideas from other women, and men, in the continuing expansion of the Tree's – Hochmah's – intelligence.

GODDESS ARCHETYPES

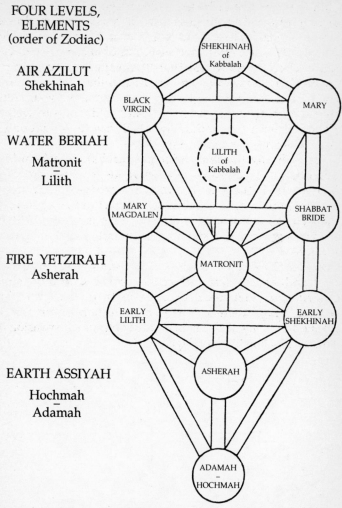

**FOUR LEVELS,
ELEMENTS**
(order of Zodiac)

AIR AZILUT
Shekhinah

WATER BERIAH

Matronit

Lilith

FIRE YETZIRAH
Asherah

EARTH ASSIYAH

Hochmah

Adamah

Labels within diagram:
SHEKHINAH of Kabbalah
BLACK VIRGIN
MARY
LILITH of Kabbalah
MARY MAGDALEN
SHABBAT BRIDE
MATRONIT
EARLY LILITH
EARLY SHEKHINAH
ASHERAH
ADAMAH – HOCHMAH

The usual qualities and relationships of the Sephirot are implicit
here.

However, Lilith, in Da'at, is the dis/connection of this Tree
with the 'male' Tree: its unknown uncontained dimension. Lilith
is the transformatory serpent coiled round the Tree – the
creature in the abyss – guardian of hidden knowledge (she
knew the secret name of God) – sexual – makes the bridge from
the ineffable to the carnal: the Da'at of one level becoming the
Yesod of the next.

She is the suppressed feminine of the Kabbalistic Tree.

FEMININE BODYLIFE AND EMOTIONAL LIFE

in
ASSIYAH

in
YETZIRAH

(Kether of Assiyah = Tipheret of Yetzirah)

HEAD and MOUTH

CROWN OF HEAD
(Tipheret of Beriah)

SHOULDERS – Muscular
control of/by Tipheret
CONNECT to ARMS, action

TEMPLES, EYES
– Centres of perceived
understanding

THROAT, HEART
– Silence

'THIRD EYE', Pineal
Gland, Brainstem, Hypo-
thalamus. Intuitive and
primitive awareness

BREASTS
(N.B. Kleinian 'Good
and Bad Breasts')

EARS and SINUS
Receptive and reactive

SOLAR PLEXUS and
LOWER BACK – motivation

NOSE and MOUTH
Breath, Inspiration, Oracular
speech, song (Malchut of Beria

HIPS and OVARIES
Movement, sexuality,
grounding. CONNECT
to LEGS

SHOULDERS
Control, socialization

WOMB

THROAT
Inner voice, silence,
impulse to utterance
of joy or grief

VAGINA, CLITORIS,
ANUS (N.B. classic
denigratory combination and
confusion of sexuality and
anality)

HEART, SOLAR PLEXUS

KETHER

BINAH

HOCHMAH

DA'AT

GEVURAH

HESED

TIPHERET

HOD

NETZACH

YESOD

MALCHUT

Central pillar: SPINE and
Kundalini energy

N.B. the importance of resisting the male tendency to see the
Tree as chiefly a mode of ascent – toward the patriarchal
divinity – over-valuing the aspiration toward transcendence.
Depth is as important as height: the descent is the way of
releasing and manifesting the divine into the world of action.

MENSTRUAL PROCESS

Four worlds

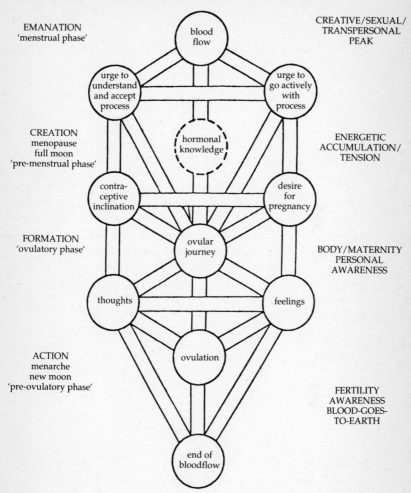

EMANATION
'menstrual phase'

CREATIVE/SEXUAL/
TRANSPERSONAL
PEAK

blood
flow

urge to
understand
and accept
process

urge to
go actively
with
process

CREATION
menopause
full moon
'pre-menstrual phase'

hormonal
knowledge

ENERGETIC
ACCUMULATION/
TENSION

contra-
ceptive
inclination

desire
for
pregnancy

FORMATION
'ovulatory phase'

ovular
journey

BODY/MATERNITY
PERSONAL
AWARENESS

thoughts

feelings

ACTION
menarche
new moon
'pre-ovulatory phase'

ovulation

FERTILITY
AWARENESS
BLOOD-GOES-
TO-EARTH

end of
bloodflow

This schema should be looked at in conjunction with the previous chart. It suggests the flexible interaction of the body's time-bound experience with emotional-spiritual consciousness; woven into it are the tensions and conflicts produced by social pressure and conditioning. Is the World of 'Emanation' the Goddess's menstrual flow ...?

This exploration is based on the many insights offered in *The Wise Wound*.[3] See Chapter 1 in particular.

BIRTH PROCESS

The perinatal energy-pattern is as charted by Stanislav Grof.[4] I use his 'Basic Perinatal Matrices' 1–4. This becomes an individual and collective pattern of creative process.[5]

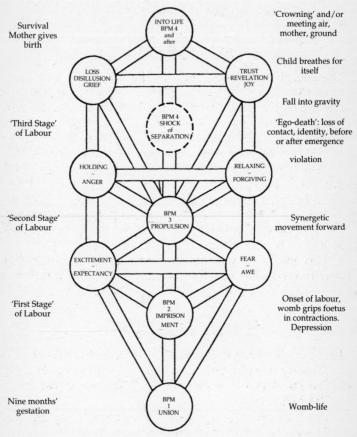

The maternal and foetal experience are represented separately here: the mother's in the outer pillars, the child's in the central column. But the foetus of course shares the mother's feelings. For more on the mother's experience, see my observations, p. 181 and p. 190.

The *descent* is made, in voluntary primal regression, or involuntary regression, dreaming, and psychosis, by those seeking to retrace the origins and meaning of their life – as far back as the mystery of conception and incarnation. (Shekhinah in Malchut.)

The Process of Dying is similar in its patterning, often repeating the individual's birth-pattern. This is described by Grof and Halifax in *The Human Encounter with Death*. Similarly Elisabeth Kübler-Ross distinguishes five stages in the process of conscious dying.[6] If Kether is the next life, beyond this, then the descent is the process of reincarnation, the soul seeking an appropriate body in Malchut.

SEXUAL PROCESS

The energy-pattern leading towards orgasm is similar to the birth pattern, and influenced by it. It is present as both vertical and zig-zag ascent: foreplay in Malchut; genital meeting in Yesod; progress via Tipheret through Yetzirah, to climax in Beriah. Da'at is the ecstatic 'little death', loss of consciousness and contact. Meeting, afterglow, desire gratified, is in Kether.

The divine Desire – cosmic Love-energy – is in Azilut. It descends with the lightning-flash, moving through the three levels to find an appropriate focus, love-objects, in Assiyah. The sexual meeting then re-connects through orgasmic progress to the divine. William Blake says men and women require of one another to be 'the lineaments of gratified desire'.

This energy-flow is vital for the freeing and channelling of spiritual/sexual energy. Tantric sexual practices aim at conservation rather than expenditure of that energy.

REFERENCES

1 For an excellent exploration of matriarchal priesthood, see *Sarah the Priestess*, by Savina Teubal (Swallow Press, 1984).
2 See *The Occult Philosophy in the Elizabethan Age*, by Frances Yates (Ark, 1983).
3 Penelope Shuttle and Peter Redgrove, *The Wise Wound: Menstruation and Everywoman* (Paladin, 1986).
4 In *Realms of the Human Unconscious* (Viking, 1975). See also the work of Frank Lake, *passim*.
5 See *Birth and Rebirth*, ed. Pirani (Self & Society, 1978).
6 Elisabeth Kübler-Ross, *On Death and Dying* (Tavistock, 1977).

LILITH
Valerie Sinason

On the sabbath
the world is renewed
Lilith has dusted the apples
swept the earth
polished the moon
and now she can rest

but Adam does not renew her
he leaves her untouched

'Lie down' says God
He ribs her. 'Be quiet and wait.
The old Adam is on the wane.
It's time for a one millennium stand.
I want grandchildren to pray to me'

It's night-time
But she won't lie down.
In that time of her month
Lilith stands like a tree
ringed in her red and silver ages
Her breasts glow like beacons
but he will not come to her

She lies, she sleeps
wrapped in her own arms
body and soul tilted
to no man's hand

He told you I was the first woman
whispered Lilith
He told you wrong.
Ask Him where your mother is
It's she who takes your body away

Adam rolls over, counts his ribs.
He is scared there is something he will lose.

The man walks across the earth
his shadow over her
wherever he goes
his shadow over her

RECOMMENDED READING

The contributors to this volume here describe those books which they have found essential to the exploration of its themes.

Begg, Ean (1985), *The Cult of the Black Virgin*, London, Arkana. A fascinating combination of Jungian mythological and symbolic analysis, and a gazetteer listing sites of Black Virgins throughout the world.

Goldenberg, Naomi (1979), *Changing of the Gods*, Boston, Beacon Press. Goldenberg gives a clear insight into the effect of the total exclusion of women from the major religions, discusses the impact of women's movements, and proposes that internal identification with the divine will follow the external Oedipal patriarchal divinity, now dying in the West.

Heschel, Susannah (ed.) (1983), *On Being a Jewish Feminist: A Reader*, New York, Schocken Books. An excellent collection of writing by leading thinkers on all aspects of Jewish life, theology, mythology and psychology as they affect women. A most imaginative and stimulating book that breaks new ground.

Hurcombe, Linda (ed.) (1987), *Sex and God: Some Varieties of Women's Religious Experience*, London, Routledge & Kegan Paul. Based on the premise that 'The erotic is the realm in which the spiritual, the political and the personal come together' (Starhawk), this collection, authoritative and passionate, has a spiritual and intellectual intensity characteristic of the emerging Goddess energies.

Hurwitz, Siegmund (1980), *Lilith, die erste Eva*, Zürich, Daimon Verlag. The author was trained by Jung, Toni Wolff and Marie-Louise von Franz. This book gives the most comprehensive account of the archetypal background to the

Lilith myth and its psychological consequences today.

King, Ursula (1989), *Women and Spirituality: Voices of Protest and Promise*, Basingstoke, Macmillan Education. An invaluable overview that ranges widely through the literature of feminine spirituality. The author is Professor and Head of the Department of Theology and Religious Studies at Bristol University.

Koltuv, Barbara Black (1986), *The Book of Lilith*, Maine, Nicolas-Hays Inc. An important guide to understanding the mythical significance of the Lilith archetype in the feminine psyche in both its destructive and creative form.

McFague, Sally (1983), *Metaphorical Theology: Models of God in Religious Language*, London, SCM Press. The author plays with models of God as Mother, Lover, Friend, showing that a 'model' has the attributes of both 'is' and 'is not' – and thereby God as Father has become, by long use and tradition, no longer model but dogma.

Patai, Raphael (1990) [1967], *The Hebrew Goddess*, Detroit, Wayne State University Press. The indispensable authoritative work on the Goddess, which gives her history in rich detail, also examining it from a psychological and mythical point of view. An exploration and celebration of the nature of deity itself: compulsive reading.

Scholem, Gershon (1969), *On the Kabbalah and its Symbolism*, New York, Shocken Books. Scholem is the leading historian of Jewish mysticism. This book contains five profound studies in Kabbalah: excellent for the psychologically minded who wish to understand the broader context of Jewish mysticsm and some of its basic ideas.

Shuttle, Penelope and Redgrove, Peter (1986), *The Wise Wound: Menstruation and Everywoman*, London, Paladin. This book never fails to impress: it has changed so many people's view and understanding of the essential feminine experience. The authors demonstrate how the ever-persistent menstrual taboos and negative conditioning have suppressed women's spiritual power and influenced whole civilizations for the worse. Scientific, psychological, historical in its approach.

Walker, Barbara (1983), *The Women's Encyclopaedia of Myths and Secrets*, San Francisco, Harper & Row. This radically enlightening work, the fruit of twenty years' labour, was justly the *Times Educational Supplement* 'Book of the Year' and is required reading for all – not just feminists – who seek the unconscious repressed bases of our culture.

Warner, Marina (1985), *Alone of All her Sex*, London, Pan Books.

This study of Mary is a great modern work of personal commitment, feminist criticism, and profound scholarliness. An outstanding achievement.

Whitmont, Edward (1987) [1983], *Return of the Goddess*, London, Arkana. A major work, describing the repression of the feminine in human consciousness and evolution, and the inevitability of its return. The author, Jungian analyst and survivor of Nazi persecution, brings to the subject realism, wide-ranging scholarship, and a vision for the future. A book to give to rationalist sceptics.

GENERAL BIBLIOGRAPHY

Albright, W.F. (1940), *From the Stone Age to Christianity*, Baltimore, Johns Hopkins University Press.

Baigent, Michael, Leigh, Richard and Lincoln, Henry (1986), *The Holy Blood and the Holy Grail*, London, Corgi Books.

Blake, William (1948 edn.), *Poetry and Prose*, London, Nonesuch Press.

Bolen, Jean Shinoda (1985), *Goddesses in Everywoman: A New Psychology of Women*, New York, Harper & Row.

Broner, Esther (1978), *A Weave of Women*, New York, Bantam Books.

Brooten, B.J. (1982). *Women Leaders in the Ancient Synagogue*, California, Scholars Press.

Cameron, A. and Kurht, A. (1983), *Images of Women in Antiquity*, London, Croom Helm.

Campbell, Joseph (1985), *The Masks of God: Occidental Mythology*, Harmondsworth, Penguin Books.

Canan, Janine (ed.) (1989), *She Rises like the Sun: Invocations of the Goddess by Contemporary American Women Poets*, California, The Crossing Press.

Cassuto, Umberto (1971), *The Goddess Anath*, Jerusalem, Hebrew University Press.

Chicago, Judy (1979), *The Dinner Party*, New York, Anchor Books.

Chicago, Judy (1982), *Through the Flower*, London, The Women's Press.

Christ, Carol P. (1987), *The Laughter of Aphrodite*, California, Harper & Row.

Cooper, Howard (ed.) (1988), *Soul Searching: Studies in Judaism and Psychotherapy*, London, SCM Press.

Daly, Mary (1974), *Beyond God the Father*, Boston, Beacon Press.

240

Driver, G.R. (1956/71), *Canaanite Myths and Legends*, Edinburgh, T. & T. Clark.

Durdin-Robertson, L. (1975), *The Goddesses of Chaldea, Syria and Egypt*, Eire, Cesara Publications.

Engelsman, Joan C. (1987), *The Feminine Dimension of the Divine*, Wilmette, Illinois, Chiron Publications.

Ellis, Marc H. (1989), *Toward a Jewish Theology of Liberation*, Maryknoll, New York, Orbis Books.

Farrar, Janet and Stewart (1987), *The Witches' Goddess*, London, Robert Hale.

Feher, Elizabeth (1980), *The Psychology of Birth*, London, Souvenir Press.

Ferguson, Marilyn (1982), *The Aquarian Conspiracy*, London, Paladin Books.

Fiorenza, Elisabeth Schüssler (1983), *In Memory of Her*, New York, Crossroads.

Fiorenza, Elisabeth Schüssler (1984), *Bread not Stone*, Boston, Beacon Press.

Gadon, Elinor W. (1990), *The Once and Future Goddess*, Wellingborough, Aquarian Press.

Graf, Hilda (1985), *Mary, a History of Doctrine and Devotion*, London, Sheed & Ward.

Graves, Robert (1948/1958), *The White Goddess*, New York, Vintage Books.

Graves, Robert and Patai, Raphael (1964), *Hebrew Myths: The Book of Genesis*, New York, McGraw Hill.

Gray, John (1964), *The Canaanites*, London, Thames & Hudson.

Green, Deirdre (1989), *Gold in the Crucible: Teresa of Avila and the Western Mystical Tradition*, Shaftesbury, Element Books.

Greenberg, Blu (1981), *On Women and Judaism: A View from Tradition*, Philadelphia, Jewish Publication Society.

Grof, Stanislav (1975), *Realms of the Human Unconscious*, New York, Viking Press.

Grof, S. and Halifax, J. (1978), *The Human Encounter with Death*, London Souvenir Press.

Halevi, Z'ev ben Shimon (Warren Kenton) (1979), *Kabbalah, Tradition of Hidden Knowledge*, London, Thames & Hudson.

Harding, Esther (1982), *Woman's Mysteries*, London, Rider.

Hillman, James (1973), 'The Great Mother, Her Son, Her Hero, and the Puer', in *Fathers and Mothers*, ed. P. Berry, Dallas, Spring Publications.

Hillman, James (1976), *Suicide and the Soul*, Dallas, Spring Publications.

Hillman, James (1983), *Healing Fiction*, New York, Station Hill

Press.

Hillman, James (1987), *Insearch: Psychology and Religion*, Dallas, Spring Publications.

Hoffman, Edward (1981), *The Way of Splendor: Jewish Mysticism and Modern Psychology*, Berkeley, Calif., Shambhala.

I Ching (1983), trans. R. Wilhelm, London, Routledge & Kegan Paul.

Keleman, Stanley (1975), *The Human Ground: Sexuality, Self and Survival*, Palo Alto, Calif., Science and Behavior Books.

Kübler-Ross, Elisabeth (1977), *On Death and Dying*, London, Tavistock Publications.

Layard, John (1975), *A Celtic Quest*, Zürich, Spring Publications.

Long, Asphodel (1985), 'Lilith – Night-Hag or Mother Goddess', in *Arachne*, No. 2 (London).

Long, Asphodel (1986), 'Canaanite Goddesses', in *Arachne*, No. 5 (London).

Long, Asphodel (1987), 'Goddesses of Wisdom', in *Arachne*, No. 6 (London).

McClure, K. (1983), *The Evidence for Visions of the Virgin Mary*, Wellingborough, Aquarian Press.

Maier, W. (1986), *Asherah, Extra Biblical Evidence*, Atlanta, Georgia, Scholars Press.

Matthews, Caitlin (1990), *Sophia – Goddess of Wisdom*, London, Mandala.

Monaghan, Patricia (1981), *Women in Myth and Legend*, London, Junction Books.

Moore, Thomas (1982), *The Planets Within*, London, Associated University Presses.

Neumann, Erich (1955), *The Great Mother*, Princeton, N.J., Princeton/Bollingen.

Nicholson, Shirley (ed.) (1989), *The Goddess Re-awakening*, Wheaton, Ill., Theosophical Publishing House.

Olson, C. (ed.) (1985), *The Book of the Goddess, Past and Present*, New York, Crossroads.

Orenstein, Gloria (1990), *The Reflowering of the Goddess*, Oxford, Pergamon Press, Athene Series.

Orenstein, Gloria (1990), *Reweaving the World: The Emergence of Ecofeminism*, Sierra Club Books.

Pagels, Elaine (1979), *The Gnostic Gospels*, New York, Random House.

Pagels, Elaine (1988), *Adam and Eve and the Serpent*, New York, Random House.

Perera, Sylvia Brinton (1988), *Descent to the Goddess: A Way of Inititiation for Women*, Toronto, Inner City Books.

Perera, Sylvia Brinton (1986), *The Scapegoat Complex: Shadow and Guilt*, Toronto, Inner City Books.

Pirani, Alix (ed.) (1978), *Birth and Rebirth*, London, Self and Society.

Pirani, Alix (1989), *The Absent Father: Crisis and Creativity*, London, Penguin Arkana.

Rank, Otto (1959), *The Myth of the Birth of the Hero*, New York, Vintage Books.

Redgrove, Peter (1989), *The Black Goddess and the Sixth Sense*, London, Grafton.

Roberts, Michèle (1984), *The Wild Girl*, London, Methuen.

Robinson, J.R. (1977), *The Nag Hammadi Library*, Leiden, Brill.

Ruether, Rosemary Radford (1983), *Sexism and God-Talk*, London, SCM Press.

Sarton, May (1978), *Selected Poems*, New York and London, W.W. Norton.

Saunders, Lesley (ed.) (1987), *Glancing Fires: An Investigation into Women's Creativity*, London, Women's Press.

Scholem, Gershon (1967), *Major Trends in Jewish Mysticism*, New York, Schocken Books.

Scholem, Gershon (1974), *Kabbalah*, Jerusalem, Keter Publishing House.

Sjöö, Monica and Mor, Barbara (1987), *The Great Cosmic Mother: Rediscovering the Religion of the Earth*, New York, Harper & Row.

Spiegelman, J. Marvin and Jacobson, Abraham (1986), *A Modern Jew in Search of a Soul*, Phoenix, Ariz., Falcon Press.

Starhawk (1979), *The Spiral Dance: A Rebirth of the Religion of the Great Goddess*, San Francisco, Harper & Row.

Stein, Diane (1989), *The Women's Spirituality Book*, USA, Llewellyn Publications.

Stone, Merlin (1976), *When God was a Woman*, New York, Harvest/Harcourt.

Stone, Merlin (1979), *Ancient Mirrors of Womanhood: Our Goddess and Heroine Heritage*, New York, New Sibilline Books.

Teubal, Savina (1984), *Sarah the Priestess*, Athens, Ohio, Swallow Press.

Trible, Phyllis (1984), *Texts of Terror: Literary–Feminist Readings of Biblical Narratives*, Philadelphia, Fortress Press.

Ulanov, Ann Belford (1971), *The Feminine in Jungian Psychology and Christian Theology*, Evanston, Northwestern University Press.

Ulanov, Ann Belford (1981), *Receiving Woman: Studies in the Psychology and Theology of the Feminine*, Philadelphia,

Westminster Press..

Von der Heydt, Vera (1976), *Prospects for the Soul*, London, Darton Longman & Todd.

Von Franz, Marie-Louise (1978), *Time: Rhythm and Repose*, London, Thames & Hudson.

Walker, Barbara (1988), *The Crone: Woman of Age, Wisdom and Power*, New York, Harper & Row.

Waskow, Arthur (1978), *Godwrestling*, New York, Schocken.

Welldon, Eudora (1988), *Mother, Madonna, Whore: the Idealization and Denigration of Motherhood*, London, Free Association Press.

Winnicott, D.W. (1971), *Playing and Reality*, London, Penguin and Tavistock.

Wolkstein, D. and Kramer, S.N. (1983), *Innana*, New York, Harper.

Woodman, Marion (1985), *The Pregnant Virgin*, Toronto, Inner City Books.

Woolger, Jennifer Barker and Roger J. (1989), *The Goddess Within*, New York, Fawcett Columbine.

Ya'qub ibn Yusuf (1989), 'The Redemption of the Shekhinah', in *Gnosis* magazine, No. 14. (Detroit).

Yates, Frances A. (1983), *The Occult Philosophy in the Elizabethan Age*, London, Ark Paperbacks.

INDEX

Sophia – Goddess of Wisdom
The Divine Feminine from Black Goddess to World-Soul
Caitlín Matthews

Honoured as the transcendent wisdom that inhabits the heavens as Bride of God, but also feared as the Black Goddess upon Earth, Sophia has been one of the few active manifestations of the Divine Feminine for the last two millennia. Now, in response to the ecological, social and spiritual needs of the twentieth century, the Goddess is re-emerging from her long eclipse, along the pathways that Sophia has kept open.

Sophia – Goddess of Wisdom is a major new book that takes the reader on a journey through time, seeking out the presence of the Goddess from pre-Christian spirituality to the present day. Drawing mainly on sources from the Western tradition the many faces of the Goddess are revealed. She is shown as the primeval Black Goddess of the earth, as Saviour Goddess, the Gnostic Sophia, World Soul, Apocalyptic Virgin and as Mother of God. We see how the foundation mysteries of the Goddess underlie the esoteric streams of orthodox religions, and trace her hermetic presence in Qabala and alchemy. Finally, we track her appearance in the realms of Goddess religion, feminist theology and the New Age movement.

This definitive work gives Sophia a voice that will be welcomed by all who seek to reaffirm the Goddess as the central pivot of creation and as the giver of practical and spiritual wisdom.

To Be a Woman
The Birth of the Conscious Feminine
Edited by Connie Zweig

A new era in women's self-awareness is about to emerge. With the fruits of feminism and individual development, women now have the opportunity to imagine and to live a kind of femininity that is consciously chosen – and that contains the benefits of our hard-won independence as well.

In this ground-breaking collection, women from many walks of life describe the key insights and experiences that can provide entry to this new level of consciousness.

This book explores:

• What it means to be a woman in a man's world for those of us who do not wish to stay at home and 'become like our mothers' or to strive aggressively and 'become like men';

• Why women in conventional marriages are initiating divorce in greater numbers than ever before;

• Why women are expressing deep disillusionment with the promises of feminism and the reality of career success;

• Why women are leaving careers and rushing to have babies late in life;

• Why women are exploring feminine spirituality and the Goddess.

The answers can be found in a woman's longing to be authentically feminine, to experience herself fully as a woman and, at the same time, to be a strong, independent individual whose power and authority are rooted within her. At a time when feminine values are on the rise, this book offers a vision of renewal.

Contributors include Marion Woodman, Jean Shinoda Bolen, Riane Eisler, Linda Schierse Leonard, Merlin Stone, Sylvia Brinton Perera and June Singer.

Dreaming the Dark
Magic, Sex and Politics
(new edition)
Starhawk

In this classic book Starhawk unites the world of nature worship and magic with the world of political organization and social activism. She intertwines the erotic with the political, and modern humanistic psychology with the ancient religion of the Goddess, to offer a transforming power that can heal the spiritual and political split between the individual and society.

Dreaming the Dark traces a path from despair in the face of cultural cruelty and the threat of global catastrophe, to inspiration, empowerment and action.

Starhawk is a witch, writer, teacher, counsellor and political activist.

'Persons of all genders, religions, and politics interested in healing self or planet would do well to avail themselves of this extraordinary text.'
The CoEvolution Quarterly

'Reading this book is in itself transformational . . . You are sure to come away from [Starhawk's] work richer, deeper, more truly transformed.'
New Age Journal

The Chalice and the Blade
Our History, Our Future
Riane Eisler

The Chalice and the Blade is a fascinating and powerful reconstruction of prehistory and history which offers new hope for the future.

Examining the past as a blueprint for the future Riane Eisler develops a theory of cultural evolution which contains two models: the dominator model, symbolised by the blade, when one half of society dominates the other, and the partnership model, symbolised by the life-giving chalice, when men and women are valued equally. Some 5,000 years before the global shift to patriarchy took place a society existed which was based on the gender holistic model. This study reveals that it was a time of great peace and contentment which has been obscured from world view, despite the fact that the Goddess culture lasted for thousands of years.

Today humankind stands at a crossroads. The lethal power of the blade, manifesting itself in the breakup of the family, environmental damage and possible nuclear holocaust, threatens global annihilation. Yet this is not our only option. We can, by rediscovering the partnership ethic and spirit of co-operation that existed in our prehistory, change our ideas and transform our culture.

' . . . both scholarly and passionate . . . essential reading.'
FRITJOF CAPRA, Physicist

'A fascinating and thorough historical account of how our culture lost its feminine values, and with it its value of life, leading us to the evolutionary crossroads we now stand at . . . Essential reading for anyone concerned about the future of humanity.'
PETER RUSSELL, author of The Awakening Earth

'Some books are like revelations, they open the spirit to unimaginable possibilities. *The Chalice and the Blade* is one of those magnificent key books . . . Raine Eisler proves that the dream of peace is not an impossible utopia . . . This book offers us the certainty that a better world is possible, if only we could remember.'
ISABEL ALLENDE

The Goddess Changes
The Ninefold Path – Faith, Experience and Knowledge
Felicity Wombwell

The Goddess Changes is a guide to working with the Goddess in a personal, individual way.

All of us go through the cycle of birth, life and death, and throughout our lives this cycle repeats itself in metaphorical ways. This process is reflected in the Goddess's sacred tasks of Spinning, Weaving and Cutting. By exploring the ancient feminine mysteries, and particularly the goddesses associated with the weaving of the thread of life, we can find a way of working with the changes that life brings.

Throughout the book the author encourages readers to accept their own personal experience of the feminine and the Goddess as valid. By giving an account of the changes she herself has been through and the way she has seen the Goddess at those times, she hopes to inspire others to work creatively with the Goddess. By changing with the Goddess in whatever way her spirit comes through, we help release her from the prison in which she has so long been kept and allow her wisdom and vision to infuse the world once more.

Symbols for Women
A Matrilineal Zodiac
Sheila Farrant

For 2000 years the symbols and interpretations of astrological signs have reflected a patriarchal system which has little connection with women's images of themselves. *Symbols For Women* examines an earlier, matrilineal system of astrology – drawing on anthropology, mythology and recent archaeological discoveries – to provide a reinterpretation of the twelve zodiacal signs which will redress this imbalance.

Sheila Farrant evokes the famous women, goddesses and societies of antiquity, relating them to our present and future times, and shows how the period of patriarchal bias has diminished many of our most popular symbols, and the consequences of this for women's self images. Tracing out, in detail, the histories of the familiar signs of the zodiac, along with their planetary rulers and restoring their femininity, she rediscovers their essential relationships and significance.

This is a challenging and informative work, full of fascinating ideas and meticulous research, accessibly written with perception and wit. It offers an exciting new perspective on our accepted understanding of the zodiac and the ways we approach it, and gives to women the chance to rediscover and be fulfilled by the full breadth and richness of their symbolic images.